MARVEL

MARVEL UNIVERSE MAP BY MAP

Senior Editor Cefn Ridout
Senior Art Editor Clive Savage
Production Editor Siu Yin Chan
Senior Production Controller Mary Slater
Managing Editor Sarah Harland
Managing Art Editor Vicky Short
Publishing Director Mark Searle

Cover by Matt Taylor

First American Edition, 2021
Published in the United States by DK Publishing
1450 Broadway, Suite 801 New York, NY 10018

DK, a Division of Penguin Random House LLC
21 22 23 24 25 10 9 8 7 6 5 4 3 2 1
001–324053–Nov/2021

© 2021 MARVEL

A catalog record for this book is available from the Library of Congress.
ISBN 978-0-7440-3979-5

DK books are available at special discounts when purchased in bulk
for sales promotions, premiums, fund-raising, or educational use.
For details, contact: DK Publishing Special Markets,
1450 Broadway, Suite 801 New York, NY 10018
SpecialSales@dk.com

Printed and bound in China

ACKNOWLEDGMENTS
DK would like to thank James Hill and Nick Jones for their text and expertise;
Andrew DeGraff, Adam Simpson, and Matt Taylor for their beautiful illustrated maps;
Tom Brevoort for his insightful foreword; Brian Overton, Caitlin O'Connell,
Jeff Youngquist, and Joe Hochstein at Marvel, and Mike Siglain and Chelsea Alon
at Disney for vital help and advice; Kathryn Hill for invaluable copy editing;
Alastair Dougall for editorial assistance; Lisa Sodeau for design assistance;
Jennette ElNaggar for proofreading; and Vanessa Bird for creating the index.

For the curious
www.dk.com

This book is made from
Forest Stewardship Council™
certified paper—one small
step in DK's commitment
to a sustainable future.

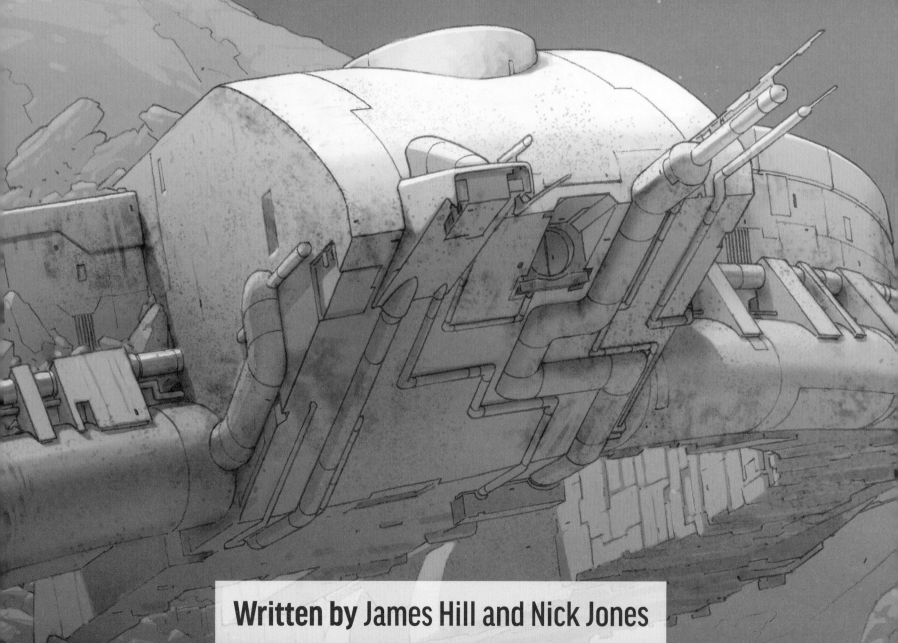

MARVEL

MARVEL UNIVERSE MAP BY MAP

Written by James Hill and Nick Jones

CONTENTS

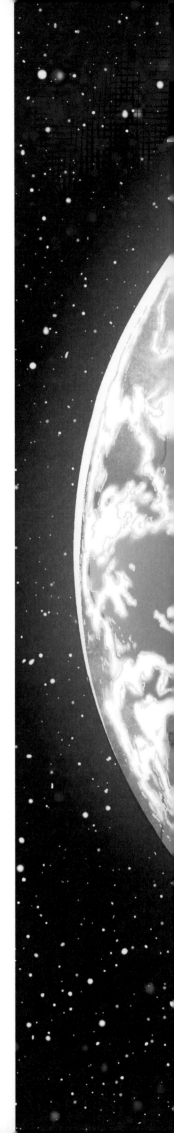

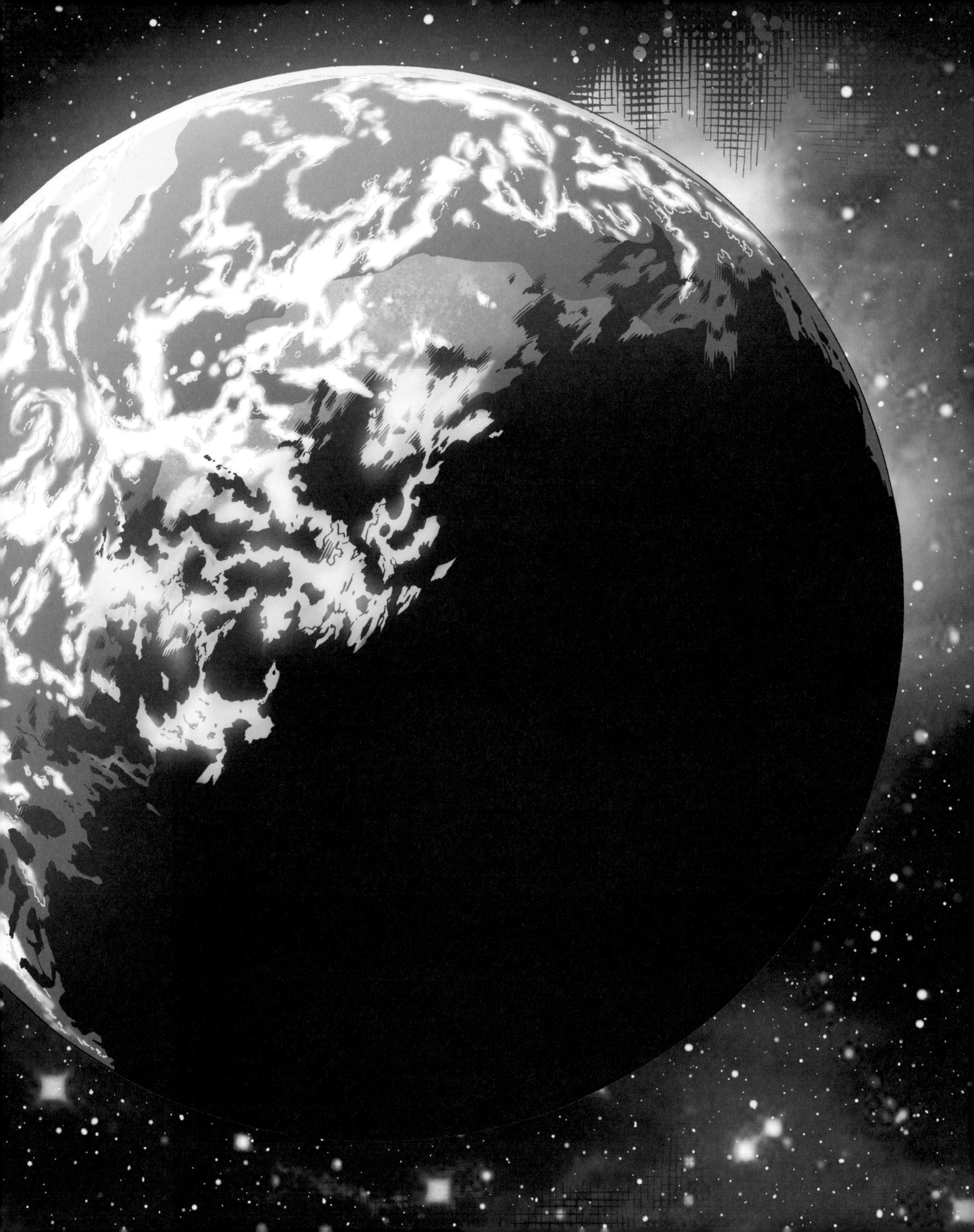

LIST OF COMMISSIONED ILLUSTRATIONS

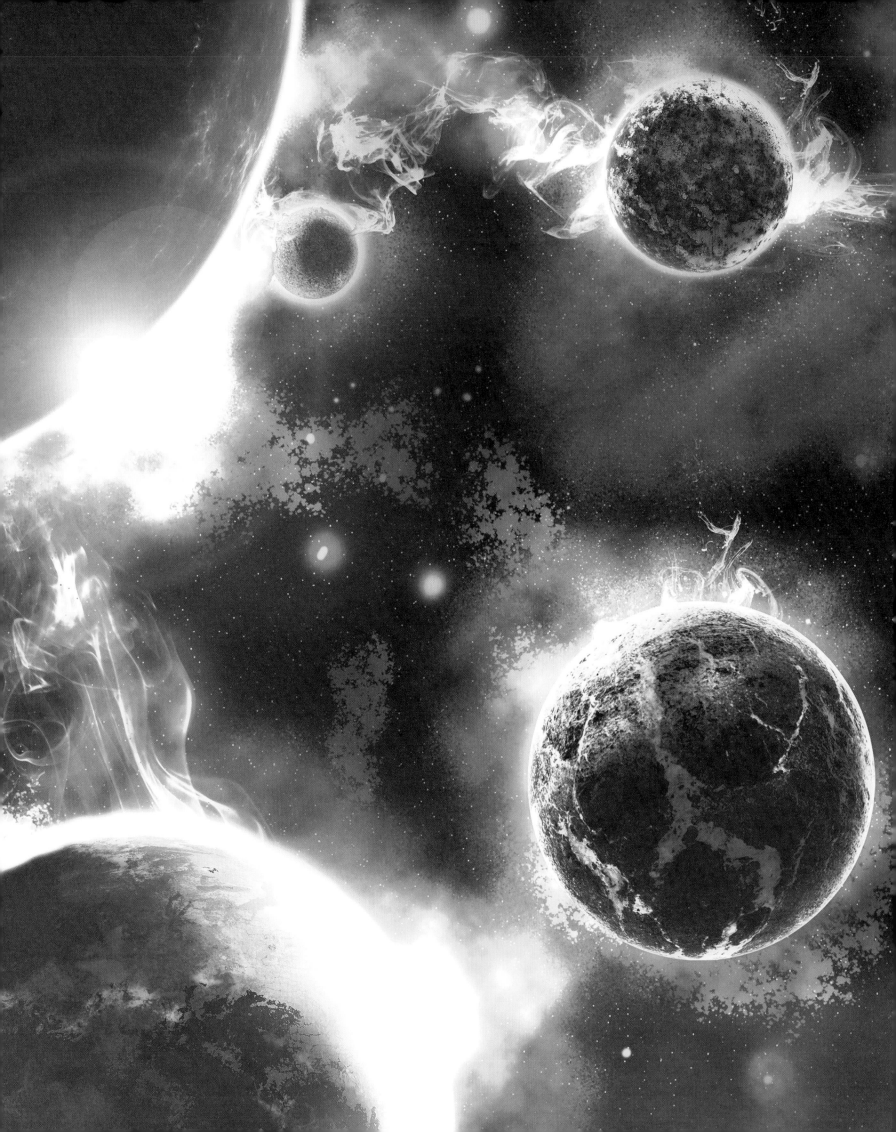

Foreword

It's become something of a cliché for people to say that the Marvel Universe represents "the world outside your window." And in fact, that description wasn't devised to describe the Marvel Universe at all, but rather 1986's New Universe. Still, the idea applies. In terms of its storytelling and its subject matter, the writers and artists of the Marvel Comics Group have always attempted to reflect the world and the times that they were living in.

This didn't start out as a plan so much as it evolved over time. Before Marvel had made its debut, most Super Heroes lived in fictitious made-up cities. And indeed, the very first issue of the flagship Marvel release, *Fantastic Four* #1, has its action taking place in the fictitious "Central City." But by the third issue, creators Stan Lee and Jack Kirby had thought the better of this, and instead headquartered their cosmic quartet in a skyscraper building in the heart of Manhattan. From then on, all of the Marvel creations tended to call New York home (with the notable exception of the Incredible Hulk, who rampaged across the Midwest, primarily in New Mexico).

This wasn't a carefully considered plan so much as it was a move to make the stories they were working on easier. Both Lee and Kirby lived in and around Manhattan and had grown up in New York. It was very familiar territory to them, and they were intimately familiar with the sorts of characters who populated the city. Indeed, they would likely run into some of them on their way to the Marvel offices. And so, instead of having to make up the details of their various characters' lives, they came naturally, instinctively. What's more, especially for characters such as Spider-Man or Daredevil, the ambiance of New York almost became a character itself in their series. Spider-Man would have felt like a very different character had he not lived in Forest Hills, Queens.

This verisimilitude wasn't lost on the growing readership, either. It was one of the ways in which the Marvel stories felt more plausible than the competition's Super Hero offerings. It's common today to hear stories of fans making their first visit to the Big Apple and being astonished to see the kinds of water towers that Steve Ditko or Frank Miller drew dot the landscape, and those visitors practically expected Spider-Man to come swinging around the next street corner.

As the Marvel Universe grew, of course, it added to its map of the world, with fanciful new environments such as Wakanda, Latveria, the Savage Land, the Negative Zone, and the star-spanning Kree and Skrull Empires. But while these territories were all the stuff of fantasy, the fact that they were situated against a world that otherwise resembled the one we lived in gave them a greater sense of reality. As these places were further developed over story after story, they each began to possess the kind of complex history and backstory that only genuine landmarks have.

Marvel Universe—Map by Map charts the topography of the Marvel Universe in loving detail, but it can be only a snapshot, a moment captured in time. Because the Marvel Universe is alive and ever-growing, and it's entirely likely that the years to come will see new environments debut and flourish, the only thing that's certain is that those new fantasy realms will exist adjacent to Poughkeepise, Susquehanna, and Schenectady. Because for all of its far-out fantasy, the Marvel Universe is truly the world outside your window.

Tom Brevoort, Marvel Senior Vice President of Publishing

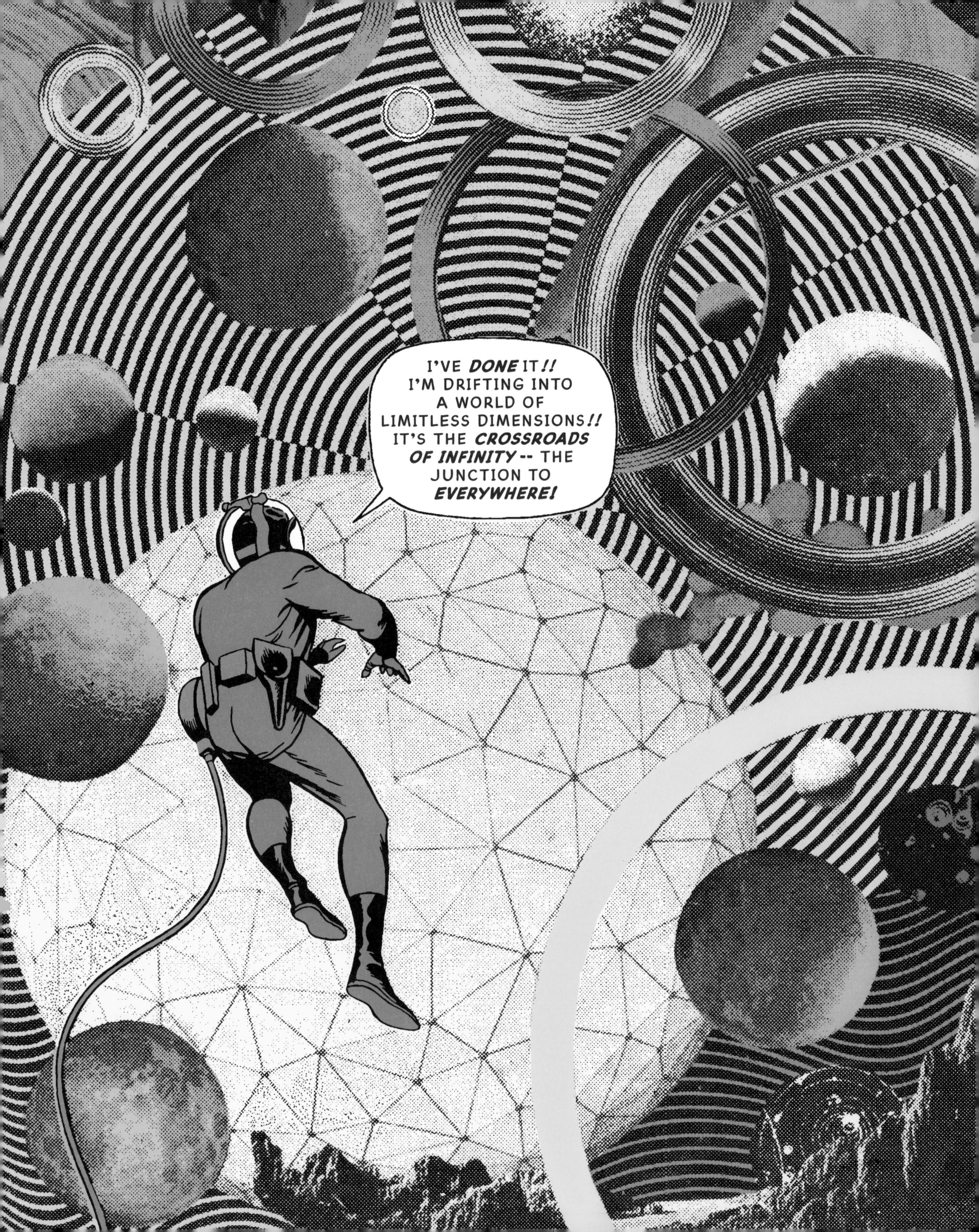
I'VE DONE IT!! I'M DRIFTING INTO A WORLD OF LIMITLESS DIMENSIONS!! IT'S THE CROSSROADS OF INFINITY -- THE JUNCTION TO EVERYWHERE!

Journeys of wonder

Beyond their obvious function as tools of navigation, maps have always empowered the imagination. Over the centuries, they have provided the armchair explorer with glimpses of unseen lands and faraway kingdoms. They have translated the world into shapes and symbols, and captured the environment in a codified fashion that can be read, understood, and, if desired, followed precisely. However, maps are not just templates for actual travel and are much more than mere lines on paper. They are windows on places yet to be personally encountered and vivid stimuli for speculation. "Yes, there is a continent to the south, but what is it like? Who lives there and what tumultuous events have shaped the landscape and forged the people?" Skilled cartography prompts such thoughts and in this way, maps have always been vistas of storytelling, providing opportunities for journeys of the mind and the promise of discovery and adventure.

Similarly, the ever-expanding Marvel Universe inspires rich and rewarding rumination. Grounded in a recognizable world since its inception in the 1960s, it has grown considerably over the decades, with each new development leading to ever greater conjecture. "How did the kingdom of Wakanda develop its advanced technology?" "What transpired when the expansionist Skrulls came upon the alien Kree in the great vastness of outer space?" "Where did the Silver Surfer's fantastic voyage across the cosmos begin?" Marvel's writers and artists have pondered these questions and mapped their fictional domain like cartographers of old drawing up their charts, carefully filling in the gaps, and expanding their scope to accommodate fresh information. After all, the very nature of story is to ask, "what happens next?" Just as the very nature of map making is to ask, "what comes next?" Every story in Marvel's history has provoked new questions and the answers have propelled readers further along a seemingly endless sea of the imagination, always heading toward a fresh horizon.

Even place names within the Marvel Universe are an invitation to wonder—and wander. Who would not want to visit the jungle environs of the Savage Land or steal into Doctor Strange's Sanctum Sanctorum? To this day, place continues to play an important role in the development of the universe, with locations helping to define, and sometimes redefine, Marvel's heroes and villains.

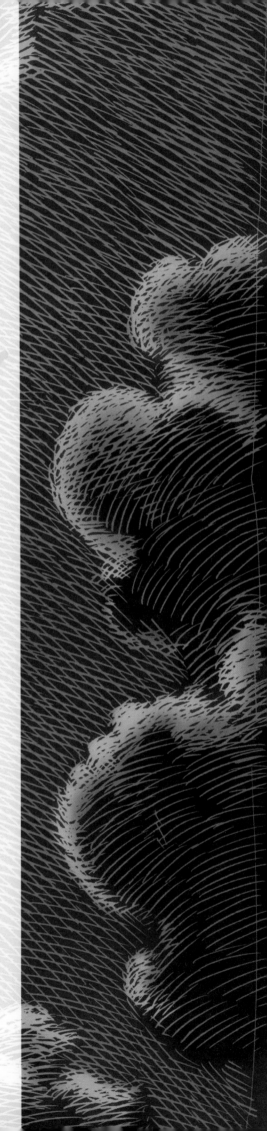

In his recent retooling of the *X-Men*, writer Jonathan Hickman transforms the island of Krakoa, a long-established feature of the mythos, into a mutant nation-state, opening up many new avenues for storytelling. And in his groundbreaking run as author of the *Immortal Hulk*, Al Ewing reveals the nightmarish Below-Place to be the bottom layer of Hell. What distinguishes this version of the infernal domain from what preceded it, is that it is intrinsically linked to the Hulk's origins—character and place knitted together to make a compelling narrative whole. Both examples follow in the footsteps of the pioneers who originally mapped this frontier while also extending the boundaries of the Marvel Universe.

Through 16 specially commissioned, beautifully illustrated maps and a compendium of carefully curated essays, *Marvel Universe: Map by Map* delineates the contours of this hugely imaginative terrain. It traverses the incredible locations and epic events that have made the Marvel Universe one of the world's most fully realized fictional creations. Starting with Super Hero Central in Manhattan, the book navigates Earth's super-powered nations as well as the arcane regions of the planet that remain steeped in myths and magic. It then reveals the hidden kingdoms and lost lands that exist in the curious hinterland between legendary belief and scientific certainty. From there, the focus shifts to outer space, to chart the rise and fall of mighty galactic empires and examines the relentless forces and powerful beings that have helped shape the cosmos. The perspective widens even further as we enter the ethereal realms of divinity and look at the significance of godly cities like Asgard and Olympus. Next, we cross the borders of the universe to negotiate those dimensions closest to the Earthly sphere, the metaphysical realms of sorcerers and mystics, and the terrifying hellscapes of devils and demons. Finally, before embarking on our return home, we catch a glimpse of alternative-reality Earths and divergent timelines that are hauntingly familiar yet shockingly different.

Marvel Universe: Map by Map is both atlas and guidebook to a wondrous universe that is forever broadening its horizons, beckoning to be explored. Every journey begins with a single step and, perhaps just as significantly, every imaginative journey can begin with a map.

Prime Earth

Prime Earth, designated Earth-616, sits firmly at the nexus of universal events and is one of the most important planetary bodies in all of creation. While it has numerous counterparts in the myriad of alternative realities that make up the Multiverse, the seemingly innocuous blue-green world is unique among the stars. Billions of years ago, its soil was infused with the cosmic energies of a dying Celestial space god and this made it a fertile breeding ground for superhuman beings and a magnet for extraterrestrial visitors. Thanks to its singular genesis, Prime Earth is a world blessed with an abundance of Super Hero protectors, including the Avengers and the Fantastic Four. It is home to scientifically advanced nations like the Black Panther's Wakanda and the Sub-Mariner's undersea kingdom of Atlantis. A voyage across Prime Earth delivers countless wondrous sights and reveals many inspirational stories.

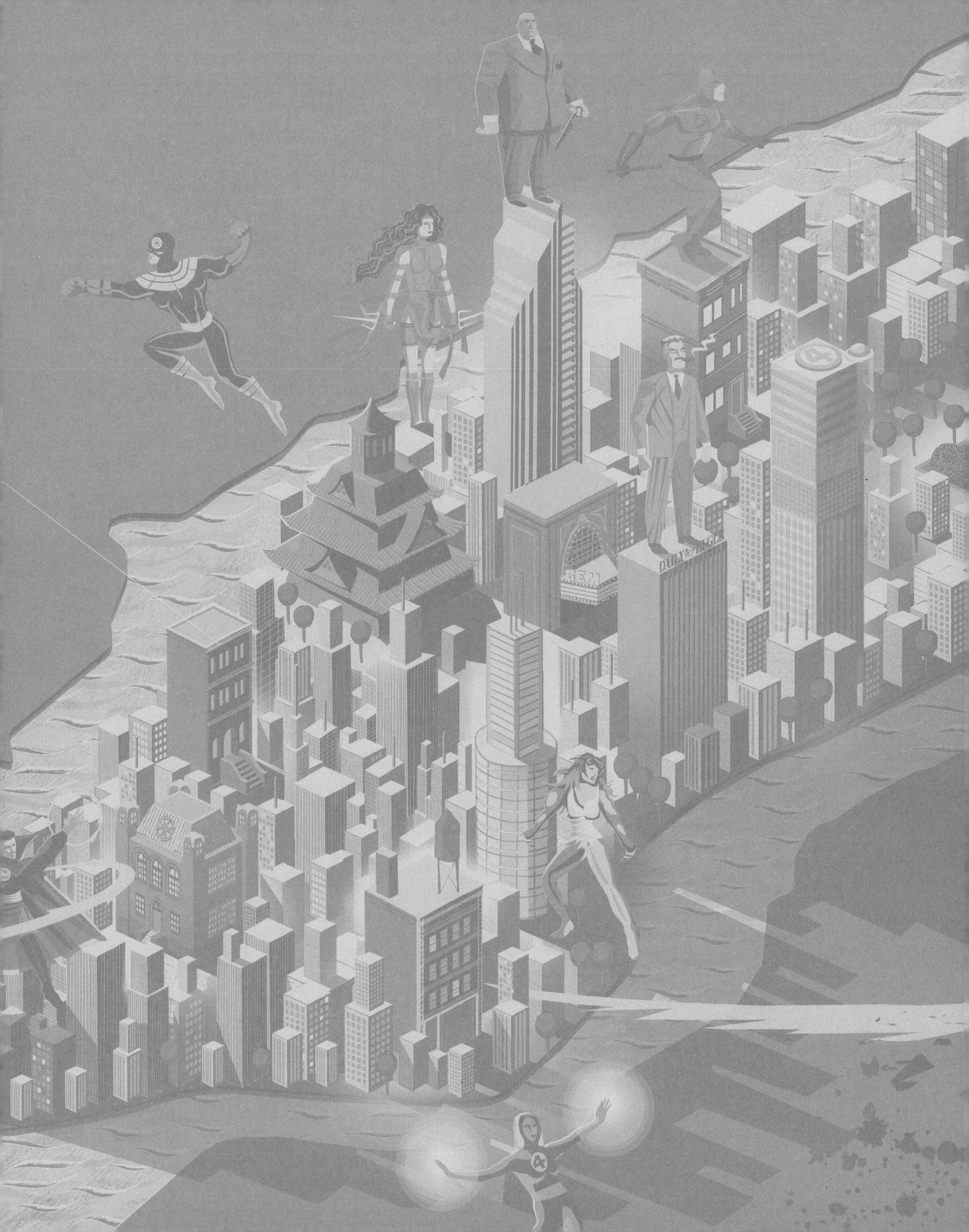
GEM
DAILY

Super Hero Central

The most densely packed borough of New York City is home to the world's greatest heroes. Manhattan Island—with its global economic and diplomatic connections—has long been the place to be if you're a member of the Super Hero community.

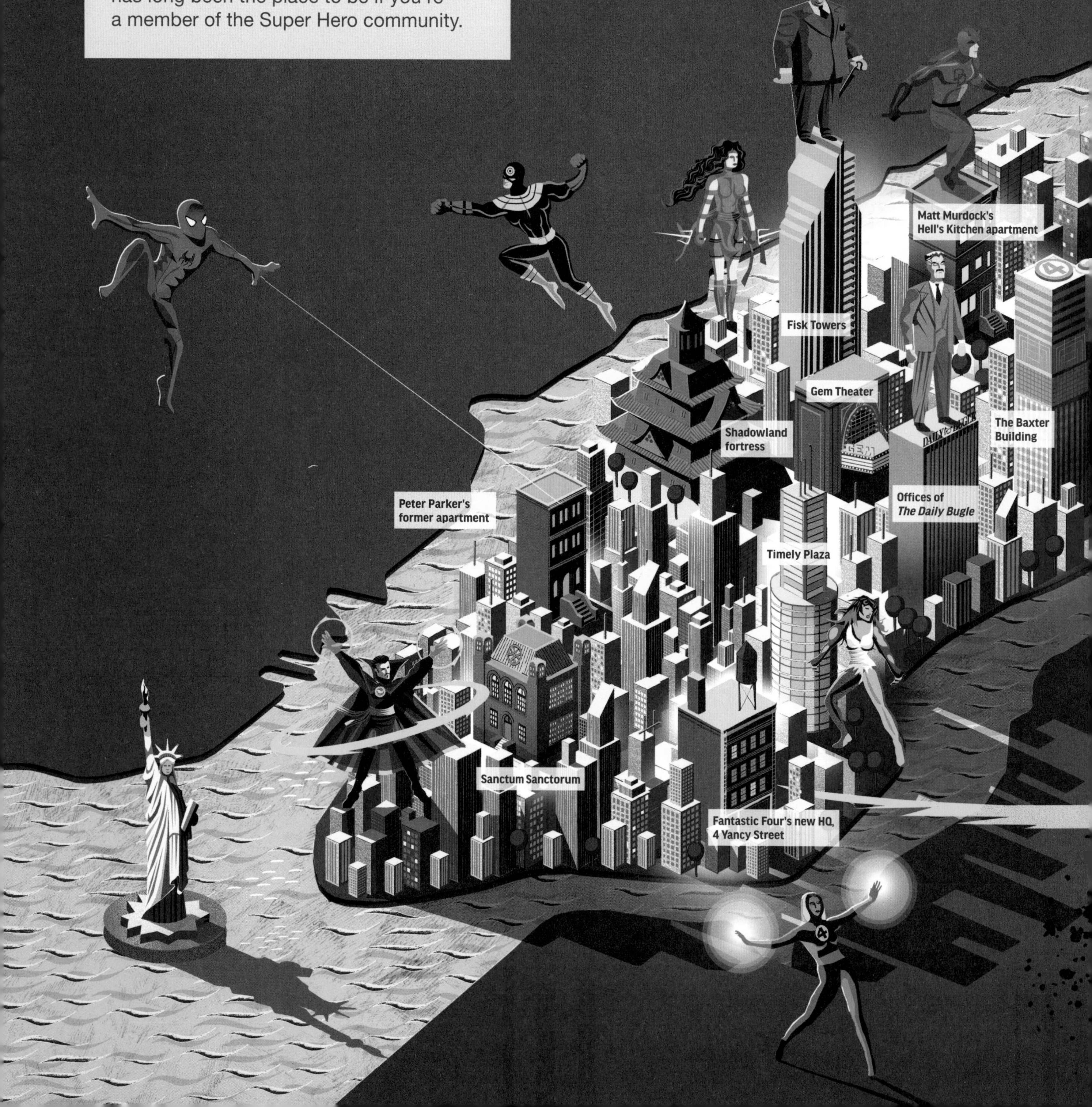
Matt Murdock's Hell's Kitchen apartment
Fisk Towers
Gem Theater
Shadowland fortress
The Baxter Building
Offices of *The Daily Bugle*
Peter Parker's former apartment
Timely Plaza
Sanctum Sanctorum
Fantastic Four's new HQ, 4 Yancy Street

Avengers Mansion

The Raft

World War II is often considered the crucible in which the first age of Super Heroes was forged. Disparate superhuman champions like Captain America, Sub-Mariner, and the android Human Torch joined forces as the Invaders, battling the enemy overseas and leading the charge against tyranny and oppression. Their example inspired many ordinary women and men—like *Daily Bugle* reporter Jeffrey Mace—to don colorful costumes and fight for justice in a much more prosaic fashion. Mace became the Patriot, one of several "home front heroes" to take on the saboteurs and fifth columnists who threatened to disrupt the United States' war effort and sow discord on American soil.

In the aftermath of the war, Mace took over the role of Captain America and joined an expanded Invaders team that went by the name of the All-Winners Squad. The group was stationed in Manhattan, and Mace witnessed firsthand the borough's postwar boom, with new buildings and new industries, powered by new technologies, springing up all around him. When the All-Winners Squad's original Times Square headquarters was destroyed in a battle with the villain Madame Death, Mace suggested a move to the Baxter Building, a 35-story tower that was currently under construction at the intersection of 42nd Street and Madison Avenue. The brainchild of entrepreneur Leland Baxter of the Leland Baxter Paper Company, the building utilized revolutionary "K-bracing" in its steel frame construction, making it the strongest skyscraper in the world. The Baxter Building was a monument to modernity. Its glass-and-steel frontage spoke to a vision of a brighter tomorrow—a bold, new era brought into being by advanced engineering and technological innovation.

In something of a contrast to this audacious mission statement, the Baxter Building's lower floors were designed to accommodate large and noisy pulp recycling machinery. The upper floors were, however, light and airy, and, thanks to Jeff Mace's friendship with fellow newspaperman Baxter, they were easily secured for the All-Winners Squad. The team moved into the still-unfinished building in early 1948 and remained tenants until the group disbanded several years later.

"It should take anything we—or our enemies—throw at it!"

Captain America (Jeff Mace)

Living on the edge
Following victory in World War II, the All-Winners Squad moved into the airy upper floors of the still-incomplete Baxter Building.
Captain America: Patriot #2, Nov. 2010

The torch is passed

The All-Winners Squad wouldn't be the last Super Hero team to use the Baxter Building as a headquarters. As a new era of heroes dawned in modern times, the Fantastic Four moved into the top five floors of the skyscraper. Reed Richards (aka Mister Fantastic) carefully supervised the extensive and costly reconstruction of the facility so that it provided not only expansive living quarters but also ample space for his cutting edge—and often bulky—scientific paraphernalia, including an access portal to the extradimensional Negative Zone. The building's top floor was retrofitted as a launch deck for the team's Fantasticar, Pogo Plane, and numerous high-powered jet cycles.

Manhattanites, characteristically blasé, did not give much attention to the reconstruction work happening at the Baxter Building, but a dramatic call to action was enough to finally wake them from their everyday distractions. Alerted to mysterious seismic activity centered around nuclear power stations, Richards summoned his colleagues—Ben Grimm, Sue Storm, and Sue's brother, Johnny—for their first official mission together as the Fantastic Four. He fired a flare from an upper window, writing the team's name in fiery letters and prompting one astonished onlooker to declare, "Those words in the sky! What do they mean?" What they meant was that the Fantastic Four had arrived to make Manhattan their home, and with Johnny Storm possessing powers remarkably similar to the original Human Torch, the flame had been passed, quite literally, from one generation of heroes to the next. The All-Winners Squad gave way to the Fantastic Four—and Manhattan, and the wider world, would never be quite the same again.

Hitting the streets
The Baxter Building was perfectly situated for the newly formed Fantastic Four to race into action at the first sign of danger.
History of the Marvel Universe #3, Nov. 2019

Home for heroes
Reed Richards believed the Baxter Building would be an ideal home and headquarters, bringing the Fantastic Four together with a fiery signal from the skyscraper's rooftop.
Fantastic Four: 1 2 3 4 #1, Oct. 2001

❝Try and think of our new home as a living building.❞
Mister Fantastic

Under siege

With the group's identities public knowledge and an iconic headquarters in Midtown, the Fantastic Four became the world's first celebrity Super Heroes. Fans would frequently gather outside the Baxter Building to catch a glimpse of their favorite superstars, and while its security systems were among the most sophisticated in the world, the headquarters also served as a magnet for some of the Fantastic Four's most intractable foes.

Doctor Doom—the despotic ruler of the European nation of Latveria and a jealous rival of Reed Richards since their shared university days—was among the first villains to strike at the building directly. Having suffered a humiliating defeat at the hands of the Fantastic Four, he approached Namor the Sub-Mariner and proposed that the duo enter into an alliance.

The Atlantean prince had fallen far since his days as a wartime hero. He had spent years lost in a fog of amnesia and, having finally regained his faculties, had been horrified to discover that his home of Atlantis had been unwittingly destroyed during a nuclear test, its people scattered far and wide. Seething with rage at this injustice, Namor had struck back at those he held responsible: the US government. This brought him into conflict with the Fantastic Four and he, too, had been recently defeated by the heroes. Persuaded that united they would be unstoppable, Sub-Mariner agreed to join forces with Doctor Doom. Together, they used a tractor beam to rip the Baxter Building from its foundations and transport it into outer space.

Doom looms large
Doctor Doom frequently plotted to take over the Baxter Building. On one occasion, the Fantastic Four recruited Daredevil and Wyatt Wingfoot to evict their unwanted tenant.
Fantastic Four #39, Jun. 1965

Trapped inside their headquarters, with their vehicles damaged during the upheaval, the Fantastic Four watched helplessly as they were pulled along behind a spacecraft piloted by Doctor Doom. However, when it became apparent that the armor-clad villain was also plotting to eliminate the Sub-Mariner, who he viewed as a potential rival, events took an even more dramatic turn. The aquatic mutant confronted his erstwhile partner, forcibly ejecting Doctor Doom from his spacecraft and going on to help return the Baxter Building to its corner plot in Manhattan's Midtown.

The jet set
The Fantastic Four taking off for parts unknown in their jet-powered Fantasticar was a regular sight in the skies above Manhattan.
FF #3, Jul. 2011

Giant appetite
When he arrived to feast on Earth's life-sustaining energies,
the alien Galactus towered over the New York City skyline.
Amazing Spider-Man #12, Feb. 2019 (variant cover)

Towering titan

While superhuman activity in and around the Fantastic Four's headquarters
became a common occurrence, shrugged off as largely inconsequential
by passersby, one event caused all of Manhattan to stop and take notice.
The cosmic devourer known as Galactus arrived from outer space to consume
the life-sustaining energies of Earth. Alerted to the precise location of the planet
by his herald, the Silver Surfer, Galactus alighted on top of the Baxter Building,
causing mass panic on the streets below. Galactus ignored the furious buzz
of activity and set about constructing an energy converter, a device that would
enable him to transform the planet and its inhabitants into an easily digestible
food source. The Fantastic Four were powerless to stop him; even Ben Grimm's
formidable strength did little to dislodge the towering extraterrestrial from the roof
of the Baxter Building. However, when he was made to see humanity's worth,
the Silver Surfer turned on Galactus and helped the Fantastic Four win the day.

Stomping grounds
The Thing grew up on the notorious Yancy Street
and was frequently drawn back to the down-and-
out, crime-ridden area.
Marvel Knights: 4 #22, Nov. 2005

"No matter where in the
universe I am, my mind is
never far from Yancy Street."
The Thing

The old neighborhood

In a very real sense, the Baxter Building was the backdrop to the Fantastic Four's tumultuous lives. In addition to Super Villain attacks, there were births, marriages, breakups, reconciliations, and even new group rosters. Throughout it all, the Baxter Building was a reassuring presence; a place that the founding members of the team all considered their true home. In the end, it was Kristoff, the vengeful son of Doctor Doom, who brought about the Baxter Building's destruction. He transported the skyscraper into outer space and then blew it up.

The Fantastic Four survived the experience, however, and went on to rebuild their lives and organization. Four Freedoms Plaza—a 45-story office block—was built on the former site of the Baxter Building. The new headquarters was even more futuristic than its predecessor, housing state-of-the-art labs and even a miniaturized particle accelerator. Of course, with such a rich history, the Baxter Building was always going to be remembered as a far more iconic structure than its replacement. And so, when Four Freedoms Plaza was itself destroyed, Richards seized upon a rare opportunity to move forward by going backward. With the aid of Noah Baxter—a visionary architect and a relative of the late Leyland Baxter—he constructed an exact replica of the Baxter Building in low-Earth orbit. He then teleported the copy into the same space in New York City once occupied by the original. The Baxter Building was back where it belonged, and, somewhat predictably, few busy Manhattanites batted an eyelid.

In the aftermath of a universal crisis that threatened to wipe out all of creation, Reed and Sue were presumed dead. The Fantastic Four was officially disbanded, and Ben Grimm and Johnny Storm moved on with their own lives. The Baxter Building passed through several hands until it was purchased by a new team of heroes: the publicity-hungry Fantastix.

Neighborhood hangout
The Yancy Street Café gave the
Thing an opportunity to dine on a
lean corned beef sandwich and
keep up with the local gossip.
Fantastic Four #539, Oct. 2006

It eventually transpired that Reed and Sue were still alive and had been exploring the vastness of the Multiverse alongside their children, Franklin and Valeria, and a group of extraordinary teens and preteens known as the Future Foundation. Returning to Earth, Reed and Sue were reunited with Ben and Johnny. However, instead of returning to the Baxter Building, the team took up residence at 4 Yancy Street in Manhattan's impoverished Lower East Side. This was Ben Grimm's old stomping ground. He had grown up on the street and had even spent a few years as a member of the notorious Yancy Street Gang. Rather than an outright criminal organization, the Yancy Street Gang was primarily a group of individuals who were determined to look out for one another and protect their community from what they saw as predatory outsiders. When Grimm found celebrity as a member of the Fantastic Four, the Yancy Street Gang felt he had turned his back on his working-class background. In retaliation, they embarked on a campaign to undermine the hero's credibility, playing countless practical jokes on him and harassing him whenever he turned up in the old neighborhood. Now, Grimm was back on a permanent basis—and he had brought the Fantastic Four with him.

Together with his genius daughter, Valeria, Reed devised a means to create pocket dimensions within 4 Yancy Street, making its interior square footage roughly twice that of the Baxter Building, while its outside appearance remained unchanged. Naturally, there was local push back, with many of the street's older residents fearing the arrival of the Fantastic Four would lead to gentrification and an inevitable spike in rents. Their fears were calmed, however, when the heroes promised to share their dimensional technology with landlords, allowing more residents to comfortably move into the area.

The Fantastic Four's new Yancy Street headquarters spoke to the group's enduring commitment to the concepts of family and home. Despite being celebrity Super Heroes—they may have once lived in a luxurious skyscraper—the Fantastic Four hadn't abandoned their roots. While the Baxter Building was a modern marvel, 4 Yancy Street was a reminder that, in every corner of Manhattan, vibrant, diverse communities still came together just as they had always done in the past.

Four into one
Reed Richards created pocket dimensions within 4 Yancy Street to make the tenement bigger on the inside. *Fantastic Four* #4, Jan. 2019

Clean up crew

The concentration of so many super-powered individuals in Manhattan threw up some unique business opportunities. Anne Marie Hoag founded an organization called Damage Control, a specialist cleanup crew that would make good any property damage inflicted on the city during superhuman battles.

The business was initially financed by Tony Stark and Wilson Fisk. Somewhat predictably, the two financiers fell out, however, forcing Hoag to secure more reliable funding from S.H.I.E.L.D. The majority of company employees were ordinary "hard-working Joes," like the straight-talking, no-nonsense foreman Lenny Ballinger, but the firm occasionally called on superhuman muscle to help move particularly heavy loads. The demigod Hercules even took a full-time job with Damage Control when he found himself "financially embarrassed" after being sued for damages by the villain Constrictor.

Renovating Super Hero HQs was supposedly a company specialty, but things didn't always run smoothly. On one particularly embarrassing occasion, Damage Control dropped a fully repaired Avengers Mansion into the Hudson River. Then a repair job at the X-Mansion in Westchester County, New York, went awry when company employees accidentally activated robots that wrecked the building.

Hardworking hero

If the Fantastic Four were the superstars of the Super Hero set—universally recognized as selfless adventurers—then Spider-Man was the hapless hero forever destined to be maligned and misunderstood. Since gaining spider-powers as a teenager, Peter Parker had struggled to balance the needs of his everyday life with the responsibilities of a Super Hero career. A native of Forest Hills in Queens, Peter had been raised solely by his aunt May following the tragic death of his uncle Ben. With money tight at home, Manhattan beckoned, promising to provide financial opportunities and help Peter give back to his beloved aunt. While still a biophysics student at Empire State University, he freelanced as a photojournalist for *The Daily Bugle*, one of the city's longest-running newspapers.

Founded in 1897, the paper had been launched as an expression of progressive ideals, a crusading organ with a mission to deliver truth on a daily basis. It fell on hard times, however, until its fortunes were revived in the modern era when purchased by lifelong newspaperman J. Jonah Jameson. The new publisher reinvigorated the floundering tabloid, making it fit to compete with rivals *The Daily Globe* and *The New York Bulletin*. Jameson was a hard taskmaster, often irascible and stubborn, but his commitment to journalistic integrity was unquestionable. Perhaps the clearest example of Jameson's ideals was the huge *Daily Bugle* logo he had built and placed on top of the company's Midtown headquarters—a visible reminder to passersby that *The Daily Bugle* was always there to scrutinize the events of the day and hold those in power accountable for their actions.

Photo opportunities

Peter Parker's history with Jameson was complex and often contradictory. The publisher recognized Parker's photographic skills, but the canny businessman refused to pay too much for any single image. Consequently, Peter lived a hand-to-mouth existence, constantly scrambling from one freelance paycheck to the next. After Jameson demanded Parker bring him pictures of Spider-Man, Peter hit upon a novel idea. He began taking photos of himself while in action as Spider-Man, using cameras he discreetly webbed into alleyway corners and other out-of-the-way places. The pictures were a huge hit with Jameson. Unfortunately, while Peter hoped the images would help secure him a reputation as New York's "Friendly Neighborhood Spider-Man," quite the opposite occurred. Invariably, Jameson would use Peter's photos as part of his campaign to undermine the public's trust in Spider-Man, resulting in countless *Daily Bugle* headlines declaring the hero a menace.

Day job
By night, Peter Parker guarded the city as the Amazing Spider-Man. By day, he worked as a photojournalist for *The Daily Bugle* newspaper.
The Pulse #3, Jul. 2004

"The city needs the *Bugle*, now more than ever."
Robbie Robertson

Jameson's animosity stretched back to when Spider-Man's heroic activities had taken the media spotlight away from the publisher's heroic astronaut son. But his vendetta wasn't wholly personal. A lifetime investigating wrongdoings and abuses of power had made Jameson deeply cynical. Experience had taught him that most self-proclaimed heroes had feet of clay. That belief, coupled with an intense distrust of vigilantes in general, meant he viewed the arachnid hero with great suspicion. Drawing on *The Daily Bugle*'s considerable cash reserves, as well as his own personal fortune, Jameson posted numerous rewards for Spider-Man's capture or information about his secret identity. He financed the building of Spencer Smythe's Spider-Slayer robots and hired numerous individuals to hunt down Spider-Man, including New York's own Hero for Hire Luke Cage, and Silver Sable, a mercenary from the cloistered European nation of Symkaria. While these misguided efforts generally failed, they would sometimes lead to Spider-Man battling super-powered individuals, such as the genetically enhanced Scorpion, right at the very heart of *The Daily Bugle* bullpen. The resulting chaos and property damage only served to further Jameson's hatred of the hero.

Living dangerously

The Daily Bugle's campaign against Spider-Man put Peter Parker in an impossible bind. His own photography was being used to undermine his heroic persona, but he needed the freelance payments if he was to make a life for himself in the hellishly expensive borough of Manhattan.

Working for Jameson was never easy, but Peter found a receptive advocate in the form of *The Daily Bugle* editor in chief Robbie Robertson. A veteran of the newspaper business, Robbie knew how to work around an overbearing publisher and, when Jameson would fire Parker for some misdemeanor, the editor would invariably rehire him.

When he began working at *The Daily Bugle*, Peter shared student accommodations with his friend Harry Osborn. He eventually moved into his own West Side apartment at 410 Chelsea Street. Cramped and somewhat run-down, the top-floor apartment suited Peter perfectly as its rooftop skylight allowed him to slip in and out of the building as Spider-Man. What was less than perfect, though, was the extortionate rent.

Busy bullpen
The Daily Bugle editor Robbie Robertson would strive to meet the latest deadline, while publisher J. Jonah Jameson would often harangue hapless employees.
The Pulse #2, May 2004

The amazing Spider-Island

Working for a mysterious benefactor, the villainous Jackal spent months slowly infecting the population of Manhattan with mutated bedbugs that gave people powers similar to those of Spider-Man. At first, many viewed this as a boon, and Manhattan was soon overrun with joyous wall-crawlers and web-spinners. However, over time, these people mutated even further—and were transformed into giant spiders the size of small cars.

With the city overrun by these monstrous creatures, it was finally revealed that Adriana Soria, the so-called Spider-Queen, was the mastermind behind the scheme. As more people were turned into arachnids, Soria's link to the extradimensional Web of Life was strengthened and her powers amplified. The island of Manhattan was just the first step in her planned conquest of the world.

An antigen to the spider-contagion was developed by Reed Richards and the scientists at Horizon Labs. Spider-Man used drone Octobots, held in storage since a failed attempt by Doctor Octopus to take over the city, to distribute the cure.

The big city
With an entire city to protect, Spider-Man often felt the weight of his heroic responsibilities, but he refused to be cowed.
Amazing Spider-Man #655, Apr. 2011

Originally an industrial area, Chelsea was on the way up, and so were property prices. Always strapped for cash, Peter was forever dodging landlady Mrs. Muggins and her seemingly endless demands for money. Events came to a head when Peter's apartment was firebombed by local hoodlums and Mrs. Muggins threatened to evict her hapless tenant if he didn't make good on the repairs.

Moving on

Peter eventually bowed to the inevitable and moved back to his Aunt May's house. After graduating college, he spent time as a science teacher at his alma mater—Midtown High School in Forest Hills.

Change also came to *The Daily Bugle*. With newspaper sales on the decline, Jameson branched out into magazine publishing, first launching *Now* and then *Woman* under the editorship of Carol Danvers. Perhaps his greatest concession to economic necessity and the readership's changing tastes was *The Pulse*— a weekly supplement to *The Daily Bugle* that reported exclusively on Manhattan's ever growing Super Hero community, including a certain costumed web-spinner.

"Look at my costume. I'll never get the soot out."

Spider-Man (Peter Parker)

Hot news
Super Villains like Electro would frequently attack the offices of *The Daily Bugle* after receiving bad press.
Amazing Spider-Man #614, Feb. 2010

When Jameson was incapacitated following several heart attacks, *The Daily Bugle* was sold to Dexter Bennett who swiftly turned the respected paper into a gossip-focused scandal sheet, renaming it *The DB!* This prompted Robbie Robertson and others to walk out and join the *Front Line*, a rival daily that had recently been established. Eventually, a recovered Jameson took back the rights to *The Daily Bugle* and gave them to Robbie Robertson, encouraging his former employee to revive the moribund title.

Robertson was joined in his new mission by many former colleagues, including reporters Ben Urich and Betty Brant, and Peter Parker, who was once again relying on his skills as a freelance photographer to make ends meet. Robertson's publishing plan was to focus on investigative journalism: to deliver the truth on a daily basis once more.

In a way, this was something of a homecoming for Peter. He was back working in the heart of Manhattan, meeting the considerable challenges of city life while continuing to operate around the clock as Spider-Man. He was, just as he had always been, an everyman hero.

Local heroes

The Amazing Spider-Man wasn't the only Super Hero in Manhattan to focus primarily on street-level crime. There were many others, including ex-con-turned-Hero-for-Hire Luke Cage. Reputedly only motivated by money—and apparently willing to work for almost anyone so long as the pay was good—Cage's selfless character would inevitably assert itself and he would frequently find himself defending the downtrodden and dispossessed for no financial reward whatsoever.

Cage initially operated out of a dilapidated movie house—the Gem Theater on 42nd Street, close to the bustling hub of Times Square. A magnet for tourists, who flocked there to experience the glamour of nearby Broadway, the area also attracted countless con men, grifters, and petty crooks. Cage's decision to base himself at the Gem Theater was no accident. While the faded dream palace certainly offered cheap office accommodations—and an occasional bed for the night— it also placed Cage at the beating heart of New York City. If bad things went down, Cage was where he needed to be to set them right and protect his community.

Cage eventually entered into a fruitful partnership with the martial artist Iron Fist and, while that association would see him travel far and wide, his commitment to his home turf was always absolute.

Tarnished treasure
The Gem Theater was home to Heroes-for-Hire Luke Cage and Iron Fist until firebombed by gangsters Señor Muerte and Señor Suerte. **Top:** *Power Man and Iron Fist* #69, May 1981; **above:** *Power Man and Iron Fist* #63, Jun. 1980

Guardian devil
The heroic Daredevil slipped out of his apartment every night to patrol the city, a crimson crusader swinging across Manhattan's rooftops.
Daredevil #2, Apr. 2019

City keep

The contrast between Cage's spartan accommodations and the apartment owned by Matt Murdock—who secretly patrolled Manhattan's streets as the hero Daredevil—could not have been starker. Located at Sutton Place in the prestigious Upper East Side, Murdock's well-appointed brownstone building was steeped in history and character.

Blinded by the same chemical accident that had given him an extraordinary radar sense, Murdock had remodeled his apartment to suit his unique requirements—both in and out of costume. The top floor was a personal art gallery containing tactile sculptures and intricate bas-reliefs. Beneath this was an extensive braille library, containing numerous documents to aid Murdock in his career as a defense attorney. Finally, adjacent to the living quarters was a hidden, soundproofed training gym where Murdock kept his Daredevil costumes and spent countless hours keeping himself in top physical condition.

The brownstone apartment was a veritable castle, a place where Murdock could retreat from his twin roles as hero and lawyer. Cloistered behind stout stone walls, he was alone in a world of his own making, safe and secure, and able to balance the demands of a complex lifestyle that had the potential to spiral out of control.

> **"**She (the city) greets me with a blast of wind and her endless angry roar.**"**
>
> **Daredevil**

Aerie retreat
Overlooking the Hudson River, Matt Murdock's brownstone home provided a sanctuary where he could briefly escape the obligations of Daredevil and take stock of the world.
Elektra Lives Again graphic novel Mar. 1990

King of New York City
Wilson Fisk posed as a legitimate
businessman, but, in reality, he ruled the
mobs, reigning over a huge criminal empire.
Kingpin #2, May 2017

Mob boss

When it was time to go into action, Daredevil would exit the brownstone
through a rooftop skylight that was activated by stepping on an
unmarked floorboard. With his hyper-senses to guide him, he would
swing across the Manhattan rooftops—a crimson-clad devil who
soared like an angel. While he often battled costumed foes, such as the
towering Stilt-Man and the deadly Gladiator, Daredevil's primary focus
was on corralling everyday crooks—the drug dealers, muggers, and
shakedown artists who were a blight on city life. This inevitably brought
him into conflict with Wilson Fisk, the so-called Kingpin of Crime.

Power politics

The Mayor of New York faced a
unique challenge. How best to keep
ordinary citizens safe in a city filled
with super-powered individuals?
For the most part, that was an easy
question to answer, especially as
the Avengers and the Fantastic Four
operated under rigorous guidelines.
In recent years, however, costumed
vigilantes and their unofficial role in
the city have become a hot topic
in mayoral elections.

After his election as mayor, former
Daily Bugle publisher J. Jonah
Jameson continued his vendetta
against Spider-Man. He formed an
"Anti-Spider Squad" to capture the
much-maligned hero and went on
to develop a new army of Spider-
Slayer robots. When these went on
a rampage, Jameson was forced to
retire from public office in disgrace.

Sometime later, the notorious
mob boss Wilson Fisk took over
the mayoralty. When the United
States fell under the sway of Hydra,
Fisk used his resources to keep
New York running as smoothly
as possible. Following Hydra's
defeat, Fisk parlayed his newfound
popularity into political power. He
was elected Mayor of New York City
on a mandate to eradicate vigilantes
like Daredevil and the Punisher.

Fisk posed as a businessman, but he was the unseen hand who controlled the mobs in New York City. His legitimate façade was so complete that he was able to maintain Fisk Towers at 439 West 38th Street, just north of the Empire State Building and a few blocks southeast of the financial district. Supposedly the headquarters for an international conglomerate, Fisk Towers dominated the skyline just as the man dominated the city's underworld. Intriguingly, Fisk's office was at the very top of the building, as if, on some unconscious level, he was trying to put as much distance between himself and the grubby world of crime from which he had emerged.

Following several serious setbacks at the hands of Daredevil, Fisk vowed revenge. His opportunity finally arrived when Matt Murdock's ex-girlfriend, Karen Page, revealed to a petty hood that the blind lawyer was actually Daredevil.

Where the heart is

The information passed through several underworld sources, moving up through the criminal food chain, before reaching the very top. With knowledge came power, but instead of attacking his enemy directly, Fisk spent the next few months slowly picking apart Murdock's carefully orchestrated life. He framed the lawyer for witness tampering and had him disbarred. Fisk then used his influence to have the IRS investigate Murdock for tax fraud and freeze all his bank accounts. With the hero at his lowest ebb both mentally and physically, Fisk delivered the coup de grâce—the destruction of Murdock's beloved brownstone. Murdock was left in shock as his castle was blown apart and reduced to a pile of rubble.

Homeless and left a broken man, Murdock sought refuge in Hell's Kitchen—his childhood neighborhood and location of Fogwell's Gym, where his father, "Battlin' Jack" Murdock had trained as a prize fighter. It was a spiritual homecoming as well as a literal one. Murdock was discovered at the gym by his estranged mother, Maggie. Now a nun, she took him in and nursed her son back to health.

From the gutters
While its upper stories touched the heavens, Fisk Towers was actually the product of underworld vice.
Daredevil #228, Mar. 1986

Fallen fortress
Wilson Fisk broke the hero and shattered his world when he blew up Daredevil's beloved brownstone home.
Daredevil #227, Feb. 1986

Shadow warriors
Luke Cage looked on in disbelief as Daredevil staked a claim to Hell's Kitchen with his brutal fortress, Shadowland. *Shadowland* #1, Sep. 2010

> **"I live in Hell's Kitchen and do my best to keep it clean."**
>
> Daredevil

Eventually, Murdock was able to strike back at Fisk. The former lawyer fed evidence of the villain's criminal activities to the press and, while it was not enough to convict the secret mobster, it dented his reputation. Fisk's tower of respectability had, at last, been undermined. For his part, Murdock was happy to make a new life for himself in Hell's Kitchen. Daredevil would no longer be an aloof knight, isolated behind stout stone walls, but part of the community he protected—a neighborhood hero.

From the shadows

This new resolve was tested when Daredevil took over the leadership of the Hand, an ancient clan of ninjas, thieves, and assassins that had been among his most implacable foes. He hoped to mold the army of killers into a force for good, but it wasn't the Hand that was changed. Daredevil slowly became darker, both in costume and temperament.

The tipping point arrived when the villain Bullseye blew up a city block in Hell's Kitchen, claiming the lives of 107 innocents. Daredevil responded by erecting Shadowland on the site of the destroyed buildings—a fortress from which he dispatched his ninjas to deliver harsh justice to even petty criminals. Wrongdoers who were lucky enough to survive an encounter with the Hand were caged without trial in Shadowland's subterranean dungeons.

All was not as it seemed, however, and it became apparent that Daredevil had been possessed by the Beast, a demonic entity worshipped by a faction of the Hand known as the Snakeroot Clan. As the Beast's influence grew, so did Daredevil's ruthlessness. In the end, the former assassin Elektra infiltrated Shadowland and—supported by a coalition of street-level heroes that included Luke Cage, Iron Fist, and Spider-Man—she fought to save Daredevil's blackened soul. As the battle raged, the Beast's power weakened and Daredevil was finally able to expunge the demon from his psyche.

Ironically, it was Wilson Fisk who proved to be the ultimate beneficiary of events. In the chaotic aftermath of the Shadowland incident, he expanded his criminal empire by subsuming the Hand into his own organization.

To the rescue
Daredevil's former lover Elektra breached the walls of Shadowland to save his soul from demon-worshiping ninjas. *Shadowland* #4, Dec. 2010

Magical site

While Daredevil and his crime-fighting cohorts were forced to confront the harsh realities of everyday street crime, Doctor Strange routinely faced evil of a far more esoteric nature. After studying under the beneficent Ancient One, former neurosurgeon Stephen Strange returned to his native New York as a Master of the Mystic Arts. He was drawn to Greenwich Village, which had long been a magnet for nonconformists and bohemians, where he purchased a three-story town house at 177A Bleecker Street. The building, which Strange referred to archly as his Sanctum Sanctorum, had long had a reputation for being haunted. This was because it had been constructed on a nexus of magical energy. Centuries before the arrival of European settlers, a Native American shaman had bound the chaos-entity Tyanon to the land on which the Sanctum Sanctorum would eventually sit.

Over the centuries, Tyanon had amassed vast quantities of mystical energy, although she was still powerless to escape her magical confinement. One of the first acts Doctor Strange performed upon moving into the building was exorcising Tyanon and securing his new home against similar mystical entities.

In many ways, the Sanctum Sanctorum was more than a physical location. Thanks to its unique history and Doctor Strange's magical presence, it acted as a gateway between the tangible world and the Mystic Realms that lay just beyond reach. It may have been physically located in Greenwich Village, but it existed in a hinterland between reality and unreality. A step through an upper-story doorway could very well be a step into the unknown. The seemingly mundane town house also served as a tangible anchor for Doctor Strange's physical form when he projected his astral body into the metaphysical void.

Bohemian façade
Behind the innocuous exterior of 177A Bleecker Street lay a secret world of mysticism.
Doctor Strange #2, Jan. 2016

Arcane artifacts

Naturally, over time, the Sanctum Sanctorum became a repository for Doctor Strange's vast array of arcane objects—a museum of magic in all but name. The third floor of the town house was where the most powerful objects were stored, including the all-seeing Orb of Agamotto and the ancient Book of the Vishanti, from which the sorcerer drew his most potent spells.

The Vishanti was a trinity of antediluvian sorcerers and they loomed large in Doctor Strange's life in more ways than one. Not only did he call upon them for eldritch wisdom, but he also used their mystical seal as a design motif in the Sanctum's upper-story window. The Window of the Worlds, as the sigil was sometimes called, drew power from the three ethereal beings and further bolstered Strange's occult defenses.

Doctor Strange's magical wards made sure that ordinary passersby didn't pay too much attention to his abode, but for those that required his aid in combating occult forces there was always a warm welcome. For a time, the house served as an impromptu headquarters for a loose coalition of outsider heroes known as the Defenders. Later, when Doctor Strange joined the Avengers, the Sanctum Sanctorum became a temporary headquarters for New York's premier Super Hero team.

Fellow travelers

Over and above Super Hero house guests, Stephen Strange shared his home and life with many different people—some were lovers and some were fellow mystics. Clea, who hailed from the Dark Dimension, proved to be both, and she remained at the sorcerer's side until circumstances drove the couple apart.

Wong, a follower of the Ancient One's teachings, was a fixture of the Bleecker Street mansion for the longest time. On the suggestion of his venerable master, the young monk had traveled to New York to aid Stephen Strange in his mission to defend humankind from the forces of darkness. While never a sorcerer himself, Wong was knowledgeable in the mystic arts, a highly skilled martial artist, and he proved invaluable as an aide-de-camp. He not only maintained the smooth running of the Sanctum Sanctorum but also ensured that Doctor Strange looked after himself as much as he did others.

Like many fellow travelers, Zelma Stanton first came to the Sanctum Sanctorum seeking a cure for a peculiar malady. A librarian from the Bronx, the young woman had been infected by Mind Maggots—parasitic creatures that would consume her life essence if left unchecked.

Sanctum sigil
Its design etched into an attic window, The Window of the Worlds' sigil empowered Doctor Strange's spells and helped protect the Sanctum Sanctorum from harm.
Marvel Tales: Doctor Strange #1, Jan. 2020

"Practicing the mystic arts in New York should be anything but dull."
Doctor Strange

Emergency surgery
Whenever eldritch beasts crossed over from their dark realms, Doctor Strange would cast them back and stitch up the wounds to reality.
Doctor Strange #1, Aug. 2018

What should have been a relatively easy consultation proved to be anything but when the highly agitated creatures abandoned Zelma to sow chaos throughout the Sanctum Sanctorum. They invaded the mystic library and began to consume the spells contained within the books. Left with no other option, Doctor Strange absorbed the manic pests into his own body, hoping his numerous mystical wards would inoculate him against any dangerous side effects. Zelma was cured completely and, recognizing her special sensitivity to the occult, Doctor Strange offered her a job as his librarian, which she happily accepted.

Brought to ruin

In her work, Zelma discovered that many of Doctor Strange's books were crumbling to dust or the incantations on the pages were mysteriously fading away. In a mystical sense, the ancient tomes were dying, as if beset by some strange ailment. It soon became apparent that the magical world was under assault from a formidable force known as the Empirikul, an extradimensional science-based cult hell-bent on eradicating sorcery from throughout the universe. In fact, it had been the Empirikul's slow movement through the magical dimensions that had earlier driven the Mind Maggots into such a frenzy and caused them to infect Zelma.

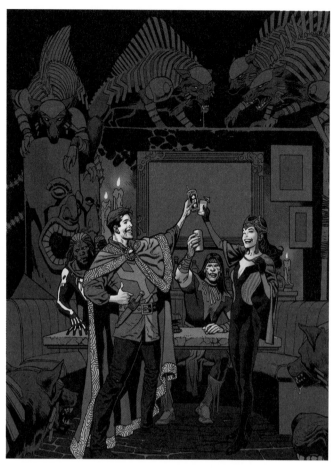

Sobering situation
Empirikul invaders dispatched Witchfinder Wolves to hunt down the mages at the Bar With No Doors.
Doctor Strange #4, Mar. 2016

Off the shelf
Doctor Strange's arcane grimoires seemingly had lives of their own until Zelma Stanton organized the chaotic library.
Doctor Strange #2, Jan. 2016

Strange responded to the threat by convening a war council at the Bar With No Doors. Traditionally, the venue was where sorcerers and mystics came together to socialize and escape the mundane world. Existing in a discrete dimension deep beneath New York City, the tavern could be accessed by magically stepping through a blank wall. Usually a hive of merriment—with barman Chondu struggling to keep up with the demands of his customers—the tavern now had a funereal atmosphere. Doctor Strange did his best to prepare his fellow magicians for what was about to happen, but calamity arrived all the same. The Empirikul army reached Earth, killing several magic users and destroying numerous icons of power. The Sanctum Sanctorum became the site of a huge battle in which the forces of magic were overrun by the forces of science.

With his home partially destroyed, Doctor Strange escaped the Empirikul, embarking on a worldwide quest to find Earth's few remaining artifacts of mystical power.

Power lines
Doctor Strange drew magical power directly from Earth's underground ley lines in an effort to expel the Empirikul.
Doctor Strange #6, May 2016

"Sanctum Sanctorum, which is Latin for 'Holy of Holies.'"
Zelma Stanton

Armed with these new weapons, he returned to the fight—seeking to expunge the Empirikul from his home. He was unexpectedly aided in this endeavor by a monstrous creation of his own making. Over the years, Doctor Strange had sustained many metaphysical injuries and his existential pain had coalesced into a physical being that became known as The Thing in the Cellar. The entity had spent decades alone in the dark, its bloated mass metastasizing as Strange suffered greater and greater deprivations. With the Sanctum Sanctorum in ruins, the creature was finally free to move into the light. Hostile and anxious to sow misery—to pass on its pain—it nevertheless joined forces with Doctor Strange to defeat the Empirikul. In the aftermath of the battle, the creature sloped off to find fresh purpose.

Later, now calling itself Mister Misery, the monster returned to bedevil Doctor Strange and his loved ones. It threatened to kill Wong and was stopped only when the Sorcerer Supreme absorbed its protoplasmic form into himself. For the first time in a long time, Doctor Strange shouldered the burden of his own terrible pain and anguish, accepting that his crusade came with a high price. In the aftermath of Mister Misery's defeat, Zelma and Wong set about helping Doctor Strange restore the Sanctum Sanctorum to its former glory.

Home for heroes

Avengers Mansion was situated only a few miles north of the Sanctum Sanctorum, but it might as well have been a world away. From the outside, Doctor Strange's town house was largely innocuous, just another old building tucked into a discreet corner of the city. The building that served as a headquarters for Earth's Mightiest Heroes was far from innocuous. Situated at 890 Fifth Avenue, right across from the green oasis of Central Park, it could not be missed.

The three-story mansion had first been commissioned by industrialist Howard Stark to serve as his New York residence. An opulent abode, it was the best that money could buy. Stark was a mover and shaker in the worlds of politics and science, and the house and its prime location spoke of his position as a global power broker. Originally intended as a family home, the mansion was repurposed when Tony Stark inherited it upon his father's death. As Iron Man, Tony was a founding member of the Avengers, and shortly after the team first came together, he refashioned the building into Avengers Mansion, providing a permanent base of operations for the team.

While the upper stories remained largely unchanged, the building's substructure was excavated to allow for multiple additional basements. The most significant change occurred about a year after the Avengers moved in, when Thor and Iron Man pushed the building back from Fifth Avenue to allow for more extensive grounds and greater privacy. As the Avengers roster expanded, a statue of the original members was erected in the gardens—a visual reminder of the team's founding principle that like-minded heroes should pool their resources to meet the gravest of threats. Eventually, the team received UN endorsement and the mansion was granted special embassy status. The Avengers was thus confirmed as the world's foremost Super Hero organization.

Monumental marvels
As the Avengers roster grew, a statue to honor the founding members was erected in the grounds of Avengers Mansion. *Avengers* #1, Feb. 1998

First class service
Iron Man, Ant-Man, The Wasp, Thor, Hulk and teenager Rick Jones, were the first Avengers to be served by butler Edwin Jarvis. *Avengers: Earth's Mightiest Heroes* #1, Jan. 2005

Moving in day
Like many heroes before him, Luke Cage made
Avengers Mansion his family home, moving in with
his wife, Jessica Jones, and daughter Danielle.
New Avengers #1, Aug. 2010

Along with a mansion, came a butler. Edwin
Jarvis originally worked for the Stark family,
and when the new residents moved into 890 Fifth
Avenue, he continued to serve, only now he
looked after numerous gods, monsters, androids,
and mutants—an ever-revolving cast of colorful
individuals, each with their own special
requirements. The heroes came and went, but
Jarvis was a permanent fixture. His ostensible role
may have been domestic, but his commitment
to the team was as strong as any of the Super
Heroes. When the Masters of Evil invaded the
mansion, Jarvis was beaten savagely, but he
refused to retire despite his many injuries.

Rebuilt

The attack by the Masters of Evil left Avengers
Mansion in disarray, and it was deemed sensible
for the team to relocate to Hydrobase, a floating
artificial island located nine miles from New York.

It quickly became clear, however, that Avengers
Mansion was much more than a headquarters.
It was a public symbol of the team, and, more
importantly, it was a place where the heroes
could come together to relax—somewhere to
simply enjoy each other's company and briefly
escape the rigors of their demanding occupations.
Just as Howard Stark had always hoped, the
mansion had become a beloved family home.

Even when the building was later destroyed by
the villain Proctor, it was replaced by an identical
replica from an alternative-reality Earth. This new
version served the Avengers well until a schism
within the ranks blew apart the team and sent the
walls of Avengers Mansion tumbling to the ground.

Wanda Maximoff, aka Scarlet Witch, was one of
the Avengers' longest-serving and most powerful
team members. In fact, she and her husband, the
synthezoid Vision, had been permanent residents
of the mansion for much of their time together.

> **"It was the best money I ever spent (on Avengers Mansion)."**
>
> Iron Man (Tony Stark)

Theirs was a fairy-tale romance, their love blossoming as they shared a home and grew to know each other as individuals and not merely teammates. Unfortunately, their story took a dark turn when the Scarlet Witch suffered a total nervous breakdown. Following the tragic loss of her children, she became increasingly unstable, losing control of her reality-warping powers. In her madness and blind rage, she struck out at the Avengers—conjuring up all manner of dire threats to send against them. Her destructive spree reached a crescendo when she took control of the Vision and forced him to crash a Quinjet into Avengers Mansion. The building was almost completely destroyed as a result, and the Founders Statue was left in pieces. Similarly shattered was the team's heroic resolve. The Scarlet Witch's machinations had left many of the heroes traumatized, and they voted unanimously to disband the team. What was left of Avengers Mansion would be shuttered and closed, and the world's foremost Super Heroes would all go their separate ways.

The big bang
The Scarlet Witch gave vent to her anguish and brought down the walls of Avengers Mansion with her magical powers.
Avengers #500, Sep. 2004

" ... those vulgarians had the audacity to foul the mansion with their presence. "

Jarvis

Honored heroes
Following the decision to disband the Avengers, New Yorkers came out en masse to honor their heroes.
Avengers: Finale #1, Jan. 2005

Lightning strike
Electro struck at the maximum-security Raft prison, prompting
a mass breakout of Super Villains from the island facility.
New Avengers #1 Jan. 2005

From the ashes

Perhaps inevitably, circumstances brought the team back together—
or at least a similar grouping of heroes. The New Avengers picked
up where the original team left off, and according to Captain
America, it was the unfathomable workings of fate that brought
the new squad together at precisely the right moment.

The Raft, a maximum-security prison for super-powered criminals,
was located on a small island a few miles offshore from Manhattan.
Run under the auspices of S.H.I.E.L.D., it was supposedly a state-
of-the-art detention facility. However, the super-charged villain
Electro easily circumvented the security systems, precipitating
a mass breakout. Heroes in the area, including Captain America,
Iron Man, Spider-Man, and Luke Cage, responded to the crisis.
Coordinating their efforts, they managed to corral 45 escaped
villains. Inspired by this remarkable achievement, Captain America
encouraged the disparate heroes to form the New Avengers.

The freshly forged team made Stark Tower, situated in the vicinity
of Manhattan's Columbus Circle, its headquarters. The gleaming
beacon of modern architecture had been created to be a personal
residence, but once again a Stark building was repurposed as a
welcoming and fully equipped home for heroes. Jarvis was even
recalled into service to help things run smoothly.

Tower of power
Tony Stark's apartment complex in the
newly built Stark Tower became the HQ
for the freshly formed New Avengers.
Siege #4, Jun. 2010

High Court action
When not besting villains, She-Hulk used her legal prowess to represent heroes like Valkyrie in court.
She-Hulk #7, Nov. 2004

Avengers reassembled
A remodeled Founders Statue showcased many reserve members of the Avengers.
Avengers #690, Jun. 2018

Justice served

As with the original team, the ranks of the New Avengers swelled with numerous heroes making use of the tower's luxurious living quarters. One resident was Jennifer Walters, aka the gamma-powered She-Hulk. With a deserved reputation as something of a party animal, She-Hulk frequently took advantage of her team privileges and brought unannounced guests to the tower. This presented a security risk and added further to the burdens placed upon an already overworked Jarvis. Events finally came to a head and, at Jarvis's urging, She-Hulk was asked to move out.

With her possessions packed into the trunk of her car, She-Hulk found herself on the streets of New York with her access to the Avengers' funds temporarily suspended. A solution to her plight came when she was hired to work for Goodman, Lieber, Kurtzberg & Holliway (GLK&H), a Manhattan-based legal company specializing in the field of superhuman law. It wasn't She-Hulk's Super Hero connections that made her an attractive hire, however, but Jennifer Walter's brilliant legal mind—and she went on to make a vital contribution to the firm. GLK&H represented numerous superhumans in court, defending them from libel and other claims. Their cases often transcended earthly jurisdictions and She-Hulk frequently found herself working for the Time Variance Authority or as an adjudicator for the omniversal being known as the Living Tribunal.

In many ways, She-Hulk's new role made her a typical Manhattanite. Here she was, struggling to meet the needs of a demanding career on top of her existing commitments. She even had a daily commute to navigate, from the company-provided apartment in Atlas Towers to the GLK&H head office at Timely Plaza. Perhaps more than any other Avenger, She-Hulk grew to understand the daily demands of living—and working—in a modern metropolitan city.

All together

The New Avengers were not the only heroes to fill the void created when the original team was dissolved. The Young Avengers, a band of heroic prodigies and protégés, stepped up to play their part. Inspired by those who had gone before them, they donned costumes of their own and ventured out to make a difference. Their commitment to continuing the legacy of the Avengers was unwavering and they even repaired the broken Founders Statue in the grounds of the abandoned Avengers Mansion. The meaning was clear: what was once broken should be restored. The message struck home and, over time, the New Avengers morphed back into a global organization with many divisions.

> **"It's not the first time our beloved mansion has been destroyed."**
>
> Jarvis

While some Avengers remained in Stark Tower, others returned to a restored mansion. Eventually, it became headquarters to the Avengers Unity Division—a squad with several former X-Men, such as Rogue and Havok, serving as members.

When two Elders of the Universe, the Grandmaster and the Challenger, chose Earth as the location for their latest gladiatorial combat, Avengers Mansion was hit hard once again. It was partly destroyed by the competing aliens, but this didn't stop the Avengers from rallying the team's reserve members and going on to win the day. In the aftermath, the Founders Statue was remodeled to feature the likenesses of all the triumphant heroes. In Jarvis's words, "Like the Founders Statue … being recast and rededicated, we take important parts of our legacy and use it to forge the future."

City living

For decades, Super Heroes have been drawn to Manhattan by fate and circumstances and an abiding commitment to protect the innocent and make the world a better place. The city's story is the heroes' story. Individual triumphs and tragedies are seen reflected in the ever-changing architecture and buildings. The heroes, like their residences and headquarters, have frequently been knocked down, but they inevitably get back up again. Earth's Super Hero Central is always evolving, but the ideals on which it stands are constant—rock solid. Manhattan is as strong as the K-bracing used to reinforce the iconic Baxter Building, as indomitable as the heroes who call it home. ▪

Island heroes
Spider-Man is just one of Manhattan's many tireless defenders who have saved the city countless times.
Ultimate End #1, Jul. 2015

Battlefield Earth

The mass breakout at the Raft detention facility was just the first of many destabilizing events orchestrated by the Skrulls as part of a secret invasion of Earth. The extraterrestrials had replaced influential world leaders and, hidden in plain sight thanks to their shape-shifting abilities, they sowed discord and precipitated a Super Hero civil war that tore the Avengers apart. Now believing Earth to be helpless, the technologically advanced aliens finally stepped out of the shadows.

The Skrulls had underestimated their foes, however, and Iron Man and Captain America set aside their differences to rally the heroes of New York City in defense of the entire planet. The stakes were so high that many Super Villains were also called up to help turn back the tide of alien invaders. Fittingly, the final battle took place on the rolling fields of Manhattan's Central Park, close to the honored site of Avengers Mansion. Iron Man led the charge against the massed Skrull army with a rousing cry of "Avengers assemble!" There was no doubt who would emerge triumphant at the end of the day.

Water world
of Vodan

Orreki Reefs

Time and Tide

One of the oldest civilizations on Earth sits at the bottom of the sea. Atlantis has endured much hardship over the centuries, overwhelmed by the relentless tides of history and buffeted by the cruel currents of fate. Can it ever reclaim its former glory?

Sunken Atlantis

Settlement of
the Sea Blades

Fabled Atlantis represented the pinnacle of human achievement in ancient times. In an era when much of the globe was under the heel of the monstrous Deviants, the continent functioned as a living library that preserved much of humanity's cultural and scientific heritage. Although it was sent crashing to the ocean floor, Atlantis survived the seismic event precipitated by the Great Cataclysm of 18,000 BCE. Miraculously, it was not only the continent's robust architecture that endured but also some of its inhabitants. A fraction of Atlanteans survived the upheaval, their bodies adapting so that they could live in an aquatic environment. What ultimately precipitated this change is unknown. Some believe it to be the result of arcane sorcery, while others speculate that advanced science was responsible for the mutation. What is certain is that the Atlanteans came into contact with natural water-breathers soon after finding themselves adrift in the Atlantic Ocean.

The Vodani was a band of aquatic extraterrestrials who had traveled some years earlier to Earth's seas through a portal from the water world of Vodan. The two peoples interacted extensively and, from this intermingling, a new race was born—*Homo mermanus*. This emergent species was instinctively nomadic, spreading out across the vast seabed, forming countless small tribes and establishing numerous underwater principalities. Centuries after this first migration, a band of nomadic barbarians returned to the submerged ruins of Atlantis. They established a permanent settlement on the site and restored many of the damaged buildings. They embraced the philosophy and science-based culture of their forebears. They referred to each other as Atlanteans and saw themselves as inheritors of a historically important legacy.

Capital city
Rebuilt by descendants of its original inhabitants, Atlantis became the economic and political powerhouse of a vast undersea kingdom.
Namor #4, Aug. 2003

Creature comforts
Atlanteans frequently commanded undersea creatures to do their bidding, employing monstrous leviathans to help create ever more lavish buildings.
Namor #12, May 2004

When still on the surface, Atlantis had been an early flowering of human civilization, a progressive and forward-looking culture. Now in the hands of its new custodians, Atlantis became the hub of a complex and ever-evolving undersea kingdom. In many ways, this was the original sin of the underwater Atlanteans. From the very beginning of their society, they harked back to a lost time, hoping against hope that the great promise of Atlantis—that which had been so spectacularly washed away by the tumult of the Great Cataclysm—could, at last, be fulfilled.

Sunken treasures

Some 500 years after the resettlement, a group of *Homo mermanus* left the city of Atlantis to establish a colony in Lemuria, another continental civilization submerged during the Great Cataclysm. These Lemurians, as they came to call themselves, discovered the Serpent Crown—a magical icon empowered by the malign Elder God Set—in the ruins of their new home. Exposure to the crown's mystical energies made the Lemurians more serpentlike in appearance than their Atlantean cousins.

Water-breathing barbarians constantly viewed Atlantis with a jealous eye, and over the centuries, they sent raiding parties to plunder the city's resources. An attack by a force from the undersea dominion of Skarka was successfully repelled by a young prince named Thakorr, but the battle left the city in a ruinous state. When he ascended to the throne as emperor, Thakorr organized a second migration from Atlantis, leading his people on a long journey to Antarctica, where they established a new home beneath the protective ice shelf. This second city grew to rival the original Atlantis in scale and splendor, its political influence extending far across the ocean floors to guarantee the safety of nomadic tribes like the Chasm People, who followed long-established seasonal migration routes from the frigid Arctic seas to the bountiful Orreki Reefs in the Pacific Ocean.

Luminescent wonder
The sunken city of Atlantis was a bright light in the inky-black depths of the ocean, the last remnant of one of the greatest civilizations on Earth.
Nick Fury #4, Sep. 2017

Bridging the chasm
A youthful Prince Namor was part of a diplomatic mission to greet the nomadic Chasm People as they arrived to spend the summer at the Orreki Reefs.
King in Black: Namor #1, Feb. 2021

Atlanteans had little contact with their human cousins for millennia, although rare sightings of *Homo mermanus* inspired sailors to regale any who would listen with colorful tales about sirens and aquatic merpeople. In the early 20th century, an encounter between ocean explorer Leonard McKenzie and Thakorr's inquisitive daughter, Princess Fen, led to romance, marriage, and the birth of a hybrid human-Atlantean child named Namor, who was also one of the world's earliest mutants. The product of two very different worlds, the young prince was never really at home in either. He had few close comrades while growing up, save for a young prince of the Chasm People called Attuma. In time, though, their friendship soured and Attuma became an implacable foe.

Thanks to his dual heritage, Namor was looked upon with suspicion by his fellow Atlanteans. What's more, he was taught by Emperor Thakorr and other members of the royal court to distrust surface dwellers. Headstrong and willful, he disobeyed his grandfather's edicts and journeyed to the surface world to investigate humankind's intentions for himself. There, he was met with paranoia and outright fear, condemned by the press as the "savage" Sub-Mariner. Living up to his name, which meant

The crown couple
Revered for finding a new home for their aquatic people, Emperor Thakorr and the crimson-clad Queen Korra were stern grandparents to a young Prince Namor.
Namor #11 , Mar. 2004

"avenging son" in Atlantean, Namor responded in kind. He attacked New York City but was rebuffed by the android Human Torch in the first of many clashes between the two powerful individuals. Recognizing a fellow outcast, the Torch eventually extended the hand of friendship, and the two formed an unlikely bond that ultimately led to Namor's decision to support the Allies against the Axis powers as a member of the Invaders Super Hero squad.

Helping secure victory in World War II brought an opportunity for Atlantis to at last take its rightful place among the leading nations of the world. A petition to join the United Nations—personally delivered by Namor—was declined, however, with the United States and the Soviet Union too preoccupied by their emerging Cold War rivalry to give the matter careful consideration.

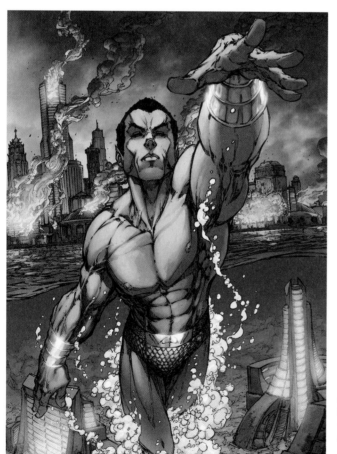

Land and sea
A human-Atlantean hybrid, Namor struggled to find his true place in the world—caught, as it were, between the surface world and the sea.
Sub-Mariner #1, Aug. 2007

Elemental foes

The aquatic Sub-Mariner and the fiery Human Torch clashed in the skies above New York City when they first met in the late 1930s.
The Marvels Project #6, Apr. 2010

Day of destiny

In response to this slight, Atlantis became even more isolationist. Tricked into believing Namor cared more about the surface world than Atlantis, Emperor Thakorr banished his grandson from the undersea kingdom. Shortly after this, Namor encountered the villain Destiny, a human telepath who used the Lemurian Serpent Crown to amplify his formidable mental abilities. Drawing on the crown's eldritch powers, Destiny was able to precipitate seismic tremors and he tested this newfound power on Atlantis—causing mass panic and destroying much of the city. He also used the Serpent Crown to cloud Namor's mind, to wipe away the Atlantean's memories and leave him adrift in a fog of uncertainty. Thanks to Destiny's power, the last thing Namor witnessed before succumbing completely to amnesia, was an image of Atlantis falling to ruin, with Emperor Thakorr crushed among the rubble.

Namor wandered the world aimlessly for many years until a chance encounter with the Fantastic Four's Human Torch awakened his repressed memories. He immediately returned to Atlantis only to find the city deserted. Further investigations revealed that the waters had been contaminated by radioactive fallout. "The humans did it, unthinkingly, with their accursed atomic tests," Namor concluded.

The Prince of Atlantis was now consumed by a terrible rage, a tsunami of anger bubbling up to overwhelm him just as it had when he first encountered surface dwellers years earlier. He was appalled that the Atlanteans had been driven from their undersea capital yet again, that a culture that had sustained itself for so long against such overwhelming odds was once more on the precipice of disaster. And he feared that he might never be able to find his people in the seemingly endless expanse of Earth's oceans.

New Atlantis

When Atlanteans were forced from their underwater city by the sorceress Morgan le Fay, many found sanctuary in Utopia, a mutant homeland established in San Francisco Bay by the X-Men. The artificial island was unstable, however, so Namor agreed to help build an enormous support pillar that would prevent the sinking of Utopia and also serve as a new home for his scattered people.

The world was growing darker by the day, with villains like Norman Osborn exploiting schisms within the Super Hero community to increase their hold on organizations such as S.H.I.E.L.D. In response, Namor believed an alliance with the X-Men would be prudent for both parties.

New Atlantis was not to last, however, and the refuge shared the same fate as the city for which it was named—washed away during a calamitous war between the X-Men and the Avengers. In the immediate aftermath of that conflict, as his people scattered across the ocean floor once more, Namor remained behind in the ruins of New Atlantis, mourning the loss of his kingdom.

Namor swore vengeance on humanity, and using an ancient trumpet to stir it from the depths, he unleashed a monstrous leviathan called Giganto upon New York City. This was the first in a series of attacks on the surface world, many of which were rebuffed by Super Heroes like the Fantastic Four.

Rising tensions

Even after finding his lost people and establishing a new capital city in the Atlantic Ocean, Namor seethed with righteous indignation, ultimately launching a full-scale invasion of the surface world. He was repelled yet again, but the incident confirmed Atlantis's outlaw status. Ostracized by the leading nations of the world, the undersea kingdom was forced to seek allies elsewhere.

"I am king of a fallen kingdom."

Namor

Coming ashore
At his most belligerent, Namor would lead raiding parties on land to discourage commercial exploitation of the seas.
The Torch #4, Feb. 2010

Tsunami warning
Over the years, Namor frequently threatened to wash away cities like New York in a tidal wave of destruction.
The Marvels Project #6, Apr. 2010

Latveria, a tiny European nation under the heel of the tyrannical Doctor Doom, became an unlikely advocate for Atlantis on the world stage. Having first joined forces with Doctor Doom against the Fantastic Four, only to find himself betrayed, Namor had no illusions about the armored despot's true nature, but he realized Atlantis could not thrive in the modern world without powerful allies. However, tensions eased following Namor's decision to join the ranks of the Avengers, and relations between Atlantis and the surface world slowly improved. Suspicion always lurked just below the surface, though, and Namor grew increasingly frustrated and angered at what he saw as humanity's contemptuous disregard for the natural world.

Rogue conglomerates like the Roxxon Energy Corporation continued to plunder the seas of natural resources with no care for international law or the environmental degradation they left behind. Namor finally snapped, and he formed the Defenders of the Deep—a team of formidable undersea warriors that included the likes of the Atlanteans Orka and Andromeda—to act as a strike force to drive surface dwellers from the world's oceans completely. Inevitably, this led to a clash with the Avengers and an even further rise in tensions between Atlantis and the leading countries of the world, particularly the United States of America.

Namor's reckless actions had branded Atlantis an outlaw nation once again: a great civilization brought to its nadir by its ruler's unremitting anger and hubris. Anticipating the worst, yet still refusing to accept any personal culpability, Namor planned for all-out war with the surface world. Seeking to bolster his armed forces, he accessed a spatial anomaly located in a trench in the Pacific Ocean known as the Mindanao Deep and traveled to the extraterrestrial water world of Vodan. There he asked King Okun to pledge his people to the Atlantean cause. The Vodani had vowed never to return to Earth, however, and they rebuffed the Atlantean's entreaties, forcibly expelling him from their aquatic realm.

Alien waters
On the water world of Vodan, Namor found an advocate in Princess Kataw, but his plea for a military alliance was rejected by King Okun.
Namor: The Best Defense #1, Feb. 2019

> "Sadly, Atlantis is used to military strikes."
>
> **Captain America (Steve Rogers)**

Back on Earth, Namor turned elsewhere for help and found enthusiastic allies in the form of underwater pirates like the notoriously violent Sea Blades. Such raw recruits helped swell the ranks of the Atlantean army to a size never before seen in the history of the undersea kingdom.

Mind games

With Namor evermore belligerent, war seemed inevitable. Events reached a boiling point when Atlantis launched a missile strike on a sleepy coastal town in the northeastern US state of Maine. Instead of carrying explosive ordnance, however, the bombs delivered a chemical compound that

transformed 3,000 individuals into water-breathers. In the face of global outrage, Namor argued that he had delivered a great boon to humanity. So long as they pledged allegiance to him, he offered the newly aquatic people permanent sanctuary in Atlantis. He went on to promise free access to his mutagenic formula, suggesting it was humanity's only way to escape the inevitable consequences of global warming and rising sea levels.

Namor's wartime comrades from the Invaders, including Captain America, reached out to their old friend but were met with open hostility and resentment. Ultimately, their investigations revealed that Namor was suffering from a deep-rooted psychosis that was the result of PTSD sustained during the war. During his time as a wandering amnesiac, Namor had been approached by fellow mutant, Professor Charles Xavier. The powerful telepath had sensed the Atlantean's distress and he hoped to ease his mental suffering. He built psychic constructs within Namor's mind that took on the form of Tommy Machan, a close friend of Namor who had been killed during the war. While this had been intended to bring comfort, it served only to traumatize Namor anew. Xavier had hoped the Machan construct would act as an inner voice of reason, but over time, that voice

Plunder palaces
Defecting from the Atlantean army, the Sea Blades became pirates, amassing stolen treasure in their beautiful city.
Invaders #1, Mar. 2019

became ever more bellicose. In fact, it was Machan's malign influence that had caused Namor to act so irrationally and aggressively over the years.

With his control slipping away, Machan tracked down the Serpent Crown and used its power to escape Namor's mind and assume control of a former naval officer named Roman Peterson. Now able to operate freely in the corporeal world, Machan set in motion a desperate plan to wipe away the surface world forever. Using a device built by Atlantean scientists, he drew water from distant Vodan to create a deluge of biblical proportions—a flood reminiscent of the Great Cataclysm of ancient times. However, with the help of his old allies from the Invaders, Namor defeated Machan and successfully turned back the tide.

Underwater warfare
Atlantis's unprovoked attack on a coastal town led to a retaliatory strike from Iron Man and Captain Marvel, which failed to breach the underwater city's force field.
Invaders #5, Jul. 2019

> "I will do anything for my people ...
> I have to do anything for them."
>
> Namor

With the immediate crisis averted, Namor returned to his sunken realm. Sitting upon his briny throne, he appeared an isolated king of an isolated kingdom. Yet again, the rest of the world viewed Atlantis with fear and suspicion. While it was an undoubted tragedy that Atlantis had been sent crashing to the ocean floor in ancient times, it was perhaps an even greater tragedy that the Atlanteans had failed to reverse their fortunes in the many years that had followed. An age-old civilization with a powerful advocate in the form of King Namor, Atlantis had nevertheless failed repeatedly to cast off the chains of history, to escape from the ocean's inky-black depths, to reclaim its rightful place in the sun. ◾

Kingdom of one
His ambitions thwarted by his own rash decisions and reckless actions, King Namor cut a lonely figure on the throne of Atlantis.
Invaders #12, Feb. 2020

Up from the depths

The brainchild of oceanographer Walter Newell, who sometimes operated as the aquatic hero Stingray, Hydropolis was an undersea biosphere located in the Pacific Ocean. It was designed to promote peace and understanding between humans and Atlanteans, a neutral venue where leaders and scientists could meet and exchange ideas. However, when the Sub-Mariner launched a fresh assault on the surface world, the dream of peaceful coexistence was shattered. Namor formed the team Defenders of the Deep and led them in a direct assault on the facility.

Created as an underwater counterpart to the Avengers, Namor's squad was comprised of former villains Orka, Tiger Shark, Echidna, and Bloodtide. They were supported by the Atlantean warrior Andromeda and the monstrous King Crab. These disparate individuals all shared an abiding, passionate devotion to the preservation of their undersea kingdom. As the Defenders of the Deep rampaged through Hydropolis, Namor raised the domelike structure from the bottom of the sea. It was clear that the time for diplomacy with the surface world was over. "The oceans of Earth are hereby off-limits," proclaimed an enraged Sub-Mariner.

Bast's Bounty

Blessed with an abundance of natural resources and protected by the panther goddess Bast, the small African nation of Wakanda thrived while its neighbors frequently struggled. In modern times, King T'Challa finally took the brave decision to share his country's material and cultural wealth with the rest of the world.

In a time lost to legend, the land that would become known as Wakanda was home to several species of mythical beasts known collectively as the Originators. These creatures lived in harmony with the natural world, but their idyll was disturbed when human settlers arrived to cultivate the region. The two groups lived in peace for a time, but when the humans started mistreating the land—taking more from it than they were willing to put back—war broke out. As violence escalated, formidable warriors emerged to battle the mighty Originators. Empowered by the faith of their fellow humans, these individuals were transformed into the Orisha, the Gods of Wakanda. The Orisha tipped the scales of battle in favor of the humans, and the Originators were eventually overpowered and banished to an extradimensional netherworld.

Of all the Orisha, the panther goddess Bast was perhaps the most protective of her human followers. In exchange for their unquestioning devotion, she shared her mystical power and offered practical and spiritual guidance. One human in particular caught the attention of Bast. Bashenga was a formidable hunter, a unifying figure in the slowly emerging kingdom of Wakanda. When a huge meteor fell to Earth, Bashenga was among the first to investigate the crash site. He discovered the meteor was made from a strange vibrating material, the radiation from which transformed people into monstrous creatures. Bashenga prayed to Bast to give him the strength necessary to defeat these newly formed "demons" and the goddess anointed him as the first Black Panther since prehistoric times. Donning ceremonial panther robes—and empowered by Bast—Bashenga slew the monsters and then went on to fully unite the peoples of Wakanda. His lineage—women and men of the fabled Black Panther Cult—would rule the country for centuries.

JABARI-
LANDS

Birnin T'Chaka

MOHANNDA

Birnin Djata

Warrior Falls

Birnin Bashenga

Necropolis

Birnin Zana

Nyanza (Lake Victoria)

Mena Ngai (The Great Mound)

CANAAN

Birnin Azzaria

Birnin S'Yan

Alkama Fields

AZANIA

NIGANDA

Big cat country
Wakanda became a culturally rich and scientifically advanced nation
under the watchful gaze of the fearsome panther goddess, Bast.
Killmonger #3, Mar. 2019

The Great Mound

The meteor crash forever changed the destiny of Wakanda. It tore up the landscape, leaving a great mound of earth in its wake. Thanks to the unique circumstances of its creation, this new mountain was laced with an otherworldly substance—a metallic ore that would be classified as Vibranium in modern times. Bashenga and the Wakandans soon discovered that Vibranium had many practical uses. It could be mined to be used as weapons and its peculiarly conductive properties meant it had numerous industrial and medical applications.

As well as being revered as a sacred site, the Great Mound, or Mena Ngai, became a catalyst for an unprecedented cultural shift. Harnessing the power of Vibranium, Wakanda developed advanced science and technology many years before other countries. The spectacular Golden City, or Birnin Zana, was established as the nation's capital, with many other regional cities sprouting up such as Birnin Bashenga in the west and Birnin S'Yan in the south. What's more, Vibranium also altered the ecology of Wakanda. The mineral seeped into the vegetation, mutating a particular locally grown herb so that it gave Bashenga's descendants enhanced powers of strength, speed, and agility when they consumed it. Potential rulers would imbibe an infusion of the Heart-Shaped Herb as their final ceremonial act before assuming the throne and donning the mantle of the Black Panther.

Fearing outsiders would seek to exploit Vibranium for corrupt purposes, Wakandans pursued an avowedly isolationist policy. They hid in plain sight, closing their borders to other nations, and when they did show themselves to the world, they made sure they appeared to be impoverished tribespeople. Protective force fields and sophisticated holographic projections were used to further enhance the illusion. Rarely did Wakanda share its resources with the outside world, but during World War II, the then-reigning Black Panther, King Azzuri, gifted a small amount of Vibranium to Captain America so that the hero could forge his indestructible shield and go on to help save the world from tyranny. For the most part, though, Wakanda jealously guarded its secret treasures, content to remain ever apart in the protective embrace of the goddess Bast and her Orisha brethren.

Good vibrations
In ancient times, a huge meteor crash in Wakanda and left behind deposits of the remarkable mineral known as Vibranium.
Black Panther #7, Jan. 1978

City of tomorrow
Birnin Zana, selected as the kingdom's capital city and the seat of the Black Panther's power, was an urban paradise centuries ahead of its time.
Black Panther: World of Wakanda #6 Jun. 2017

Modern times

Decades after Azzuri's passing, his grandson, T'Challa, was expected to inherit the kingdom. Having been educated overseas, the prince was less religiously devout and more at ease in the outside world than any of his predecessors. When he finally ascended the throne—and assumed the mantle of the Black Panther—he decided to open up Wakanda to the rest of the world. Inspired by his grandfather's friendship with Captain America and intrigued by the proliferation of new Super Heroes— particularly those in the United States of America—T'Challa invited the Fantastic Four to Wakanda. He did this to learn firsthand about their heroic mission and to test his own mettle in combat against super-powered opponents. T'Challa came close to defeating the Fantastic Four until the heroes were helped to victory by their companion Wyatt Wingfoot. Despite the unorthodox introduction, T'Challa and the Fantastic Four become close friends and allies— with the Black Panther later serving as a member of the team when Reed and Sue Richards temporarily stepped back from active duty.

On one of his missions abroad, T'Challa fought alongside Captain America and was nominated to take his place in the Avengers when Cap took a leave of absence from the team. The Avengers became T'Challa's second family, a band of sisters and brothers who shared his heroic ideals and in whose company he could briefly let go of the burdens of statecraft and simply enjoy the powers and abilities of the Black Panther. This caused some in Wakanda to grumble that T'Challa was neglecting his sacred duties, that the king had abandoned his kingdom. Inevitably, the tethers

Leaving home
Believing his people had much to offer the rest of the world, T'Challa frequently ventured beyond the borders of Wakanda.
Black Panther: The Sound and the Fury #1, Apr. 2018

"Since the time of Bashenga, we've controlled our destiny as few other nations have."

Black Panther (T'Challa)

of leadership always drew T'Challa back to his ancestral lands. In a very real sense, the king could never truly escape the great pull of Wakandan history—and the obligations it placed upon him.

Located near Lake Nyanza, outside of Birnin Zana, Necropolis was a city of ancient mausoleums—the place where Wakandans had entombed their fallen leaders since the time of Bashenga. It was also a conduit to Bast's mystical realm and, because of this, the spirits of deceased Black Panthers were able to use Necropolis as a gateway to cross back to the material plane. These dead queens and kings formed a spiritual council that was only too willing to give T'Challa advice or to admonish him if they felt he had strayed too far from Bast's teachings. They were a link to Wakanda's rich cultural history and a reminder to T'Challa that he was only the latest in a long line of rulers.

Access all areas
Necropolis was generally closed to outsiders, but King T'Challa gave the Fantastic Four's Reed Richards a rare tour of the decrepit city.
Fantastic Four #608, Sep. 2012

Sound and fury

As Wakanda slowly opened up to the world, new threats emerged. While T'Challa was happy for his country to take a constructive role in world affairs—he accepted a seat in the United Nations General Assembly—he followed in the footsteps of his forebears and refused to share the secrets of Vibranium. Historically, this refusal had prompted unscrupulous individuals to take matters into their own hands. One such person was Ulysses Klaue, whose father had learned about the secret energy source during World War II. An outlaw physicist, Klaue believed it would enable him to build a vast arsenal of sonic weapons. He plotted incessantly to invade Wakanda and his first assault proved deadly. T'Challa's father, T'Chaka, was killed during the violent incursion, and although Klaue escaped, his brazen act cost him dearly. As he retreated, his right hand was broken beyond repair by a warrior's spear.

Spiritual inquisition
T'Challa was frequently asked to justify his actions by the spirits of his ancestors—the Black Panthers who had ruled Wakanda in the past.
New Avengers #18, Jul. 2014

Fallen son
Killmonger felt betrayed by Wakanda and sought to usurp
T'Challa's rule, even challenging the king to ritual combat
at Warrior Falls. *Killmonger* #1, Feb. 2019

Some years later, Klaue returned to Wakanda with a sonic converter device. When the weapon proved useless against the kingdom's defenses, Klaue used its energies to turn himself into a being of living sound. Brandishing a sonic emitter in place of his shattered hand, he took the name Klaw and embarked on a campaign to depose King T'Challa and steal Wakanda's Vibranium.

While Klaw sought to plunder Wakanda, a man named Erik Killmonger sought to conquer it—to turn the kingdom from the benevolent path it had been following during T'Challa's reign. Born N'Jadaka, Erik Killmonger was a Wakandan boy who was orphaned during Klaue's initial attack on his country. He was snatched from his homeland by one of Klaue's mercenary accomplices and raised outside of Wakanda's borders, cut off from the land of his ancestors and the benevolence of Bast that was his birthright.

Believing he had been abandoned to a cruel fate by an uncaring nation, Erik seethed with anger and resentment. In the end, he slew his abductor and set off to forge a new life for himself in the West.

After graduating from the Massachusetts Institute of Technology with several science and engineering degrees, Erik Killmonger spent time as an underworld operative— learning the deadly martial arts skills he would need to make his fellow Wakandans pay in blood for their seeming indifference to his pain. During this time, he was visited in his dreams by K'Liluna, the forgotten Wakandan goddess of war. K'Liluna was Bast's sister, cast out of the Orisha centuries earlier for advocating unending conflict between Wakanda and its less powerful neighbors. Now she appeared before Erik Killmonger and recruited him as her avatar, urging him to sow chaos in her name.

When T'Challa announced Wakanda's existence to the world, Erik Killmonger embraced the opportunity to finally return to his homeland. He was met with open arms by his king and was promised a bright future as a member of the country's scientific community. From his position of privilege, Erik Killmonger plotted to turn Wakanda's largely defensive weapons against the rest of the world. He failed in the attempt, however, and escaped justice by fleeing across the border. He would return time and again to plot the overthrow of King T'Challa. On one occasion, the foes fought a bitter battle at the site of the majestic Warrior Falls—a natural arena that had long served as the venue for ritual challenges to the Black Panther's authority. Erik's seeming victory was short lived, however, and T'Challa soon reclaimed his throne.

> "We are Wakandans, the only unconquered warriors on this planet."
>
> Erik Killmonger (N'Jadaka)

Tumultuous times

Despite T'Challa's best intentions, Wakanda inevitably became embroiled in global power politics. The Latverian monarch Doctor Doom fomented a coup by Wakandan extremists as cover for a bid to steal 10,000 tons of Vibranium from Wakanda's national vault.

The takeover was initially successful, but T'Challa's sister, Shuri—who was serving as queen regent during one of her brother's longer absences— swiftly regained control of the country and led a counterattack against Doctor Doom's forces.

Resolute ruler
Serving as queen during her brother's frequent absences, Shuri was always prepared to do whatever was necessary to defend Wakanda.
Captain America: Sam Wilson #12, Oct. 2016

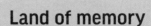

Land of memory

The past is ever present for the people of Wakanda, impacting their everyday lives in many tangible ways. Thanks to the unbroken lineage of the Black Panther Cult, the nation can trace its ancestry back through millennia. Furthermore, some gifted individuals and shamans can relive the past by entering the Djalia—a spiritual realm formed from Wakanda's collective memory.

While comatose after sustaining injuries in battle, King T'Challa's sister, Shuri, spent a prolonged period in the Djalia. There, a griot spirit taking the form of her mother, Ramonda, taught Shuri how to access the knowledge of countless generations of Wakandans and how to harness new supernatural abilities such as animorphism and transmutation.

Sometime later, when the mythical Originators returned to bedevil Wakanda, Shuri took T'Challa into the Djalia. Sitting astride a winged panther-beast, he glided through the land of memory on a vision quest to learn the truth about the original inhabitants of Wakanda and how they had been supplanted by humans in an ill-fated war during ancient times.

Deadly deluge
During a wider conflict between the X-Men and the Avengers, the Sub-Mariner
brought down the towers of Birnin Zana with a deluge of biblical proportions.
Avengers vs. X-Men #8, Sep. 2012

Sometime later, when the Avengers and the X-Men clashed over how best to manage an existential threat from the otherworldly Phoenix Force, Wakanda found itself on the front line in an all-out Super Hero war. King Namor of Atlantis was an ally of the X-Men, and empowered by the Phoenix Force, he unleashed a tsunami upon Wakanda, causing much devastation. Shuri responded fiercely—launching an equally destructive retaliatory strike on Atlantis.

When cooler heads prevailed and peace was finally restored, it brought with it a revolutionary call for change. The citizens of Wakanda now demanded a much greater say in the direction of their country. Recognizing that his people had sacrificed much in recent times, T'Challa agreed to oversee Wakanda's effective transition to a constitutional monarchy, offering to share his power with a democratically elected people's council.

Of course, Wakanda continued to face threats from both within and without, but a fresh challenge captured T'Challa's imagination like no other. Before her untimely death in childbirth, his mother, N'Yami, had been the head of a research group tasked with creating a Wakandan space force. N'Yami had hoped to develop spacecraft powerful enough to take her fellow scientists to far distant stars on a quest to locate the source of the Vibranium meteor that had fallen to Earth. Now her son vowed to fulfill that dream. T'Challa dispatched a team of Wakandan astronauts into outer space, watching with undisguised pride and admiration as the explorers left on a potentially one-way trip into the unknown.

> "The outside world doesn't know us at all. It is time for me to change that."
>
> **Black Panther (T'Challa)**

Under T'Challa's rule, Wakanda had opened up to the rest of the world, and with this bold step into the cosmos, the kingdom now announced its presence to the rest of the universe.

The people of Wakanda had enjoyed the benefits of peace and security for untold generations. They had luxuriated in the many riches provided by the benevolence of the goddess Bast and delivered through the power of Vibranium, becoming the most scientifically advanced and culturally sophisticated nation on Earth. T'Challa's decision to embrace change brought pain and strife but also a realization that Wakanda could not stand apart in the modern world. Its treasures were worthless if kept hidden—progress could not be hoarded—and Bast's bounty wasted if not shared. ▓

To the stars
To fulfill his deceased mother's cherished ambition, King T'Challa dispatched Wakandan explorers into outer space to search for the source of Vibranium.
Black Panther #1, Jul. 2018

Mighty and adored

Recruited from every tribe of Wakanda, the Dora Milaje was an elite sisterhood of warriors formed in ancient days to protect the line of Bashenga from assassination and other outside threats. Over time, the group became largely ceremonial, but it was reformed by King T'Challa in recent years with a far more serious intent. Nakia and Okoye became the first Dora Milaje to serve under T'Challa, and they were soon joined by dozens of other remarkable individuals.

Following an intense training regimen, each member of the sisterhood became skilled in the use of both ancient and modern weapons, as well as schooled in the arts of war and espionage. The warriors accompanied the king overseas and were the first line of defense against attack. Over the years, the Dora Milaje has served valiantly against such foes as Doctor Doom and the Titan, Thanos.

As she rose through the ranks, Okoye became King T'Challa's trusted right arm, eventually taking command of the Agents of Wakanda, a squad formed to support the global peacekeeping efforts of the Avengers.

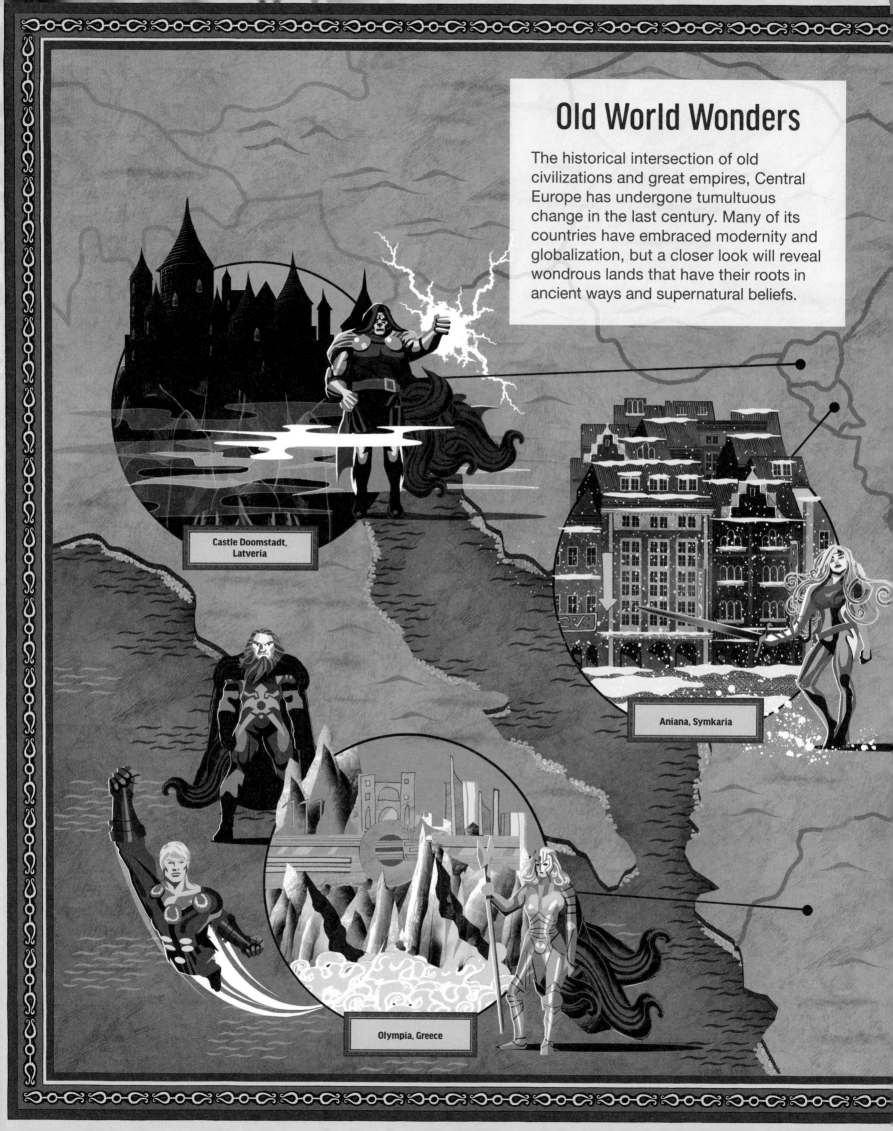

Old World Wonders

The historical intersection of old civilizations and great empires, Central Europe has undergone tumultuous change in the last century. Many of its countries have embraced modernity and globalization, but a closer look will reveal wondrous lands that have their roots in ancient ways and supernatural beliefs.

Castle Doomstadt, Latveria

Aniana, Symkaria

Olympia, Greece

Castle Dracula, Transylvania

Mount Wundagore, Transia

Discreetly tucked between Hungary in the west and Romania in the east, the tiny kingdom of Latveria has, in modern times, become one of the most powerful and feared nations on the face of the planet. Founded in the 14th century by Rudolfo Haasen, Latveria was ruled by the sadistic Fortunov family for much of the 20th century. The tyrants persecuted their citizens relentlessly, paying particularly cruel attention to members of the Romani Zefiro clan, who they dismissed as superstitious peasants. While many of the Zefiro were indeed practitioners of sorcery, they generally used their ancient wisdom in benevolent ways—acting as healers and herbalists. Cynthia von Doom was one such witch. However, after witnessing the relentless hounding of her people, she turned away from white magic and embraced the dark arts. Foolishly, she entered into a pact with the Hell Lord Mephisto. The demon granted Cynthia enough magical power to strike directly at King Vladimir Fortunov's troops. Unfortunately, her spells ran out of control and caused the death of many innocent children in a nearby town. Captured by soldiers, Cynthia was put to death—her soul condemned to endure an eternity of torment in Mephisto's infernal domain.

March to victory
Victor von Doom led an uprising to remove Latveria's cruel monarch, augmenting his revolutionary army with robotic soldiers. *Books of Doom* #6, Jun. 2006

Iron fists
As his grip on power strengthened, Doctor Doom became increasingly ruthless, as dictatorial as the rulers he had replaced. *Doctor Doom* #1, Dec. 2019

Cynthia left behind a young son, Victor, who escaped Fortunov's security forces and eventually found sanctuary in the United States. Accepting a scholarship from State University, Victor von Doom developed a reputation as one of the greatest scientific minds of his generation. He was also a secret practitioner of magic, having inherited his late mother's arcane spell books. Determined to free Cynthia's soul, Doom sought to combine the power of sorcery with that of science. After years of work, he developed a machine that would open up the gates of Hell and prepared to step through. However, Doom's scientific calculations were flawed and the device exploded, leaving him horribly scarred.

Psychologically unwilling to accept the loss of his handsome features, Doom hid his face behind a steel mask. He eventually built a suit of high-tech battle armor and returned to his homeland. There he inspired a revolution that toppled the Fortunov regime. He took the fallen king's cloak as his own and declared Latveria to be under the absolute rule of Doctor Doom.

Infernal pact

Impressed with Doom's ruthless nature and prowess in battle, Mephisto agreed to a pact. Doom would be granted an opportunity to redeem his mother's soul on one particular day each year. However, if Doom failed in his repeated rescue attempts, he would pay a high price indeed—the love of his people. Over the years, as Doom was thwarted by Mephisto time and time again, his fellow Latverians grew increasingly hostile, their admiration transformed into hatred.

Doctor Doom was branded a dictator by the outside world, but some realized his rule was preferable to the other alternatives. Caught between great international powers, Latveria might have been swept away had it not remained strong and its borders inviolate. At least under Doom's rule, the country prospered, becoming a scientifically advanced nation with a robust economy. Doom chose a medieval castle as his seat of power. Originally called Castle Sabbat, the 16th-century fortress was built upon a hilltop that overlooked Latveria's capital city. It was renamed Doomstadt (as was the capital itself), and, like much of the country, the ancient structure was given a modern makeover by Doctor Doom. The solid stone walls were augmented with force fields and defensive lasers and many of the medieval chambers were transformed into state-of-the-art laboratories. A nuclear reactor was even built into one of the turrets to provide enough power for the entire edifice as well as the bustling city down below.

Medieval modernity
Concealed behind Castle Doomstadt's medieval walls was a modern scientific research facility, replete with cutting-edge equipment. *Dark Avengers* #4, Jun. 2009

"Good people of Latveria … rise up! This is the new day of Doom."

Doctor Doom

Impregnable
Thanks to Doctor Doom's advanced weapons systems, Latveria can successfully defend itself from outside attack. Even the mighty Galactus was deterred from his voracious needs on one occasion. *Fantastic Four* #5, Feb. 2019

Blood-soaked

While Latveria enthusiastically embraced the modern age, neighboring Transylvania seemed forever locked in the past. In many ways, it was as immortal and unchanging as the fiend who would become its most infamous citizen.

Transylvania was a bleak transit point between more powerful neighbors, a land soaked in blood since medieval times. In the 15th century, a Wallachian prince named Vlad Dracul became notorious for opposing the invading Ottoman Empire and leaving the bodies of his enemies impaled on spikes as a warning to others. In 1459, Dracul was captured by the Turkish warlord Turac and delivered into the grisly care of a vampire, the Romani gypsy Lianda. After succumbing to her bite, Dracul was transformed into a vampire himself. He was consumed not only by a supernatural bloodlust but also a hunger for conquest. The man who once sought to defend his country from invaders now plotted to become an invader himself—vowing to deliver the scourge of vampirism to every country on Earth. Calling himself Count Dracula, he selected a medieval castle in Transylvania as his main base of operations. From this fortress, which became notorious throughout the land as Castle Dracula, he consolidated his power and set in motion numerous schemes to extend his influence overseas.

For the most part, Dracula operated in the shadows. He was a whisper, a legend, a myth— a ghostly figure from a distant land that few people would be able to identify with certainty on a map. However, as the world grew smaller, Dracula became increasingly embroiled in global affairs. His ambitions and actions brought him onto open conflict with many of the world's Super Heroes, most notably the X-Men. However, instead of being chastened by these bruising encounters, and the inevitable defeats that followed, Dracula seemed emboldened. He was determined to become a powerful figure on the world stage with Transylvania the capital of an expansionist vampire empire. On one occasion, he even entered into a nonaggression pact with Doctor Doom's Latveria so that he could launch a full-scale invasion of Great Britain. Although he eventually abandoned Transylvania, finding fresh sanctuary in the lethal radioactive zone around Chernobyl, Count Dracula continued to cast a long and grim shadow over his adopted homeland.

A forsaken place
The Lord of the Undead doesn't take kindly to uninvited guests, as Old Man Logan found to his cost upon entering the forbidding Castle Dracula in search of a lost friend. *Old Man Logan* #15, Feb. 2017

> **"**(I am) a towering god of night … fit to wreak my dreadful will upon the quivering continents.**"**
> **Count Dracula**

Wild country

Unlike many of its neighbors, the tiny Balkan country of Symkaria embraced the tumultuous change of the 20th century to become a progressive and forward-looking nation. Threatened with invasion during World War II, it joined forces with Latveria to drive off the Axis forces. Likewise, in the postwar years, the country fought hard to remain independent of the USSR and the Warsaw Pact. Independence meant everything to the people of Symkaria and they were respected the world over as a nation of proud individualists. Harnessing this fighting spirit, Ernst Sablinova established the Wild Pack—an organization dedicated to bringing international war criminals to justice.

When Sablinova's daughter, Silvija, took over the organization, she transformed the Wild Pack into a more general mercenary operation, providing security services for a clientele of small nations and rich individuals. Calling herself Silver Sable, she became a regular fixture in the murky world of international espionage, hiring superhumans like the Sandman to help provide support on many of her clandestine missions. Given official sanction by the government, Silver Sable and the Wild Pack became Symkaria's number one export, earning more for the country than any other business or economic activity.

Ever mindful of her country's precarious location, surrounded by far greater nations, Silver Sable maintained friendly relations with Doctor Doom. She dined with the Latverian dictator once a year to discuss affairs of state and mutual interest. As Symkaria's position on the world stage became more tenable, Silver Sable disbanded the Wild Pack. However, she recently reformed the team to free Symkaria from the grip of the tyrannical Countess Karkov, who had risen to power.

International intrigue
The Symkarian capital Aniana was a notorious hub of espionage activity, even drawing Steve Rogers to its snow-filled streets on a mission for the Secret Avengers.
Secret Avengers #19, Jan. 2012

Silver service
Silver Sable offered her security services to clients around the globe, including the wealthy citizens of neon-lit Hong Kong.
Amazing Spider-Man #25, May 2017

Science and sorcery

A tiny dot on a crowded map, the country of Transia is by no means insignificant. It is, in fact, home to one of the most important supernatural nexus points on the face of the entire planet—a mountainous site of power that has been coveted by gods and mortals alike. Approximately 11,000ft (3,300m) tall, Mount Wundagore towers over the Transian capital city of East Transia.

In ancient times, long before the birth of humanity, the Elder God Chthon retreated to the cavernous interior of the mountain where he penned the Darkhold, his fabled treatise on the laws and potency of black magic. Millennia later, sometime around the 6th century CE, the sorceress Morgan le Fay and her cult of medieval Darkholders sought to subdue Chthon and take his power as their own. They were unable to control him, however, and so they mystically bound him within Mount Wundagore. The Elder God's malign essence seeped into the clay and wood of Wundagore, infusing the land with potent supernatural energies. On particularly stormy nights, the mountaintop was seen to glow with power, prompting nearby villagers to cross themselves and pray for their futures.

In addition to being a place of magical power, Mount Wundagore was also considered a site of great scientific interest, its rocks infused with rare minerals and elements. Drawn to the mountain in the early part of the 20th century, geneticist Herbert Edgar Wyndham established his Citadel of Science among its towering peaks. Wyndham had long hoped to tame the power of evolution and, cut off from the rest of the world atop Mount Wundagore, he set about his illicit genetic research. With no hint of irony, he referred to himself as the High Evolutionary and proceeded to use the mountain's natural resources to help perfect a life-changing procedure that transformed animals into highly evolved beings that he christened New Men.

Top of the world
The High Evolutionary studied complex evolutionary patterns in his mountaintop Citadel of Science.
Spider-Woman #4, Nov. 2020

Unnatural selection
Hoping to speed up the evolutionary process, the High Evolutionary once joined forces with the ancient Evolutionaries to test the mettle of Earth's superhuman community.
New Warriors #10, Nov. 2014

The High Evolutionary was eventually alerted to the threat of Chthon by a disciple of Morgan le Fay. Anticipating the Elder God might one day escape his confinement within the mountain, Wyndham had his New Men trained in the arts of combat and chivalry. Dubbed the Knights of Wundagore, they patrolled the skies above the mountain, ever alert for signs that Chthon had awakened from his mystic slumber.

To preserve his aging form, Wyndham created an all-encompassing exoskeleton. Just as Wyndham's body deteriorated so, too, did his mental acuity. Over time, he grew increasingly unstable, desperate to find ways to defend against Chthon's possible return. He sent the Knights of Wundagore out to search for beings of power. One such raiding party returned from war-torn Serbia with twin babies who had been born recently to a powerful witch. The High Evolutionary experimented on the children, hoping to draw supernatural power from them. However, the better part of Wyndham's nature asserted itself, and he eventually returned them to the care of their aunt and uncle. The twins—Wanda and Pietro Maximoff—would go on to develop mutant capabilities and join the ranks of the Avengers as the Scarlet Witch and Quicksilver. Because of her time spent on Mount Wundagore, Wanda became particularly sensitive to supernatural energy and was thus able to wield chaos magic with considerable skill and force.

Although circumstances frequently took the High Evolutionary away from Transia, he would always return home, inevitably drawn back to the majestic Citadel of Science sitting atop the miraculous mountain of magic.

Shimmering chivalry
Snow Queen, an evolved white tiger, led her fellow Knights of Wundagore on patrols through the Transian mountains, seeking signs of the demonic Chthon's return.
Uncanny X-Men #488, Sep. 2007

"Here we can build a place of wonders."
High Evolutionary

Aloof defenders
Committed to defending humanity, the Eternals built Olympia using advanced technology to hide the city from prying eyes.
Eternals #7, Mar. 2007

Eternal city

Some 500 miles (800km) southwest of Transia lies Greece. Hailed as the birthplace of modern civilization, the country is steeped in history and myth. While much has been written about the progressive nature of Ancient Greece, there is still one secret that has yet to be fully revealed to the world. Nestled among the mountains of northern Greece—and hidden from the sight of ordinary women and men within an artificially constructed echo-dimension—is the golden city of Olympia. This is home to the Eternals of Earth, an offshoot of humanity created by the spacefaring Celestials in prehistoric times. To test the human genome's adaptability, the Celestials accelerated the evolution of a handful of primitive protohumans, gifting them the ability to manipulate matter at the molecular level and thus develop numerous superhuman capabilities. After being irradiated with cosmic energy, these miraculous beings became immortal—reborn in perfectly formed clone bodies after each successive death. Calling themselves the Eternals, they established the city of Titanos as their home. When this was destroyed, Prime Eternal Zuras ordered the construction of a new city in Greece.

Olympia was even more grandiose than its predecessor, with glistening towers, wide open boulevards, and many high-tech wonders. For millennia, it served as the Eternals' capital city, where disparate immortals would gather to discuss matters of global importance.

To ease communication, the Eternals established a Uni-Mind, merging together to create a single being that resembled a giant pulsating brain. In this form, they could make unanimous decisions almost instantaneously. The rite of the Uni-Mind was considered sacred, and so the Eternals built the Tower of the Uni-Mind at the heart of Olympia, with other buildings radiating out from this central landmark. When invited to form the Uni-Mind from the Hall of Ascent, the Eternals would levitate above the tower, slowly morphing into their gestalt form.

Highfliers
Over the centuries, Eternals like the glider Ikaris and the speedster Makkari have raced from Olympia to disrupt the diabolical plans of the monstrous Deviants.
Eternals #7, Mar. 2007

> "Gather, Eternals! Zuras calls and bids you all to answer."
>
> **Zuras**

Network hub
The city of Olympia was constructed as part of a complex transportation network, allowing the Eternals to teleport to any place on Earth instantaneously.
Eternals #1, Mar. 2021

Caretakers

The Eternals saw themselves as the guardians of Earth, defending the planet's human population from another species created by the Celestials—the Deviants. While the Eternals were angelic, the Deviants were grotesque, their unstable genome producing generation after generation of monstrous individuals. The Deviants' intent was as ugly as their appearance, and they plotted incessantly to enslave their human cousins. This forced the Eternals to frequently leave their glorious city in order to protect humankind from the machinations of the Deviants. Many Eternals became experienced warriors, most notably Zuras' daughter, Thena, and the golden-haired Ikaris, who was championed as a "living arrow" thanks to his direct nature and fortitude in battle. On their forays into the wider world, the Eternals were frequently mistaken for divine beings, the peoples of ancient Greece and Rome often confusing them with the true Gods of Olympus.

To supplement their capital, the Eternals built smaller cities around the globe. Polaria was established in the Ural Mountains (within modern-day Siberia) and Oceania in the Pacific Ocean. The cities were linked via a computerized intelligence known as the Machine. Among its many tasks, the Machine was responsible for maintaining the Network, a series of subdimensional threads that allowed the Eternals to teleport over vast distances in the blink of an eye. This made Olympia the hub of a mass transit system with links to almost any other location on Earth— a secret highway enabling the Eternals to come and go as they pleased and avoid detection by the unsuspecting mass of humanity. ▪

The fallen kingdom

Titanos was the first city ever erected by the Eternals. Located in what is now Canada's Northwest Territories, the habitat was hidden from prying eyes in a temporal pocket situated two seconds before and three seconds after any particular moment in time. Consequently, Titanos was a window on the past and the future, filled with portals to other eras.

Foremost among the city's inhabitants was Kronos, who believed the Eternals should use their gifts to aid humanity. He was opposed in this by his own brother, Uranos, who wished to conquer the Earth. The brothers fell into open conflict, and the resulting civil war left Titanos in a ruinous state. Kronos emerged triumphant, however, and went on to lead his people into a new age. Sometime later, he was killed in a laboratory explosion that also destroyed the rest of Titanos.

Zuras, Kronos's son, assumed the mantle of Prime Eternal and established a new home for his people in Greece. Decades later, Zuras was apparently killed by the Titan Thanos, who used the Eternal's teleport network to flee to ruined Titanos. The warrior Ikaris gave chase and a fierce battle ensued.

Lost Lands

The unexplored regions and dark recesses of planet Earth are home to an astounding number of hidden kingdoms. These forgotten continents and remote islands have evolved in splendid isolation and spawned many unique environments and ecologies. Such places are whispered of in legend and shrouded in mystery, visited by only a few hardy souls and dismissed as fiction by many disillusioned skeptics. There is the prehistoric splendor of Ka-Zar's Savage Land, the mysterious mutant island named Krakoa, and the Mole Man's rugged Monster Island. These secret places are filled, in equal measure, with wonder and peril. Towering monsters bestride the landscape, primordial creatures soar in crystal clear blue skies, and heroic individuals defend their homelands from unscrupulous outsiders. Cut off from the rest of the world for centuries, these lost lands are now ripe for exploration and study.

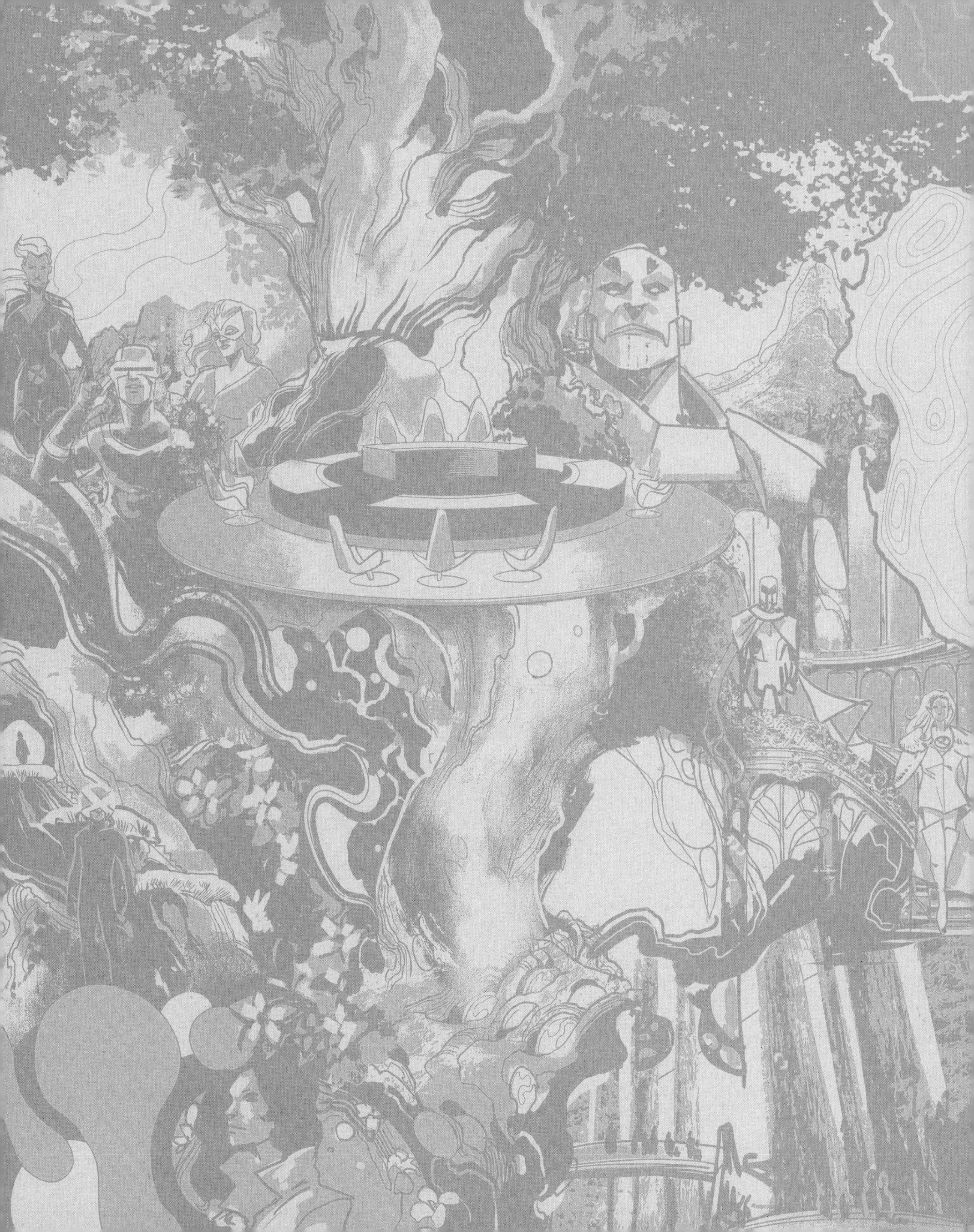

Marguerite Bay

War Room X

Thunder Falls

Eternity Mountain range

Sauron's Citadel

Mystic Mists

Skull Island

Tribal lands of the Man-Apes

The Fall People's
hunting grounds

Magneto's citadel

United Nations/S.H.I.E.L.D.
monitor station

Primal Kingdom

Isolated at the bottom of the world,
the Savage Land is a window on
the primordial past. It is a verdant
paradise where small bands of
humans compete with huge herds
of dinosaurs, their primal struggle
played out under the watchful gaze
of Ka-Zar and Shanna, custodians
of the so-called Hidden Jungle.

City of Sylanda

Dinosaur Graveyard

Mutates citadel and village

Ka-Zar and Shanna's treehouse

The Great Rift

Thunder lizards
Against a backdrop of erupting volcanoes, the Savage Land was a place
rich in flora and fauna that had once thrived in prehistoric times.
X-Men: The Hidden Years #1, Dec. 1999

Located at the base of the Palmer Peninsula in Antarctica, the Savage Land is largely cut off from the rest of the world by a ring of active volcanoes. In the distant past, otherdimensional beings called the Beyonders chose the region as the location for a grand scientific experiment. Fascinated by Earth's evolutionary process, the Beyonders planned to preserve prime examples of its uniquely diverse flora and fauna in one easily accessible area.

The Beyonders contracted the alien Nuwali to bring their lavish game reserve to life, and powerful terraformers were used to transform the frozen Antarctic landscape into a tropical paradise, with the local volcanoes helping to maintain the warm microclimate as time went on.

From the Triassic to the Pleistocene eras, the Nuwali stocked the Savage Land with plentiful creatures. As the rest of the world evolved, with mass extinction following mass extinction, the Savage Land became home to many lost species—a last holdout for Earth's first flush of primal life.

However, when the Beyonders grew bored with the Earth, the Nuwali were forced to abandon the project. In their place came the ancient Atlanteans, whose scientists discovered the Savage Land during their explorations and were entranced by the vast array of prehistoric wildlife thriving within. Like the Beyonders, they were curious about the evolutionary process and performed genetic experiments to create human-animal hybrids, such as the lizardlike Vala-Kuri.

Natural selection
Over millennia, the raptors evolved in
ways not seen in the outside world.
Savage Wolverine #2, Apr. 2013

Survival of the fittest

When Atlantis was washed away by the flood of the Great Cataclysm, the Savage Land was finally free to develop naturally. The early civilizations established by the hybrid tribes fell into ruin as the jungle reasserted itself. Evolution in the Savage Land was, it seemed, red in tooth and claw, and the isolated pockets of humanity were at a distinct disadvantage in any direct competition, especially with huge saurians such as the *Tyrannosaurus rex*. However, tribes like the Fall People managed to survive by respecting the land and carefully maintaining the natural order of things.

Cosmic beings and Atlanteans aside, the first recorded outsider to arrive in the Savage Land was a 15th-century sailor who was washed up in the territory after miraculously surviving a shipwreck. Delirious and wandering aimlessly, he crossed into the country of the Sun People, a warlike tribe who worshipped the sun god Garokk. He came upon a cup of mysterious liquid on a shrine and quenched his terrible thirst by drinking it. Outraged at this perceived insult to Garokk, the Sun People attacked the sailor and drove him from their lands. Sometime later, the sailor awoke in England with no memory of how he had returned home. As the years passed, the man discovered he no longer aged and that his body was slowly and alarmingly turning to stone. Eventually, he became a living representation of Garokk, the bizarre metamorphosis brought about by the strange liquid he had imbibed decades earlier. In modern times, now referring to himself as the Petrified Man, he returned to the Savage Land to help quell a terrible war of conquest launched by the Sun People in the name of Garokk.

Inevitably, the Savage Land could not remain hidden from the rest of the world forever and two geographical expeditions in the first half of the 20th century mapped the kingdom and set the stage for what was to follow. The Shackleton expedition in 1909 and the Goodman mission in 1938 were purely scientific endeavors, but their findings revealed that the Savage Land was rich with natural resources and, to some unscrupulous individuals, that meant ripe for exploitation.

During World War II, submariners from Germany and Britain found themselves stranded in the Savage Land. Unaware that the wider conflict in the outside world had ended, the two crews continued to wage war. Hostilities were so entrenched that even the descendants of the original survivors carried on fighting each other for subsequent decades. During this time, they also taught modern languages to many of the indigenous peoples, with English eventually becoming a common tongue for many tribes of the Savage Land.

Sticks and stones
Much like Neanderthals, the Man-Apes hailed from a time when violent clashes were commonplace.
Savage Wolverine #2, Apr. 2013

Stone-age visage
After drinking a mystical potion, an unlucky sailor took on the petrified appearance of the sun god Garokk.
Avengers #12, Jul. 2013

Savage Land survivors

A British nobleman and scientist, Lord Robert Plunder was particularly intrigued by the Savage Land. On an expedition to the region, he discovered a rare element that emitted energy waves that destroyed other metals. Plunder realized this "anti-metal" could be dangerous in the wrong hands and he fervently sought to keep his discovery a secret. It was to no avail, however, and when a criminal cartel learned of the anti-metal's existence, it put pressure on Plunder to reveal the exact location of the valuable hoard.

Seeking to escape his persecutors, Lord Plunder fled to the Savage Land with his young son Kevin. Unfortunately, the Savage Land lived up to its name, and father and son were attacked by Maa-Gor and his tribe of Neanderthal-like Man-Apes. Robert was slain and Kevin faced a similarly grisly fate. At the last moment, though, the boy's life was saved by the arrival of a Smilodon he later named Zabu. Like Kevin, the saber-toothed tiger had good reason to hate Maa-Gor. He was the last great cat in the Savage Land, his species hunted to the point of extinction by the bestial Man-Apes. Zabu rescued Kevin from Maa-Gor's war club and, with the boy astride his great back, bounded into the nearby Mystic Mists.

Sole survivors
An orphaned boy and the last living Smilodon were brought together by shared grief, eventually becoming the Savage Land's resolute defenders.
Marvel Comics Presents #5, Mar. 2008

"In the Savage Land, the hunter is oftentimes the hunted."

Ka-Zar

Unstill waters
Danger often lurked just below the surface in the Savage Land. Even the most peaceful-looking lagoon might harbor a monstrous leviathan waiting to strike.
Empyre: Avengers #3, Oct. 2020

Jungle life

Hidden from the superstitious Man-Apes by the eerie haze permeating the Mystic Mists, Kevin and Zabu formed a close, almost mystical bond. The two orphans became spiritual brothers. Kevin grew to manhood in the Mystic Mists while the unusual gases slowed Zabu's aging. By the time Kevin was an adult, the Smilodon was still in the prime of life. As he took a more active role in the affairs of the Savage Land, protecting it from outside interference, Kevin was nicknamed Ka-Zar—which meant "son of the tiger" in the language of some tribes.

While Ka-Zar's devotion to the Savage Land was unstinting, he nevertheless longed for the life he had lost. In his mind, the outside world took on an almost mythical quality. He longed to enjoy the benefits of the "civilized" world once more and so, whenever the opportunities presented themselves, he journeyed to the United States of America and the United Kingdom. There he met and befriended numerous costumed adventurers, including Spider-Man and Daredevil.

Inevitably, Ka-Zar was always pulled back to his adopted homeland. If he wasn't there to protect it, who would defend the Savage Land from the rapacious appetites of the conglomerates and corporations who would strip it of its natural wealth and unique identity? The answer to that question came in the form of Shanna O'Hara, perhaps better known as Shanna the She-Devil.

An expert zoologist and an avowed environmentalist, Shanna took up the cause of the Savage Land. Ka-Zar and Shanna fell in love and were eventually married. As he grew accustomed to family life—and particularly after the couple had a son named Matthew—Ka-Zar found his wanderlust diminishing. He finally accepted the Savage Land as his true home. It may not have been the land of his birth, but it was where he belonged.

Setting down roots
After their marriage, Ka-Zar and Shanna built a treetop home in anticipation of starting a family.
Empyre: Avengers #3, Oct. 2020

Dropping in
During the Secret Invasion of Earth, Spider-Man recruited Ka-Zar and his family to help foil a scheme by alien Skrulls to weaponize the Savage Land's anti-metal.
New Avengers #41, Jul. 2008

Mutant visitors

The X-Men were frequent visitors to the Savage Land. After first traveling to the region to investigate whether Ka-Zar was a mutant like themselves, they were repeatedly drawn back to the Hidden Jungle. Over the years, some team members came to view the Savage Land as something of a vacation spot, a place where they could come to relax and enjoy time away from their responsibilities as mutant heroes. Wolverine, in particular, considered the Savage Land his spiritual home, believing it to be the one place on Earth where he could give free rein to his animalistic instincts and fully be himself.

Following a particular humiliating defeat at the hands of the X-Men, the outlaw mutant Magneto also established a presence in the Savage Land. He built a towering citadel and, like so many before him, experimented on local tribespeople, converting them into evolved superhumans who were subservient to his will. These Mutates, as they became known, included the froglike Amphibius, the hyper-intelligent Brainchild, and the mesmerizing Lorelei. During another clash with the X-Men, the machines that maintained the Mutates' powers were destroyed and Magneto's citadel was left in disarray.

City living
The warlike Sun People erected the City of the Sun God and trapped other Savage Land inhabitants inside, until Ka-Zar and a band of visiting X-Men tore down the walls.
Uncanny X-Men #116, Dec. 1978

Consequently, the Mutates reverted to their less-evolved forms. Sometime later, however, Magneto returned to the Savage Land to empower the Mutates once again. His plan was to create an entire army of Mutate followers, but when the scheme was frustrated by the Avengers, Magneto left his creations to their fate. The Mutates returned to Magneto's former citadel in an effort to figure out where they belonged in the hierarchy of the Savage Land. Perhaps inevitably— given their natural malleability and formidable superhuman abilities—they fell under the thrall of one would-be conqueror after another, most notably Priestess Zaladane of the Sun People and the voracious energy vampire known as Sauron.

> **"It ain't called the Savage Land for bein' a nice place."**
> **Wolverine**

Tooth and claw
On a visit to the Savage Land, Wolverine was attacked by cybernetically enhanced dinosaurs under the command of the reptilelike Hauk'ka people.
Uncanny X-Men #456, Apr. 2005

Magnetic south
Hounded by human authorities, Magneto, the mutant Master of Magnetism, frequently sought sanctuary in the Savage Land.
Uncanny X-Men #19, May 2017

Born Karl Lykos, Sauron was the son of a renowned explorer. While accompanying his father on an expedition, he encountered a flock of Savage Land pteranodons. Bitten by the creatures, Lykos was infected with a virus that altered his genetic makeup. As a result, he now needed to drain energy from other living creatures in order to survive. Lykos kept his condition a secret, generally siphoning energy from pets and other small animals. When forced to feed from fellow humans, he took only a minimal amount of energy, leaving his victims disorientated and with no memory of the experience.

In adulthood, and now a qualified doctor, Lykos was asked to attend the mutant Havok who had been injured while fighting alongside the X-Men. After treating the hero's wounds, Lykos gave in to temptation and siphoned off some of his unique energy. This was the first time Lykos had fed from a mutant, and it precipitated a miraculous transformation. The doctor was turned into a human-pteranodon hybrid, with powerful wings and a hypnotic stare. Taking the name Sauron, Lykos clashed with the X-Men but was roundly defeated and forced to flee. He sought sanctuary in his father's abandoned base camp at Tierra del Fuego—off the coast of South America's southernmost tip—and found his way to the Savage Land through a labyrinth of tunnels.

Faithful followers
Abandoned by Magneto, the Mutates joined with Ka-Zar and the X-Men to battle the reptilian would-be conquerors, the Hauk'ka.
Uncanny X-Men #457, May 2005

Preserving the past

For over 700 years, the leaders of the Zebra Tribe urged the peoples of the Savage Land to unite, but for all that time those calls went unanswered. However, in modern times, with the stability of the Savage Land threatened by outside forces, the disparate peoples of the Savage Land finally came together to form a United Council of Tribes.

The Sun People, the Sylandans, and many other groups agreed to speak with one voice. In a lavish ceremony, which included the symbolic marriage of a woman of the Fall Tribe to a Saurian (pictured above), the council was convened under the stewardship of Arwandi of the Zebra Tribe.

Top of the agenda was the encroachment of outside business interests such as the Roxxon Energy Corporation. Under the pretense of offering food aid, Roxxon had gained a foothold in the Savage Land and was preparing to strip it of its natural resources. In the end, Arwandi took the unprecedented step of addressing the United Nations Assembly in person and was successful in having his homeland declared a region of special scientific interest. Roxxon was sent packing and the Savage Land's prehistoric splendor was preserved for future generations.

Tower of technology
Magneto's War Room X was
located in the Savage Land.
The tower was eventually
destroyed by the Master
of Magnetism himself.
Uncanny X-Men #11,
Oct. 2016

> "The Savage Land is
> closed to outsiders."
>
> **Ka-Zar**

Call of the wild

Thanks to his recent mutation, Sauron was particularly well adapted for
survival in the Savage Land, and he made many attempts to conquer
the Hidden Jungle, sometimes recruiting the Mutates to his cause.
Invariably, though, he would be defeated by Ka-Zar or the X-Men.
Sauron was not the only individual to experience the intense lure
of the Savage Land. Magneto felt a similar pull, and after seemingly
renouncing his violent ways, he built a new base of operations in the
region for his own squad of X-Men. War Room X was a soaring edifice
that cut through the tangled jungle canopy—but, like many high-tech
outposts established in the Savage Land, it was a temporary addition
to the landscape. The building was destroyed when the hero
Psylocke—fearing her former leader was reverting to his old ways
and leading his followers down a dark path—confronted Magneto.

Similarly, bases established by the likes of the United Nations and
S.H.I.E.L.D. (Strategic Homeland Intervention, Enforcement, and
Logistics Division) were frequently left in ruins, overrun during violent
flare-ups or sent tumbling to the ground by stampeding dinosaurs or
earthquakes. It was as
if the Savage Land itself
was somehow asserting
its dominance, intent on
wiping away every last
trace of outsiders and
their disruptive influence.

The super-scientist
known as the High
Evolutionary was
fascinated by the Savage
Land's unique ecology.
At first, he seemed to
be a benevolent figure,
drawn to the wilderness
to further his knowledge
of evolution. He even
helped restore the ancient
climate-controlling
machines when they failed
on one occasion. Over
time, though, he became
increasingly unhinged—

Pteranodon terror
Transformed into Sauron after consuming
mutant life energies, Doctor Kyle Lykos
found freedom in the Savage Land.
New Avengers #5, May 2005

convinced that the Savage Land held the key to unlocking humanity's superhuman potential. He plotted to use genetic material harvested from the Savage Land to forcibly evolve every person on the planet. Fortunately, his mad scheme was discovered and thwarted by a team of Avengers and he was expelled from the Hidden Jungle.

Despite frequent visits from outside heroes, Ka-Zar and Shanna remained the Savage Land's most staunch protectors. While investigating reports of an entombed extraterrestrial known cryptically as the Dark Walker, Shanna was mortally wounded. To save Shanna's life, priests from a shamanic tribe bathed her in a mystic pool and bound her life-force to the ecology of the Hidden Jungle. In a sense, Shanna became the Savage Land.

So long as the Hidden Jungle continued to flourish, so, too, would Shanna. She was attuned to the land itself and could access its history and channel its power through magical means. Sometime later, with Earth under assault from plantlike aliens known as the Cotati, Shanna shared her spiritual connection with Ka-Zar, and together the couple were able to command a small army of dinosaurs to drive the invaders from the Savage Land.

For years, Ka-Zar and Shanna have selflessly dedicated their lives to the preservation of their adopted homeland. Due to their spiritual connection, they are now more than mere defenders of the Savage Land, they are the living embodiment of the jungle itself—primal beings linked to a primal kingdom. ◾

"I am the Savage Land."
Shanna the She-Devil

Savage She-Devil
Bonded to the Savage Land by magical means, Shanna drew on the strength of the ecosystem itself to expunge the alien Cotati from her home.
Empyre: Avengers #3, Oct. 2020

Monster Volcano

Caldera (collapsed volcano)

Caldera (collapsed volcano)

Mystic Cave

Temple of Monsters

Cave entry to Subterranea

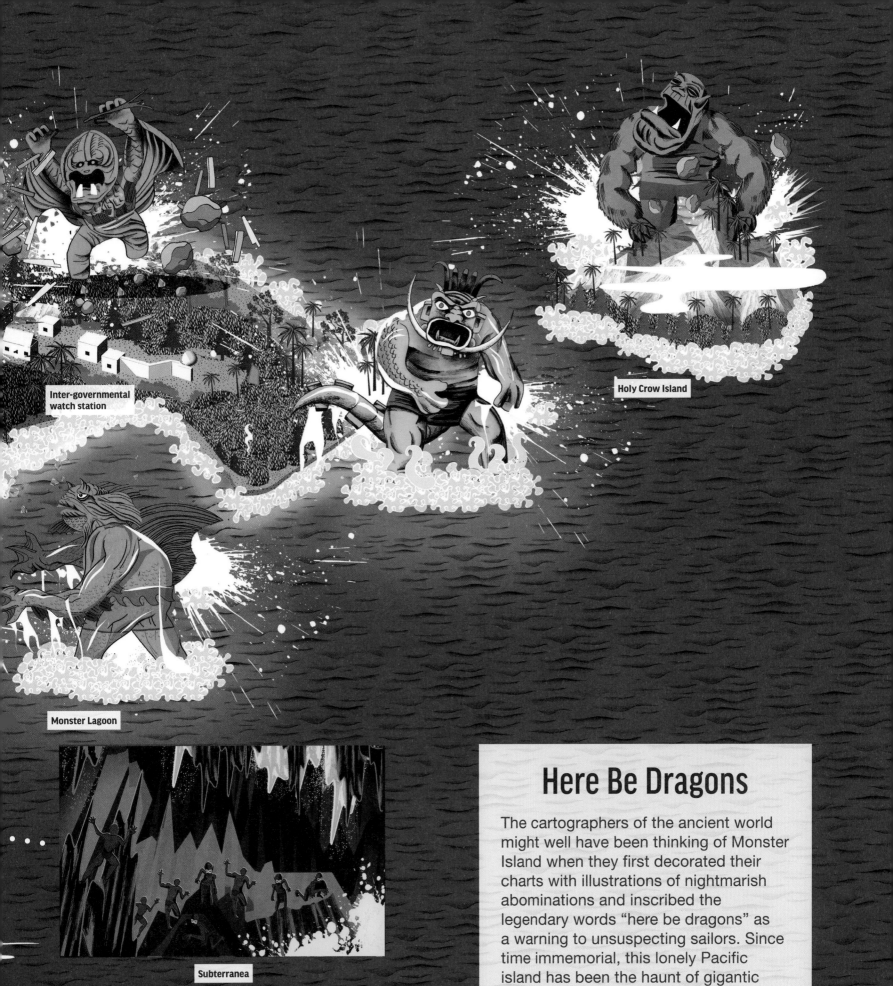

Inter-governmental
watch station

Holy Crow Island

Monster Lagoon

Subterranea

Here Be Dragons

The cartographers of the ancient world
might well have been thinking of Monster
Island when they first decorated their
charts with illustrations of nightmarish
abominations and inscribed the
legendary words "here be dragons" as
a warning to unsuspecting sailors. Since
time immemorial, this lonely Pacific
island has been the haunt of gigantic
beasts, an unspoiled Eden where
creatures roam and monsters dwell.

Island of lost souls
Those brave souls that venture onto Monster Island are
often entranced by the striking beauty of the tropical
surroundings—until the kaiju emerge from their lairs.
Marvel Two-in-One #2, Mar. 2018

Located in the north of the Pacific Ocean, Monster Island is considered to be one of the most dangerous places on Earth. At first glance it appears to be a veritable paradise, replete with cool lagoons and sun-drenched beaches. To many it would seem the perfect vacation spot, but a closer inspection reveals various threats lurking in the dense jungle and in the deep shadows of the volcanic mountain range.

Behind the Temple of Monsters, on the central plateau, something stirs. Huge claws erupt from beneath the soil and a mighty behemoth heaves into view. It is Giganto. Sharing a name with the infamous Atlantean leviathan, this giant creature is supremely adapted for tunneling through compacted earth. Rocks are no hindrance, and even enormous boulders can be crushed to dust in seconds. As he pulls himself free of the earth and stands, Giganto stretches to his full height, his spiky hide glistening in the sunlight. He raises his head, opens his vast maw and issues an ear-splitting bellow. The call is answered from some miles distant. From the west, a distinctive screech is heard, a shared note from three voices echoes across the isle. This is the morning call of Tricephalous, an enormous three-headed dragon who takes wing daily to patrol the skies above his home and serve as Monster Island's gatekeeper.

"I had heard there was a giant three-headed creature guarding this isle."
Mister Fantastic

Haven of horror

Over in the bay, a huge dorsal fin cuts through the still, blue water, announcing the arrival of the amphibious Gigantus. He has spent the night scouring the ocean depths for the tons of fish he needs to consume to power his mighty frame. As he strides onto the land, the waters roil up and a huge wave crashes down onto the beach, sweeping inland to destroy a vast tract of jungle. Shaking himself dry, Gigantus is oblivious to the destruction caused by his return home. Such tumult occurs frequently on Monster Island and is beneath the notice of the volcanic isle's gargantuan inhabitants.

A short distance away from Gigantus, a monster born of the imagination bathes in the sea. X, the so-called "Thing That Lived" is the creation of comic book writer Charles Bentley. The creature was first conjured into being when Bentley used an enchanted typewriter to script one of his popular short horror stories. Hunted relentlessly by his monstrous creation, the writer was only able to escape death by smashing the typewriter to pieces—sending X back into the ethereal realm of make-believe. Years later, X was brought back to life by a young manga artist called Tomi and has since found sanctuary with the other beasts on Monster Island.

Similarly, the Brute That Walks is a monster who came into being because of the hubris and reckless nature of a particular individual. Scientist Howard Avery imbibed a steroidlike serum of his own invention to impress a woman who he secretly loved. The potent concoction did, indeed, enhance his physique, but it also transformed Avery into a hirsute beast. Captured by the authorities, the Brute was deposited on Monster Island, where he now spends his days safeguarding the Mystic Caves, his enormous stature and powerful muscles impressing no one.

Monster Island is the habitat of many grotesqueries. It is the raucous domain of giant beasts, kaiju in the modern parlance, but how did the island come to be and how did so many remarkable and fearsome creatures arrive at its shores?

Making waves
The creatures of Monster Island, such as Vandoom's Monster, frequently bathe offshore, making the entire region a no-go area for international shipping.
Monsters Unleashed #2, Apr. 2017

Monsters unleashed
Giant beasts often jostle for position on Monster Island. Among them are the Crawling Creature (center), red-skinned Tim Boo Ba, and visiting alien-dragon, Fin Fang Foom.
Monsters Unleashed #2, Apr. 2017

Going underground

In the Antediluvian past, the Celestials created the Deviants as part of the grand evolutionary experiment that also produced the Eternals. While the godlike Eternals were perfection given human form, the Deviants were imperfect creatures, their genetic code so unstable that it produced weaker and weaker aberrations over time. However, their malign intelligence and native cunning more than made up for their lack of physical prowess. Thanks to their advanced technologies, the Deviants managed to conquer much of the ancient world—with Atlantis surviving as one of the few free outposts of humanity.

During the tumult of the Great Cataclysm, the Deviants were forced to retreat deep below ground where they established the kingdom of Subterranea. They longed for a return to the light, however, and schemed incessantly to conquer the surface world. Using advanced genetics, they created Mutates—monsters that they intended to use in the vanguard of a new army.

The Deviants lived beneath unsuspecting humanity for millennia, their network of secret tunnels giving them access to almost any place on Earth. One point of egress was Monster Island, and the Deviant Mutates would occasionally slip free of their underworld confinement and stride across the land. Glimpses of these colossal creatures gave birth to myths and legends that echoed down the ages to modern times.

In the middle of the 20th century, the Deviant warlord Kro sought to foment a global conflict that he believed would allow his kind to finally emerge from the darkness. He sent the Mutates of Monster Island to destroy American and Soviet bases, hoping the Cold War rivals would blame each other for the devastation and launch retaliatory nuclear strikes. As fortune would have it, the scheme was foiled—and the world was saved—by a band of self-styled monster hunters led by the Eternal Makkari and the ageless adventurer Ulysses Bloodstone.

What lies below
Few have explored the gem-encrusted caverns of Subterranea save for the Fantastic Four, who mapped the hidden kingdom on their missions underground.
Fantastic Four #575, Mar. 2010

Kingdom of the blind

The monster hunters met at the world-famous Explorers' Club in New York City and one of their conversations was overheard by a would-be adventurer named Harvey Rupert Elder. Harvey was a small man in more ways than one. Having been spurned because of his somewhat unconventional appearance, he had developed an abrasive personality. The world treated Harvey Elder with contempt and he responded in kind. He was obsessed with the Hollow Earth theory and came to believe he would find peace from his tormentors only somewhere deep underground. "The people of the surface world mocked me," he declared. "Finally, I could stand it no longer! I decided to strike out alone to search for a legendary new world. A world where I could be king."

As luck would have it, Harvey's eavesdropping at the Explorers' Club revealed to him the exact location of Monster Island. He made his way there and subsequently stumbled upon an entrance to Subterranea. Unfortunately, his jubilant cries precipitated a rock slide.

Blinding beauty
Home to the Deviant Moloids, Subterranea is littered with priceless diamonds, the light from which blinded Harvey Elder and set him on the path to becoming the Mole Man.
Incredible Hulk #1, Dec. 2011

Hapless Harvey found himself tumbling through miles of underground passageways. He came to rest in a cavern filled with huge diamonds, the glare from the gems robbing him of most of his sight. Harvey wasn't alone in the dark, however, and he soon encountered a group of Deviant-created subterraneans. The Moloids were a docile slave race and, having been abandoned by their creators long ago, they became Harvey's willing servitors.

With both the Moloids and the Mutates at his command, and his underground realm festooned with abandoned Deviant weaponry, Harvey's thoughts turned to vengeance. At last, here was a chance to get back at all those who had scorned him. Calling himself the Mole Man, Harvey launched a sustained assault on the surface world. He ordered one of the largest and most powerful Mutates, who he dubbed Giganto, to destroy nuclear power stations across the world. This brought him into conflict with the recently formed Super Hero team the Fantastic Four. In their first recorded mission, they tracked down the Mole Man to his lair on Monster Island. After losing a brief scuffle, the villain detonated Monster Island and was believed to have died in the explosion.

Chaos in the underworld
Seeking revenge against those who had wronged him, Mole Man unleashed the monstrous Giganto and clashed with the Fantastic Four.
Fantastic Four #575, Mar. 2010

Monstrous menagerie

The island endured, however, and so did its self-appointed guardian. The Mole Man survived the partial destruction of his home and returned numerous times to battle the Fantastic Four and other heroes such as the Avengers. Over time, he became less belligerent. So long as he was left in peace, the Mole Man was content to remain on his isle and care for his menagerie of massive beasts. Eventually, the population increased, with monsters of all types finding a home alongside the Deviant Mutates. Even some extraterrestrials, such as the dragonlike Fin Fang Foom, found a warm welcome on Monster Island during their frequent intergalactic sojourns to planet Earth.

As tensions with the outside world decreased, the United Nations established a cryptozoological watch station on Monster Island, giving inquisitive scientists access to some of the rarest creatures in all of creation.

> "I am … ruler of Monster Island and all of Subterranea."
>
> **Mole Man**

The Mole Man was the undisputed master of Earth's behemoths for a long time. His control was seemingly absolute until an 11-year-old boy emerged as an unexpected rival for the unofficial title of king of all monsters. Kei Kawade was an avid kaiju fan, spending much of his free time drawing pictures of his favorite monsters in action. When he was exposed to the transformative Terrigen Cloud and his latent Inhuman genes were activated, Kei's monster obsession took a decidedly bizarre turn. He found he could summon up any monster—and command it to do his bidding—by simply drawing it in his sketchbook.

Kei's ability proved invaluable when Earth came under attack from alien leviathans. Calling himself Kid Kaiju, he conjured up many of Monster Island's denizens, including Fin Fang Foom and Gigantus.

Cosmic conqueror
Fin Fang Foom was an alien who sought to conquer Earth many times and who later found a place of refuge on Monster Island.
All-New X-Men #12, Aug. 2013

> "No place on Earth will give you safety … when Fin Fang Foom strikes!"
>
> **Fin Fang Foom**

The boy ordered the titanic terrors to fight the invaders. The aliens outnumbered Earth's defenders, however, and it was only when Kid Kaiju created monsters from his own imagination that the tide of battle turned and victory was eventually secured.

In the aftermath, Kid Kaiju sent some of the original behemoths back to Monster Island. The enormous creatures were once again free to bask in the sunlight, free to roar and screech as they marched and flew across the land, and free to reassert their dominance as the mighty masters of their island home. ▪

Drawing up a storm
Kid Kaiju brought to life his own group of giant monsters: the robotic Mekara, the android Aegis, the dragon Slizzik, energy-based Hi-Vo, and the insectoid Scragg (clockwise from top).
Monsters Unleashed #1, Jun. 2017

Devolution in the dark

Seeking to further his illicit studies into evolution, the High Evolutionary secretly built a vast metropolis in the depths of Subterranea. The so-called Forever City was powered by a bizarre contraption called an Ascension Engine, a device the scientific genius believed would propel the city's genetically engineered inhabitants further up the evolutionary ladder. However, while the engine did indeed increase the intelligence of anyone within the vicinity of its projection field, it also caused them to devolve physically. Consequently, the High Evolutionary soon cut short his experiment and abandoned the Forever City to the perpetual darkness of Subterranea.

Decades later, with the power of the Ascension Engine building, Mole Man's Moloids found themselves drawn to the city. As they passed through its gates, their intelligence was increased to superhuman levels, while their bodies degenerated into a grotesque parody of the human form.

An unexpected side effect of this change was that these beings could not breed true. Their offspring were Moloid in appearance and thus considered inferior. The pariah children were banished to the city's catacombs until the Mole Man and the Fantastic Four set aside their differences to rescue them.

The Grove

Quiet Council chamber

House of X

Moira MacTaggert's No-Space

Arak Maw

House of M

Arbor Magna

Carousel

The Grove

Transit (main)

Arbor Magna

House of X

House of M

Carousel

Mutant Homecoming

A sentient landmass, Krakoa was born when a violent schism tore apart mutantkind's first and only homeland. Its symbiotic connection to Earth's mutant population completely severed, the island spent centuries adrift in pain and confusion. In modern times, however, the mutants returned, bringing with them renewed hope for the future.

Millennia ago, the immortals Apocalypse and Genesis founded the first mutant enclave on a sentient island called Okkara that lay to the south of the vast Pacific Ocean. The intention was to create a safe environment for mutants to perfect their many and varied superhuman abilities and thus prove themselves worthy of ruling the planet. All was well at first, with the mutants of Okkara developing a vibrant and expansive culture.

At some point, Apocalypse and Genesis conceived four children—two daughters and two sons—who went on to help their parents test the mettle of Okkara's mutants as the Four Horsemen: Famine, Death, Pestilence, and War. Okkara's singular perfection was not to last, however, and the land was literally cleaved in two by the dark god Annihilation. Using the magical Twilight Sword, she cut Okkara in half, creating two separate islands: Krakoa and Arakko. Annihilation's demonic horde then poured through the chasm between the sundered lands, intent on subsuming the entire world into the nightmarish realm of Amenth. Apocalypse and the mutants did their best to defeat the extradimensional invaders, but theirs was a losing battle.

In the end, the island of Arakko was pushed through the portal into Amenth. A large army of mutants, led by Genesis and the Four Horsemen, went with it to continue to harry the enemy in its own bleak domain. Apocalypse remained behind on Krakoa in order to prepare and strengthen mutantkind in case the Amenthi horde should ever return. As the immortal pursued his mission around the globe, Krakoa was left alone, mourning the loss of Arakko and the mutants who had once called the twin islands home.

> "The Twilight Sword of the enemy tore the world asunder, and what was one became two."
>
> **Krakoa**

Demon pit
Long ago, Annihilation wielded the Twilight Sword, cutting Okkara in two and creating a portal through which spilled Amenthi demons.
Powers of X #4, Nov. 2019

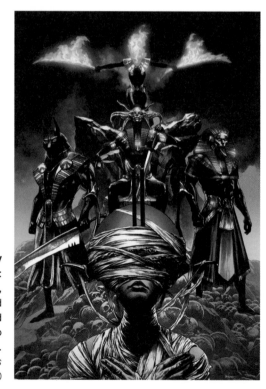

Fearsome family
Clockwise from left: Death, War, Genesis, Famine, and Pestilence braved a literal hell to protect mutantkind.
X of Swords: Stasis #1, Dec. 2020

Dream land
For centuries, Krakoa's outward appearance was that of a typical island in the Pacific Ocean. In reality, the sentient isle had fallen into a restless sleep.
House of X #5, Nov. 2019

Back to life

Krakoa remained in a fitful slumber for many centuries. In 1945, it was chosen by the United States government to serve as a sight for an atomic bomb test. The explosion awakened Krakoa to full sentience once more. It also damaged a nearby troop plane carrying Sergeant Nick Fury and his team the Howling Commandos, forcing the veteran war heroes to parachute onto the irradiated island. Angry at being awoken, Krakoa tormented Fury and his men—manifesting as a huge creature made of vegetation. Eventually, Krakoa made itself understood to Fury, and the two sides struck an accord. The island agreed to absorb the deadly radiation from the men in exchange for Fury's promise to keep Krakoa's true nature a secret.

Decades later, the mutant telepath Charles Xavier detected Krakoa's mental emanations and sent a team of X-Men, led by Cyclops, to the Pacific Ocean to investigate. The heroes were captured by Krakoa, who fed on their mutant energy to sustain its still-weakened form. In a desperate move, Xavier then convinced his friend Doctor Moira MacTaggert to send four of her own mutant students to the island. They managed to free Cyclops, but the other mutants remained trapped on Krakoa.

After arriving back in the United States, Cyclops joined with Xavier to scour the globe for undiscovered mutants. They found several, including the Kenyan Storm and the Russian Colossus, and forged a new team of international heroes. Under Cyclops's command, the new X-Men flew to Krakoa and successfully rescued the original squad. During the confrontation, Krakoa was pulled free of Earth's gravity and cast into the vacuum of outer space. The island was eventually discovered by the extraterrestrial Stranger and held captive for a time until freed and returned home by the quantum-empowered hero Quasar. Once again in the waters of the Pacific Ocean, Krakoa slipped back into a restless slumber, dreaming of the days when it had purpose and a vibrant population to protect and nurture.

Enemy territory
In the waning days of World War II, Sergeant Fury and the Howling Commandos found themselves on Krakoa, fighting against the island itself.
Journey into Mystery: The Birth of Krakoa #1, Nov. 2018

Homecoming

Some time after this, Charles Xavier and the mutant supremacist Magneto put aside their personal differences to work together to solve the problems that bedeviled mutantkind. For decades, mutants had been persecuted by both governments and individuals. Their powers set them apart from ordinary humans and they were, in equal measure, hated and feared. By forming his heroic X-Men, Xavier had hoped to demonstrate that mutants could be a force for good in the world, while Magneto had used terrorist means to further the interests of his people. Throughout the years, any attempt to establish a permanent mutant base, like the creation of Utopia in San Francisco bay, had met with disaster.

Now Xavier and Magneto pooled their resources and set in motion a far-reaching plan to establish a legitimate mutant nation-state on Krakoa. Their mission came about at the urging of Moira MacTaggert. Secretly a mutant, the geneticist had a remarkable ability to reincarnate. Upon her death, she would be reborn in utero with full awareness of her prior incarnations. In this manner, she had already gone through nine lives, amassing considerable knowledge and experience. The cumulative effect of this was that she had immense foresight into possible future events and had come to the conclusion that hostility between humanity and mutantkind was inevitable. In fact, in some of Moira's previous lives, she had seen the conflict become even more entrenched, with humankind melding with a malign machine intelligence to become post-human and even more hostile. Thanks to her unique perspective, Moira

Warm welcome
Professor Xavier flew mutant linguist Doug Ramsey to the Pacific Ocean to meet Krakoa and learn more about the island's history.
Powers of X #4, Nov. 2019

Cause for celebration
Professor Xavier and Magneto joined forces to create a mutant homeland on Krakoa—a move celebrated by the island's fresh arrivals.
Powers of X #6, Dec. 2019

As the population exploded, Krakoa provided a bounty of miraculous flowers that were used in a variety of ways. One bloom grew teleport gateways that provided instant transportation to anywhere in the universe. Another flower grew self-sustaining habitats, which were all connected via Krakoa's island consciousness. The most elaborate of these was Carousel, a vast exterior space filled with tree houses, which became home to numerous mutant families and was used for increasingly extravagant celebrations as the new nation slowly became a reality. Both Xavier and Magneto created their own habitats, which they dubbed the House of X and the House of M, respectively.

Some habitats were cut off from Krakoa's consciousness and Moira established a residence in one such place. Her No-Space was located deep underground, connected to the House of X via a secret portal. Much of the world believed Moira dead, victim to the mutant-killing Legacy virus, and she maintained this charade to help foster the birth of the Krakoan nation unhindered. Only Xavier and Magneto knew of Moira's crucial role in their master plan.

For security reasons, habitats for growing Krakoan flowers were established off the island, most notably in the prehistoric wilderness of the Savage Land. A secret base was also set up on the planet Mars for the processing of three particularly important blooms. These flowers were used as the main ingredients for a trio of revolutionary medicines that extended human life, maintained mental health, and acted as an all-purpose, adaptive antibiotic.

In exchange for Krakoa's miraculous gifts, it was agreed that the new mutant populace would donate a minimal amount of its psychic energy in order for the island to maintain its own robust health.

Communing with nature
With his innate ability to communicate in any language, Doug Ramsey was able to connect with Krakoa's consciousness.
Powers of X #4, Nov. 2019

knew things had to change if mutants were to survive as a species. It seemed saving the world as heroes, or dominating it as dictators, produced only the same tragic results in the end. A new way forward was required, and Moira convinced Xavier and Magneto to work together to establish a sovereign and inviolate mutant homeland.

Putting down roots

The first step in the plan was establishing communication with Krakoa. For this purpose, Xavier recruited Doug Ramsey, who had previously operated as the mutant hero Cypher. Ramsey possessed an intuitive ability to understand any form of language, be it written or spoken. He opened up a dialogue with Krakoa, slowly learning of the island's ancient history and developing an understanding of its current distress.

Over the course of several months, Krakoa and Doug established a deep bond and prepared the way for the arrival of the island's new inhabitants. Together they created a mutant language—different to Krakoa's native tongue, which only Doug could discern—which was imprinted telepathically into the minds of new arrivals.

Secret sanctuary
Hoping to remain anonymous, Moira MacTaggert maintained a hideout, dubbed No-Space, among the roots of Krakoa's trees.
House of X #6, Dec. 2019

World stage

When he deemed the time was right, Xavier decided to telepathically address the world, offering the global community access to the Krakoan medicines in exchange for official recognition of the new mutant state. The announcement shook the world, prompting even more mutants to flock to the island through strategically placed gateways, swelling the population to nearly 200,000. Some nations dismissed the offer out of hand and others even tried to assassinate the mutant leaders and steal the drugs for themselves.

Ultimately, the United Nations agreed on terms and granted Krakoa sovereignty. Naturally, the mutant medicines would not be provided free of charge, and after signing trade deals with more than 100 individual countries, Krakoa's national income rose exponentially. In the blink of an eye, the international order had been upended and the world changed irrevocably.

Among the fresh arrivals on Krakoa was Apocalypse. In recent years, he had been an avowed foe of the X-Men, and there were many, like Wolverine, who still believed he could not be trusted. Krakoa recognized him instantly, however, and greeted him with a flock

In the Grove
Under the watchful gaze of Krakoa, who manifested as a towering tree, the Quiet Council convened for the first time.
House of X #6, Dec. 2019

Back to the beginning
After time away from his original home, Apocalypse returned and was greeted by Krakoa and its new mutant citizens.
House of X #5, Nov. 2019

of birds, joyous that he had returned after so many millennia. While he was still unaware of Apocalypse and Krakoa's full history, this was enough for Xavier, who welcomed his former enemy home with a handshake. Other rogue mutants, who had previously used their gifts in pursuit of selfish ends, followed Apocalypse's lead and relocated to Krakoa. They were given unconditional pardons and the full protection of the state so long as they agreed to renounce their belligerent and criminal ways.

At some point, Krakoa spread its consciousness to the Atlantic Ocean. It created a small chain of five islands, including the Pointe, which served as a base of operations for the new country's security team X-Force, and Danger Island, which served as a training facility for all mutants.

With so many disparate voices vying to be heard, the Quiet Council was convened as Krakoa's governing body. It was subdivided into four sections named after the seasons, with each section consisting of three permanent members. Xavier, Magneto, and Apocalypse, the historical leaders of mutant society, comprised Autumn. Former terrorists Mister Sinister, Exodus, and Mystique were Winter. Spring, whose focus was primarily economic, consisted of entrepreneurs Sebastian

Shaw and Emma Frost, along with Xavier's onetime student Kate Pryde. Finally, former X-Men Storm, Jean Grey, and Nightcrawler were Summer, which was formed to embody the most heroic and noble aspirations of mutantkind. In addition to the council proper, Cypher and Krakoa also attended meetings—which were held in a natural amphitheater known as the Grove—to represent the interests of the island itself and promote the needs of the nation as a whole.

One of the Quiet Council's first acts was to write the three main tenets of law: mutants must make more mutants; mutants shall not murder humans; and the island of Krakoa must always be respected.

Resurrection protocols

Central to Xavier and MacTaggert's grand experiment was the concept of resurrection, a complex scientific process by which any fallen mutant could be brought back from the dead. Shortly after the foundation of the mutant nation, Xavier called on five uniquely gifted mutants— Hope Summers, Tempus, Proteus, Elixir, and Egg—to help him develop the procedure. Pooling their talents, the Five were able to generate biological husks in which viable clone bodies of dead mutants were grown. When hatched, these bodies were matured to the exact age of the deceased at the time of their passing. The final stage of resurrection involved the implanting of an individual mutant's memories and personalities, data that Xavier had spent years collecting via his super-computer Cerebro. Literally the backup file for thousands and thousands of mutants, this information was referred to in reverent terms as the Cradle, and five copies were made and stored in secret locations.

New statesmen
Former mutant heroes and villains agreed to set aside differences and come together to govern Krakoa as the Quiet Council.
Powers of X #1,
Sep. 2019

Flower power

Krakoa's transport gateways were made possible thanks to the unique properties of a specific bloom nurtured on the island. Since they shared a Krakoan consciousness, genetically identical pairs of these flowers could form organic wormholes between each other. This allowed for instantaneous transport to almost any location on Earth and beyond. In the months preceding Xavier's announcement of the mutant nation-state, flowers were planted in strategic locations around the globe, including Central Park in New York, the Arc de Triomphe in Paris, and Jubilee Gardens in London. By the time the outside world was aware of the new status quo, Krakoa's mutant population could be anywhere they wanted in a matter of mere seconds.

In addition to the terrestrial gateways, portals were also grown on Earth's moon, the planet Mars, and the throneworld of the intergalactic Shi'ar Empire.

Back on Krakoa, the gateways all opened up in Transit, a centralized hub that was carefully monitored by the mutants Cypher and Sage. New arrivals were screened telepathically and Krakoa ensured that only mutants could pass through the portals at will.

Immortal mutants
Professor X's crowning achievement was the Hatchery,
a place where mutants could be endlessly reborn.
House of X #5, Nov. 2019

Considered a sacred ritual, resurrection was performed in an underground chamber known as the Hatchery, which was formed from the roots of a gigantic fruit-bearing tree called the Arbor Magna.

Reunification

Shortly after Krakoa made its presence known to the world, a portion of lost Arakko inexplicably reappeared and merged with the larger island. Krakoa's separation anxiety was eased, but many were concerned about this unexpected turn of events. Under orders from Xavier, Cyclops took his adult children, Rachel and Nate, to investigate the new landmass that the Krakoan authorities had dubbed the Arak Coral. There they discovered the Arak Maw, an active volcano containing a long-abandoned gateway.

It was later revealed that the gateway connected to the ethereal kingdom of Otherworld and, somewhere beyond that realm, the remaining half of Arakko and the hellish lands of Amenth.

While on Arak Coral, Cyclops and his family encountered a mysterious individual who called himself the Summoner and who possessed an ability to bring forth hordes of eldritch beasts. Miscommunication led to a brief altercation in which the mutant heroes were almost overwhelmed by the intruder's monstrous creatures. Thanks to Rachel's telepathic powers, however, the two parties were eventually able to understand each other and agreed on a truce. Cyclops took the Summoner to be a confused and lost soul, little suspecting that the newcomer was on a mission of grave importance.

Explosive reunion
When a portion of lost Arakko materialized in the Pacific Ocean, it merged with Krakoa.
X-Men #2, Jan. 2020

"I mean to save all of my children. Those of Krakoa … and those of Arakko.**"**

Apocalypse

The Summoner was actually Apocalypse's grandson, born to War some three centuries earlier in Amenth. He had endured much suffering in his long life and had traveled to Earth with a dire message for his grandfather—the walls of Arakko had been breached, and the mutant defenders were at the point of being overrun by the Amenthi horde. On hearing the news, Apocalypse promised to smite the demons and unify Krakoa and Arakko no matter the cost.

For centuries, Krakoa had been dormant and its existence meaningless since the loss of its original mutant population. Now, thanks to the workings of MacTaggert, Xavier, and their allies, the island had been reunited with its people. The lost land was lost no longer. The mutant homecoming had been a joyous event, and remarkably, it promised to be just the prelude to a far more significant occurrence—the reunification of the twin islands of Krakoa and Arakko.

Battling beasts
While exploring Arak Maw, Cyclops and his children, Nate and Rachel, were almost overwhelmed by other-dimensional beasts.
X-Men #2, Jan. 2020

The Cosmos

Immeasurable and infinite, much of the universe remains unknowable. However, among the countless galaxies that comprise the cosmos, some have given up their secrets. In the Andromeda Galaxy, the shape-shifting Skrulls established one of the oldest known empires, expanding out of their native Drox System, while the Xandarians of the Tranta System formed the peacekeeping Nova Corps. In the Large Magellanic Cloud, in the Pama System, the Kree used stolen Skrull technology to build their own empire, whereas the Spartoi created a more modest domain from their native Sparta System. Light-years away in the Shi'ar Galaxy, the Shi'ar absorbed numerous inhabited worlds into their Imperium, while a mighty Intergalactic Empire of Wakanda arose in the Benhazin System. Wakanda's origins lay in the Milky Way, home to the heroes of Earth, Thanos of Titan, and the mysterious Blue Area of the Moon. Beyond this swirling celestial cluster lies the savage world of Sakaar, Ego, the Living Planet, and many other stellar wonders.

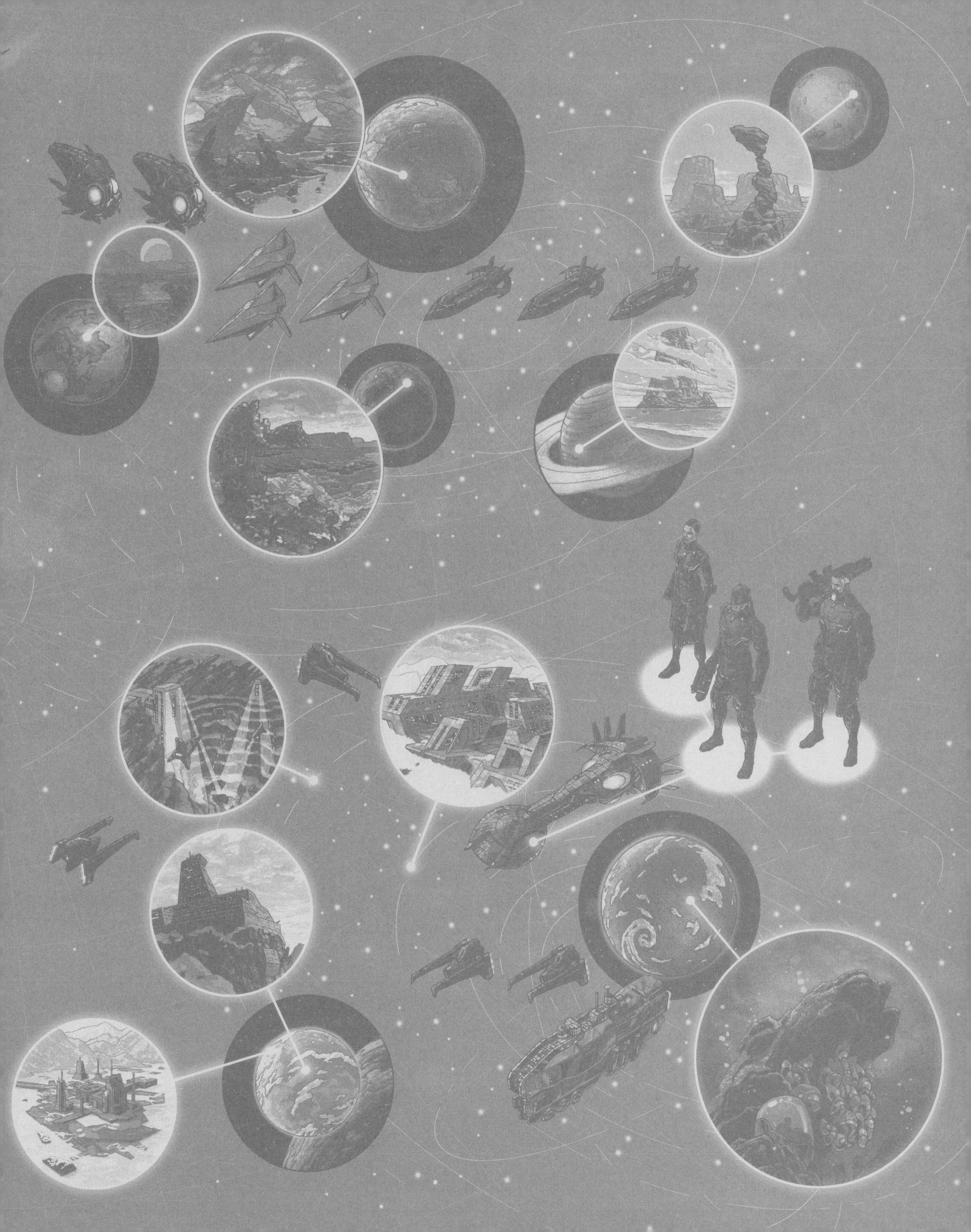

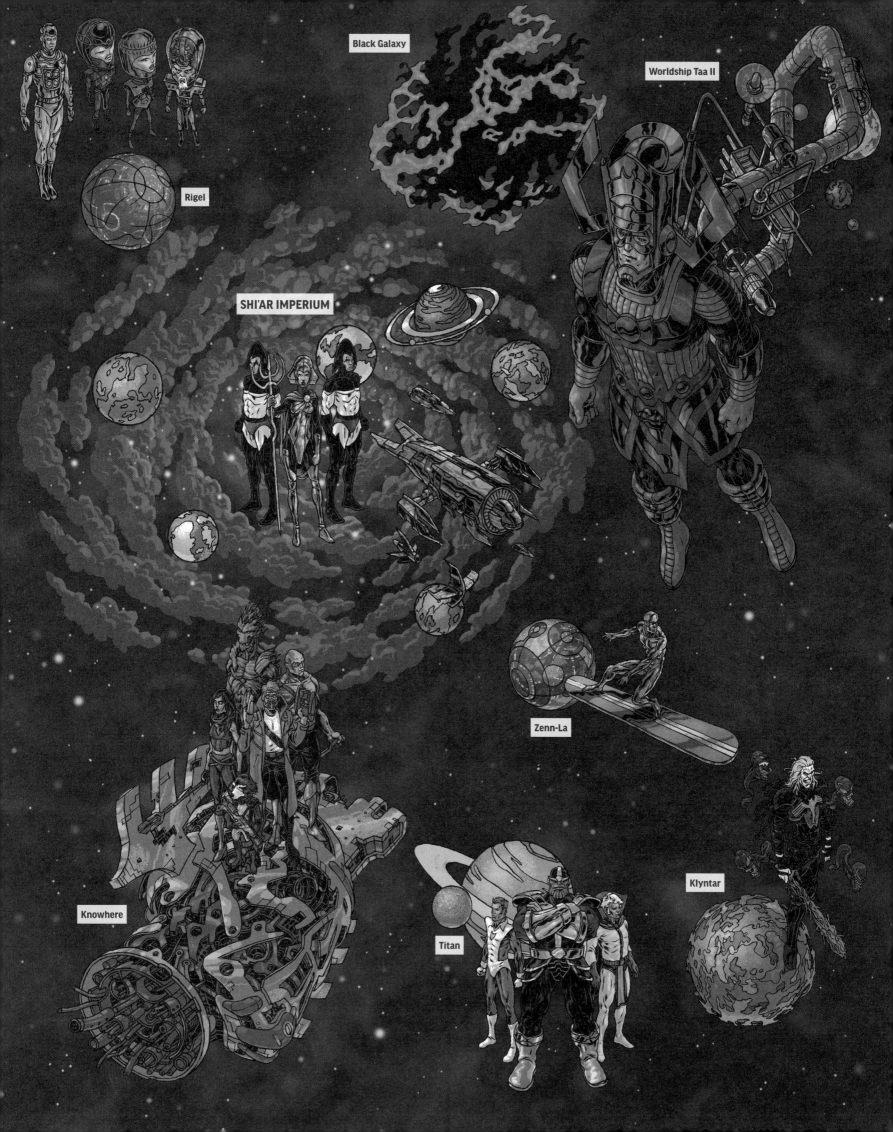

Black Galaxy

Worldship Taa II

Rigel

SHI'AR IMPERIUM

Zenn-La

Knowhere

Titan

Klyntar

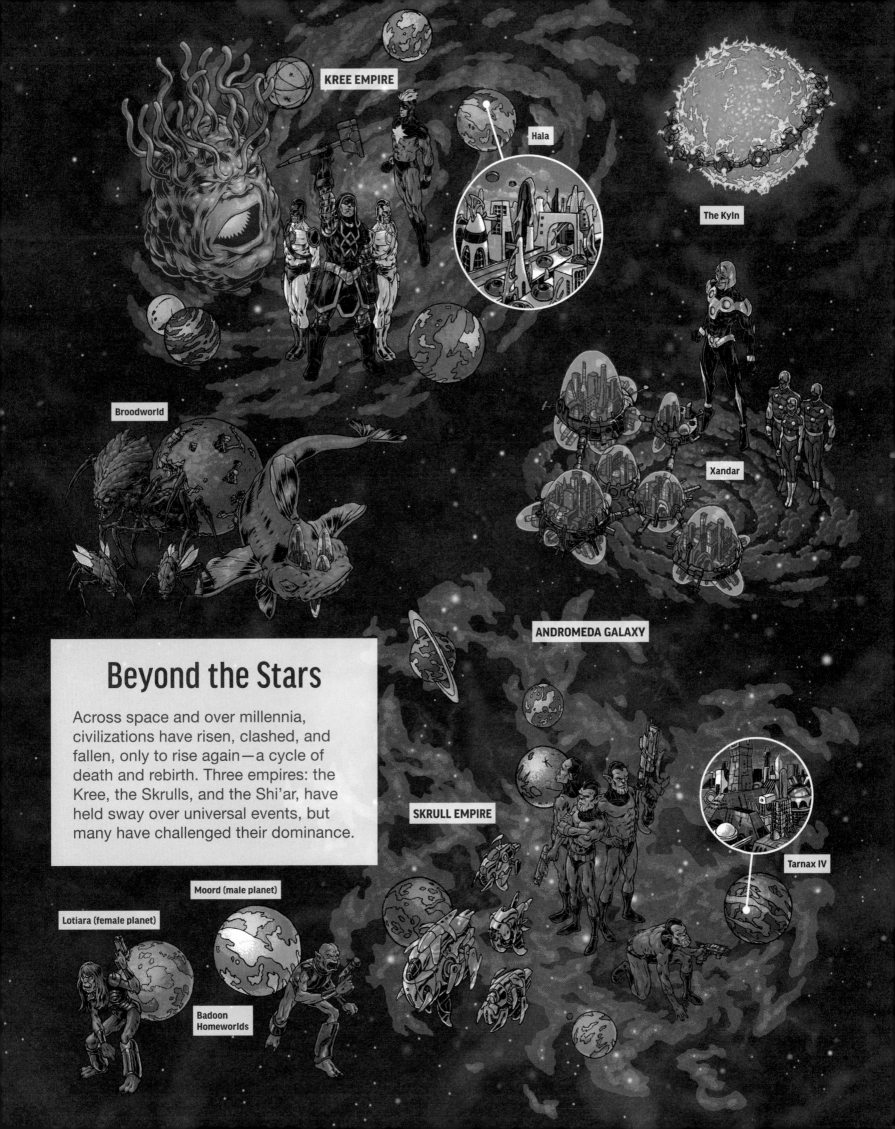

KREE EMPIRE

Hala

The Kyln

Broodworld

Xandar

ANDROMEDA GALAXY

Beyond the Stars

Across space and over millennia, civilizations have risen, clashed, and fallen, only to rise again—a cycle of death and rebirth. Three empires: the Kree, the Skrulls, and the Shi'ar, have held sway over universal events, but many have challenged their dominance.

SKRULL EMPIRE

Tarnax IV

Moord (male planet)

Lotiara (female planet)

Badoon
Homeworlds

Celestial interference
Near-omnipotent space gods the Celestials intervened in the genetic development of many species, including the Skrulls.
Incredible Hercules #117, Jul. 2008

Like mankind and all other humanoid life-forms, the origins of the Skrulls, Kree, and Shi'ar are clouded in mystery. Some believe they were the descendants of the ancient Xorrians; others, the creation of the Builders—thought to be the oldest known race in the universe. But while the truth of their beginnings is disputed, what is certain is that their empires have been instrumental in much that has occurred in the universe.

Native to the Andromeda Galaxy, the reptilian Skrulls originated on the planet Skrullos in the Drox System. Millions of years ago, the Skrulls' ancestors were visited by the Celestials, godlike beings known for tampering with the development of numerous species. The genetic experiments conducted by these mysterious cosmic entities resulted in a number of variants of the Skrull race: the long-lived Skrullian Eternals, equivalent to Earth's powerful Eternals; Normal—or Prime—Skrulls whose genes were programmed to benevolently mutate once the variant reached maturation; and Deviant Skrulls, who developed shape-shifting and mimicry abilities. Aided by their powers, and led by the warrior Sl'gur't, the Deviant Skrulls wiped out virtually every other variant, leaving them the dominant Skrull species. A sorcerous subspecies of the Deviant variant was also hunted but fled to the Dark Nebula star system.

Over time, the Skrulls developed a technologically advanced society, one that would become spacefaring. Their shape-shifting abilities proved beneficial as they began colonizing worlds across the Andromeda Galaxy, allowing the Skrulls to assume the forms of the species they encountered and become assimilated into their societies. In this way, the Skrulls established an interstellar empire, with a new homeworld, Tarnax IV.

At this juncture in their development, the Skrulls were not especially aggressive or militaristic, preferring instead to establish bonds with the societies of these new worlds through mimicry and trade. That was destined to change, however, as the Skrulls' expanding empire took them outside the Andromeda Galaxy, initially to the Large Magellanic Cloud, where they encountered the cosmic race known as the Kree.

Seat of power
With the expansion of their empire, the Skrulls established a new throneworld, Tarnax IV. It was, however, eventually destroyed by Galactus.
Road to Empyre: The Kree/Skrull War #1, May 2020

Hala forever

Hailing from the planet Hala in the Large Magellanic Cloud's Pama System, the Kree, like the Skrulls, were experimented on by the Celestials, but the two subspecies produced—Kree Eternals and Deviants—did not rise to prominence. The Kree were originally a blue-skinned species, but over time, a group with skin coloring similar to that of humans emerged, and since then the two variants have existed side by side. Outwardly humanoid, the Kree was a barbaric race possessed of superior strength and stamina, due to Hala's heavy gravity and a high percentage of nitrogen in the atmosphere. The Kree shared Hala with another sentient race, the peaceful, plant-based Cotati, with whom they had little contact.

Like the Skrulls, the Kree were destined to establish an interstellar empire in their native galaxy, but in this they owed a debt to the Skrulls. When the Kree were still at a relatively primitive stage, Hala was discovered by the spacefaring Skrulls, led by Emperor Dorrek. He offered up Skrullian knowledge and technology in exchange for loyalty but, keen to avoid dissent, was adamant that the Kree and the Cotati could not both represent Hala in the growing empire. He devised a test: 17 representatives from each species would be transported to two barren planetoids and left for a year to fend for themselves. The Cotati were deposited on an unnamed planetoid, while the Kree were placed on Earth's moon.

Furnished with an artificial atmosphere—what would come to be known as the Blue Area of the Moon—and equipped with a variety of tools, the Kree began to build, making full use of their strength and the near-constant daylight. By the time the year was up, the colonists had erected a colossal shining city, an incredible achievement that duly impressed the visiting Skrulls. However, when the 17 Kree were returned to Hala, they learned that in fact the Skrulls favored the efforts of the Cotati, who had transformed their planetoid into a garden paradise. Enraged, Morag, the leader of the Kree colonists, led his people in a frenzied assault on the Cotati, wiping them out completely—or so it was believed.

> "Skrulls may deal with barbarians, but we do not condone barbarianism!"
>
> **Emperor Dorrek**

War and peace
Dorrek's contest exposed the true nature of the Kree—aggressive and industrial—and the Cotati—peaceful and at one with nature.
Road to Empyre: The Kree/Skrull War #1, May 2020

Sore losers
When the Kree lost the Skrulls' competition, they turned their ire on the Cotati, then on the Skrulls, stealing their technology.
Road to Empyre: The Kree/Skrull War #1, May 2020

Capital Kree
The Kree homeworld of Hala was dominated by a gargantuan capital city-state, Kree-Lar, and was guarded by robotic Sentries.
FF #6, Sep. 2011

Waging war

Having destroyed the Cotati, the Kree informed their Skrull benefactors that the problem of who would represent Hala had now been solved. Outraged, Dorrek declared that Hala would forever be excluded from the Skrull Empire, prompting the Kree to slaughter the party of Skrulls and seize their starship and technology. Decades later, having constructed an armada, the Kree launched an assault on the Skrulls in the Andromeda Galaxy, igniting the Kree-Skrull War.

The war between the two species raged for millennia, ranging across thousands of worlds, but it also proved a boon to both sides. The Skrulls became more militaristic to counter the threat, while the Kree were able to greatly expand their fledgling empire into a vast dictatorship, conquering countless worlds and establishing a new planet, Kree-Lar, as their seat of power. Judgelike Accusers would uphold the Kree Empire's laws and robotic Sentries would enforce them. Guiding them in this was their Supreme Intelligence, or Supremor, a huge computer intellect comprising the greatest minds of the Kree race.

One group of Kree rejected the majority's increasingly warlike ways, however. Shunned by the wider society, this small, pacifist sect developed telepathic abilities via meditation, which led them to a hidden group of Cotati who had grown from seed pods dropped by their slaughtered brethren. The Priests of Pama, as they became known, protected the Cotati and were eventually able to spirit them away from their hideout, secreting them on numerous planets—among them Earth, specifically the jungles of Vietnam. Many years later, these Earthbound Kree and Cotati would be instrumental in the selection and training of the Avenger-to-be, Mantis. They primed the young woman to join with a Cotati— in the form of the deceased Avenger the Swordsman— and assume the mantle of the Celestial Madonna.

Supreme being
Appearing as a disembodied head, the artificial intelligence known as the Supremor was created a million years ago to impart wisdom to the Kree population.
Guardians of the Galaxy #25, May 2015

Lady Madonna
From childhood, Mantis's telepathic abilities were honed in preparation for her role as Celestial Madonna.
Giant-Size Avengers #4, Jun. 1975

Toward Titan
Passing Saturn en route back to Earth in a ship built using Kree technology, the Eternal Uranos and his followers were pursued by a Kree armada.
What If? #27, Jul. 1981

Earth in their sights

Even before the Priests of Pama hid the Cotati on Earth, the Kree had their eyes on the planet. A Kree outpost on Uranus was raided by the belligerent Eternal Uranos and his fellow human Eternals—evolved, like the Kree and the Skrulls, by the Celestials—who had been exiled from Earth. Discovering all manner of Kree technology on the planet, the outcasts planned to build a spaceship and return to Earth in order to obliterate their brethren. In the event, the renegade Eternals' destruction of the outpost's guardian Sentry alerted the Kree, who dispatched a fleet of warships to intercept Uranos's craft.

This incident had two distinct consequences. After the Kree had destroyed Uranos's vessel, they retrieved a single Eternal from the cold clutches of space. The Supreme Intelligence had believed humanity to be tree-dwelling savages and so was surprised by the genetic superiority of the specimen. He allowed the Kree to conduct their own genetic experiments on mankind, resulting in the race known as the Inhumans. Meanwhile, Uranos and a small band of Eternals also survived the Kree attack and made their way to one of Saturn's satellites. Suitably chastened by their folly, they determined to build a new world to rival the Earth city of their birth, Titanos, naming it Titan. Their descendants would be called Titans, and one in particular would profoundly impact the universe: Thanos.

As the age of heroes began on Earth, the Kree became evermore involved in the planet's affairs—and vice versa. After the Fantastic Four accidentally destroyed a Kree outpost on a remote island, along with the Sentry guarding it, the Supreme Intelligence dispatched the Accuser Ronan to pronounce sentence. The Fantastic Four defeated Ronan, prompting the Supremor to send Kree Captain Mar-Vell to Earth on a covert mission to assess humanity's capabilities. Instead, Mar-Vell became one of Earth's greatest protectors, fighting alongside the Avengers before succumbing to cancer and passing on the mantle of Captain Marvel to Earth's Carol Danvers.

Mar-Vell to Marvel
Kree Captain Mar-Vell was branded a traitor by his people after he allied himself with Earth's heroes, becoming Captain Marvel.
Lords of Empyre Emperor Hulkling #1, Sep. 2020

"Unknown and unsuspected, I hold the fate of a planet within my hands!"

Captain Marvel

Enter the Shi'ar

The war between the Kree and the Skrulls wasn't just confined to the two species. The other great intergalactic power, the birdlike Shi'ar, was also sucked into the conflict and would be a major player in other wars. A humanoid species descended from avians, the Shi'ar hailed from a planet they called Aerie in the Shi'ar Galaxy. From there they struck out and established an empire, co-opting almost every world and culture in their galaxy into their Shi'ar Imperium. To maintain order, super-powered individuals were selected from across the empire to join the Imperial Guard, with an elite corps, commanded by Gladiator, to protect the majestor (emperor) or majestrix (empress). A young empire compared to those of the Kree and the Skrulls, the Shi'ar shared

Insect invasion
Reportedly the universe's first natural predators, the Brood emerged from a dark galaxy and infested the planet Sleazeworld—a nightmarish place hiding unimaginable horrors in its depths.
Incredible Hulk #94, Jun. 2006

Imperial unrest
Even in Trelleri—a retreat for the Shi'ar High Council and royalty—majestrix Lilandra Neramani was aware that danger was ever-present.
Uncanny X-Men #481, Feb. 2007

a common, albeit remote, ancestry with another relatively young empire, the Spartoi, who hailed from the planet Spartax in the Large Magellanic Cloud, and who formed a loose alliance with the Shi'ar.

The fate of the Shi'ar became inextricably intertwined with that of Earth when the mutant X-Men, along with galactic outlaws the Starjammers, helped prevent the mad Emperor D'ken from gaining full control of the powerful M'kraan Crystal. This allowed D'ken's younger sister Lilandra to become majestrix instead. Sometime later, under the sway of the near-omnipotent Phoenix Force, the X-Men's Jean Grey consumed a star within the Shi'ar Galaxy, D'bari IV, causing the deaths of millions and briefly allying the Shi'ar, the Kree, and the Skrulls in the face of her threat.

Subsequently, Lilandra's sister Deathbird, in her efforts to usurp the majestrix, allied with the Shi'ar's enemies the Brood—a parasitic, insectoid species, typically commanded by a Brood Queen, who established a base on the planet Broodworld (aka Sleazeworld). Later still, Vulcan—Deathbird's husband and brother of the X-Men's Cyclops and Havok—seized control of the Shi'ar Imperium, igniting a devastating War of Kings between the Shi'ar and the Kree, who, at that time, were ruled by the Inhumans.

Negative impact
Annihilus, insectoid ruler of the antimatter Negative Zone, has repeatedly tried to invade the positive universe.
Annihilation Scourge Alpha #1, Jan. 2020 (variant cover)

Annihilation overload
Annihilus's most overwhelming assault was the Annihilation Wave, an unstoppable fleet of insectoid warships that decimated the planet Xandar and the Nova Corps.
Annihilation: Prologue #1, May 2006

Waves of annihilation

In truth, war has ever been a cosmic constant, but the frequency of conflicts only seemed to increase as time wore on. One of the most devastating was the Annihilation Wave instigated by Annihilus, despotic ruler of the Negative Zone. Assembling an armada of horrific insectoid starships crewed by countless bugs, Annihilus launched a tsunami of destruction across the universe, prompting multiple species to unite against the onslaught.

One of the earliest casualties of that conflict was the Nova Corps, an intergalactic police force based on Xandar in the Andromeda Galaxy. Also known as the Xandarian StarCorps, its source of power was the Nova Force, a near-limitless energy source controlled by an artificial intelligence called the Worldmind. Though the Nova Corps was almost completely wiped out by Annihilus's forces—save for Earth's representative, Richard Rider—it was subsequently reconstructed and has proven remarkably resilient in the face of similar disasters.

No sooner had the Annihilation Wave been turned back than another catastrophic conflict erupted, as the techno-organic species known as the Phalanx took advantage of the postwar chaos by invading the Kree Empire, cutting it off from the rest of the cosmos via an energy barrier. Originating in an unknown host galaxy, over which they had complete control, the Phalanx was led on this occasion by Ultron, a malevolent AI created on Earth. After attempting to subjugate all living things by infecting them with a techno-organic virus transmitted via a giant Babel Spire on Hala, the Phalanx was eventually defeated through the combined efforts of multiple individuals and various empires.

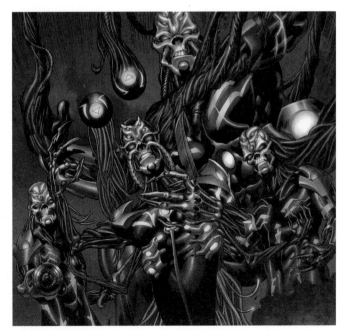

Techno terrors
Humanoid in appearance with six eyes and weapons that extended from their limbs, the Phalanx communicated via a hive mind.
Annihilation: Conquest Prologue #1, Aug. 2007

Guardians together

The Annihilation: Conquest, as the war with the Phalanx was known, was the catalyst for the formation of a ragtag group of galactic misfits, many of whom had also fought together against the Annihilation Wave. Taking their name from a far-future band of freedom fighters, these self-styled Guardians of the Galaxy were brought together by half-human Peter Quill, with a mission to protect the people of the cosmos from all threats. Hailing from Earth, Quill was the son of a human woman, Meredith, and a Spartax prince, J'Son. Quill's heritage propelled him into a life of misadventure among the stars under the alias Star-Lord.

The rest of the Guardians' origins were as disparate as their motivations for banding together. Also originally from Earth, Drax was once a human named Arthur Douglas, until he was murdered by Thanos and transformed into a powerful new being whose sole purpose was to destroy the Titan. Gamora, too, had a connection with Thanos—she was adopted by him and trained as an assassin after her people, the Zen-Whoberians, were wiped out. Groot, a member of the treelike *Flora colossi*, was exiled from his homeworld Planet X, prompting him to briefly turn his anger on the unwitting people of Earth before he mended his ways. During the Annihilation: Conquest, he formed a close bond with the raccoonlike Rocket, a genetically altered former warden of Halfworld, a quarantined colony for the insane in the Keystone Quadrant. Other guardians included Adam Warlock,

Knowhere
The head of a Celestial—said to have been severed by the abyssal god Knull—now served as an interdimensional scientific center.
Infinity Countdown #4, Aug. 2018

On guard
Groot, Gamora, Star-Lord, Rocket, and Drax the Destroyer constituted the core lineup of the Guardians of the Galaxy.
Guardians of the Galaxy #1, May 2013

a cosmic adventurer who had been originally designed by the scientific cabal known as the Enclave to be the perfect human, and Phyla-Vell, the artificially created "daughter" of Kree warrior, Mar-Vell.

The Guardians initially based themselves on an interdimensional hub built out of the severed head of a Celestial, which they dubbed Knowhere. With Mantis and Cosmo—a telepathic canine who was sent into space as a test subject by the Soviet Union, but who ended up as Knowhere's head of security—as the team's support staff, they battled a variety of galactic threats. These included the Universal Church of Truth, a religious empire that worshipped Adam Warlock's future evil alter ego the Magus; the Badoon, a devious reptilian race separated along gender lines; and the Chitauri, an insectlike species who were lured to attack Earth by Captain America after he had been corrupted by the powerful Cosmic Cube.

The Chitauri wave
Lured by a twisted doppelgänger of Captain America, the Chitauri force that attacked Earth almost rivaled the Annihilation Wave in size and savagery.
Guardians of the Galaxy #27, Jul. 2015

War upon war

The war with the Chitauri was just one of the many galactic conflicts in which the Guardians became entangled. They were key protagonists in the War of Kings and played a peripheral role when the ancient Builders, who claimed to have created most life in the universe, assembled a vast fleet and set about destroying multiple worlds in an effort to wipe the slate clean and start over. Fortunately, the universe's various empires and Earth's Avengers united to defeat the menace, while the Guardians helped defend Earth from Thanos, who had taken advantage of the Avengers' absence by invading the planet.

For a time, the Guardians fell foul of the Spartax Empire, specifically Star-Lord's father, J'Son, who had risen to become the Spartoi's king. After being rejected by his people and deposed by his son, J'Son took on a new identity, Mister Knife, and sought out an ancient artifact that conferred cosmic power on its owner, known as the Black Vortex. When J'Son took his revenge on Spartax by turning the planet's entire population over to the Brood to be used as hosts, the Guardians and their allies the X-Men used the power of the Black Vortex to defeat him.

The clash with J'Son paled in comparison to the conflict that came after, however. Having averted the existential threat of the Builders, the empires and civilizations of the universe were soon faced with an even greater catastrophe. A series of incursions were set in motion by the extradimensional Beyonders, causing universes to collide and destroying every alternate reality. Despite the best efforts of the Guardians and Earth's heroes, all that could be saved were remnants of the lost realities. These were forged into a single patchwork planet named Battleworld. Ultimately, it was left to the Fantastic Four to reconstitute the Multiverse using the Beyonders' own power.

Mirror, mirror …
The Celestial-created Black Vortex helped users realize their cosmic potential.
Guardians of the Galaxy & X-Men: The Black Vortex Omega #1, Jun. 2015

The Negative Zone

Parallel to the regular universe is an area where all matter is negatively charged. This antimatter Negative Zone was first discovered by Reed Richards of the Fantastic Four, but it is believed to be at least as old as the positive universe. However, unlike its counterpart, the Negative Zone was home to just one indigenous intelligent species: the Tyannans. A lionlike, humanoid race, they explored the farthest reaches of the Negative Zone, seeding planets as they went. One such world was Baluur, where a powerful individual named Blastaar rose to become king and establish an empire.

The most significant creation of the Tyannans was an unintentional one, however. When a Tyannan ship crashed on the barren world of Arthros, its captain decided to seed the world before he and the crew starved to death. Millions of years later, a sole Arthrosian insectoid evolved to intelligence: Annihilus. The Negative Zone empire he established soon outstripped even that of his great rival, Blastaar, and after encountering the Fantastic Four, he set his sights on the positive universe.

Light versus dark

As with the war with the Beyonders, the seeds of many of the conflicts that convulsed the cosmos were sown long in the past, and such was the case with another war that erupted soon after the Beyonders' assault. When the universe was new, a primordial being came into existence: Knull, the God of the Abyss. A creature of the dark, this self-styled King in Black was offended by the light that had begun to infect creation and raged against its brilliance. He established a race of Symbiote predators and constructed a throneworld from which to rule the void, named Klyntar.

Eventually Knull was imprisoned within Klyntar. Billions of years later, he escaped, destroying the planet and unleashing a horde of Symbiote Dragons on the galaxy. Laying waste to countless worlds, his army of darkness eventually reached Earth, where his Symbiote Dragons formed a sphere around the planet, cutting it off from the sun. With the world plunged into seemingly eternal night, Knull's Symbiotes began possessing many of the heroes who valiantly struggled against the onslaught.

Knull had reckoned without his opposite number, however—the so-called God of Light—against whom he had fought at the dawn of time. This primordial entity was also known under another name: the Enigma Force. In its Uni-Power form, the Enigma Force possessed a succession of hosts, transforming them into Captain

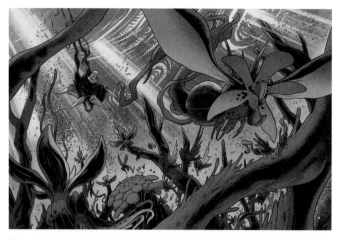

Planet of the Symbiotes
Little was known about the Symbiote homeworld Klyntar until the Guardians of the Galaxy were taken there by Agent Venom (Flash Thompson). *Guardians of the Galaxy* #23, Mar. 2015

Universe, protector of the cosmos. Freed from the planetary prison it had been confined to by Knull, the Enigma Force sought a new host—Eddie Brock—to stop the King in Black. As the antihero Venom, Eddie had long been a host for one of Knull's Symbiotes, and his part in the struggle against the Abyssal God proved pivotal.

Yet as devastating as the war against Knull and virtually all the other cosmic conflicts were, they were minor compared with the most persistent blight the universe has ever known, Thanos.

King in Black
Awakened from his slumber in Klyntar, Knull, God of the Abyss, brandished his sword All-Black and unleashed across the cosmos mayhem with his Symbiotes. *King in Black* #1, Feb. 2021

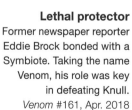

Lethal protector
Former newspaper reporter Eddie Brock bonded with a Symbiote. Taking the name Venom, his role was key in defeating Knull. *Venom* #161, Apr. 2018

Magus vs. monster
An alternate future version of Adam Warlock, the Magus tried to subvert Warlock to ensure his own existence, but was opposed by Thanos.
Warlock #11, Feb. 1976

Thanos rising

Born to Mentor and Sui-San on Titan, and thus a distant descendant of the Eternals who had originally colonized the planet, Thanos was shunned by his fellow Titans due to his malformed and mutated appearance. He developed an unhealthy obsession with the personification of Death, prompting him to murder first two of his classmates then others, including his own mother. After fleeing retribution, he later returned and decimated Titan as a tribute to Death.

These acts were merely a prelude to what would evolve into a remorseless campaign of death and destruction on a cosmic scale. Thanos's love of Death led him to a fascination with objects of power. Initially he focused his attention on the Cosmic Cube, which brought him into repeated conflict with his own brother, Starfox; with the Kree warrior Captain Marvel; and with Drax the Destroyer, who unrelentingly pursued him. Thanos subsequently became fixated on the immensely powerful, reality-altering Infinity Gems, over which he tangled with Adam Warlock. Collecting all six gems and forging an Infinity Gauntlet, Thanos used his new omnipotence to extinguish half of all life in the universe as a tribute to Death, before an all-out assault by Earth's heroes allowed Warlock to wrest control of the gauntlet and undo Thanos's atrocity.

Pursuing his own agenda, the Mad Titan allied for a time with Warlock in the Infinity Watch, alongside, among others, his adopted daughter, Gamora, and his mortal enemy, Drax. Charged with safeguarding the Infinity Gems, the group was soon pitted against Warlock's alter ego the Magus, who was attempting to replace all reality and its denizens with warped doppelgängers. Thanos continued to work with Warlock on occasion after the Magus was defeated, but his obsession with power just as frequently took him down darker paths.

Fighting fist
Perhaps the most powerful weapon ever created, the Infinity Gauntlet was forged by Thanos to house the six Infinity Gems.
Guardians of the Galaxy #8, Feb. 2009 (variant cover)

"I hold the galaxy in my palm—ready to crush it like an eggshell!**"**
Thanos

A Titan's travels

One such path led Thanos to the Kyln, a maximum security penal facility built into the mysterious energy cascade known as the Crunch. It was here, on the eve of Annihilus's Annihilation Wave attack, that Thanos first encountered Peter Quill, a portentous meeting given what was to transpire. For not only would Thanos play a vital role in Annihilus's impending Annihilation Wave, but later, when Quill formed the Guardians of the Galaxy, the Titan and the Guardians' paths would repeatedly cross.

When Annihilus launched his invasion, Thanos joined forces with the Negative Zone ruler, until Drax caught up with the Titan and tore out his heart. This was not the first time Thanos had been slain only to be resurrected, and it would not be the last. In this instance, after he was reborn, Thanos briefly allied with the Guardians of the Galaxy against an invading force from the Cancerverse (led by an alternate version of the original Captain Marvel, Mar-Vell), though to his own nefarious ends.

Later, during the war with the Builders, Thanos took advantage of the Avengers' absence by launching an invasion of Earth with his own army, the brutal Black Order. Comprising Corvus Glaive, Ebony Maw, Proxima Midnight, Supergiant, and Black Dwarf, their attack turned out to be a ruse. Thanos was in fact searching for his estranged son, Thane, an Eternal-Inhuman hybrid who he intended to murder. It transpired that Thane was hiding in Orollan, an offshoot Inhuman city situated in the Eternal Chasm in Greenland.

Time and again, the Mad Titan would cause chaos across the galaxy, seeking power and dominion over the living and the dead. However, there is one immensely powerful being who has had arguably an even greater impact on the cosmos, an entity who predates the universe itself: Galactus, the World-Devourer.

A prison for gods
Created by Galactus from the galactic energy barrier dubbed the Crunch, the Kyln became home to some of the cosmos's worst criminals.
Annihilation: Prologue #1, May 2006

New order
Transdimensional being Black Swan joined Thanos's Black Order after original member Supergiant was killed. *Black Order* #1, Jan. 2019 (variant cover)

A world of wonders
Taa had been a place of technological
marvels and miracles until the universe
collapsed into the Big Bang, destroying it.
Fantastic Four #522, Mar. 2005

The hunger awakens

A wandering cosmic giant with an insatiable appetite that can
be sated only by feasting on the energy of planets, Galactus has
crisscrossed the universe in search of sustenance, leaving only
the lifeless husks of worlds in his wake. Some call him a force for
balance in the cosmos; most merely fear his arrival.

   Galactus was originally Galan, an explorer from the planet Taa in
the universe that existed before the present one. Taa was a paradise,
but it was also doomed by a creeping plague, for which Galan found
there was no cure. In a final futile gesture of defiance, Galan and a
small crew flew a starship into the heart of the universe's largest sun.
All onboard were killed—save one. Galan was bonded to an abstract
entity called the Sentience of the Universe as the cosmos collapsed.
His ship rocketed out of the Big Bang into a new universe, where it
crashed on a planet. Seen by a Watcher—a race of impartial observers
charged with recording events but never to interfere—Galan struggled
to contain the energies coursing through him. After blasting off again,
he transformed his ship into an incubator, drifting for centuries until,
orbiting the planet Archeopia, his vessel was attacked.

   This assault was the catalyst for Galan to be reborn as Galactus.
Consumed by a ravenous hunger, he destroyed the attacking ships,
then fed on Archeopia, destroying it. However, moved by the carnage
he had caused, he vowed to reconstruct the planet, spending millennia
fashioning the ruins into a huge worldship, Taa II. From this base,
Galactus set about sating his hunger, seeking out planets upon which
to feed. As time passed, he realized that he needed scouts to locate
suitable worlds for him. He enlisted a series of heralds, selecting a
succession of beings and imbuing them with the power they would
need for their task. The greatest of these was the Silver Surfer.

The Infinity Gems

Before recorded time, all of reality
was part of a single living entity
known as Nemesis. Infinite and
forever, consigned to a lonely,
desolate existence, Nemesis
decided to end her existence;
but her power could not be
extinguished so easily, and her
core was reincarnated in the form
of six Infinity Gems. Each precious
stone granted mastery of an aspect
of reality: Power, Time, Space,
Reality, Mind, and Soul.

   The first to be discovered was the
Soul Gem, which was grafted onto
a newly reborn Adam Warlock by
geneticist the High Evolutionary.
Later, all six gems were gathered
by Thanos during a reality-spanning
quest that saw the Titan seizing
them from six Elders of the
Universe: the In-Betweener,
the Champion, the Gardener,
the Runner, the Collector, and the
Grand Master. Since that time,
the gems have been used by many
individuals, including Captain
America—who tried to stop the
Beyonders' incursions with them—
and Gamora—who temporarily
used them to create a pocket
dimension known as Warp World.

The Power Cosmic

Forging a path among the stars, the Silver Surfer has had an indelible impact on peoples and events from the major to the minor. He was born Norrin Radd on the planet Zenn-La in the Deneb star system, an idyllic nirvana where war, crime, and illness had been eliminated. But despite living in a paradise and having the love of his partner, Shalla-Bal, Norrin still hungered for more. Long ago, the denizens of Zenn-La had explored the stars, their heroes were the astronauts who had journeyed to a thousand galaxies; but by Norrin's time, Zenn-La's citizens had withdrawn, never to venture forth again. Alone among his people, Norrin dreamed of exploring the universe, little realizing that he would soon get the chance and unaware that it would cost him his love and his home.

When Galactus arrived at Zenn-La, Norrin struck a bargain: to prevent the cosmic giant from consuming the planet and to spare its population, Norrin would act as a herald, seeking out suitable worlds as substitutes. In return, he would have to leave behind the only home he had ever known. After being imbued with the Power Cosmic by Galactus, Norrin now had the ability to soar among the stars. He bade farewell to Shalla-Bal and Zenn-La, before embarking on a solitary life as a herald under the name the Silver Surfer.

The Silver Surfer served Galactus faithfully for decades, aiding him in the destruction of hundreds of worlds and abetting in the deaths of millions, little realizing that Galactus had tampered with his psyche to abate the guilt he would have otherwise felt. Then, one fateful day, he led his master to Earth, and both their destinies were forever altered.

Adventure ahead
Norrin Radd's love, Shalla-Bal, sensed that he yearned for more than she or Zenn-La could give him—the unseen worlds beyond the farthest stars.
Silver Surfer #1, Aug.1968

Paradise planet
Zenn-La was a nirvana; but as a consequence, its people had lost the spirit of adventure and exploration.
Silver Surfer #1, Jun.1982

Command of power
The Silver Surfer was imbued with a portion of the Power Cosmic— a limitless energy source granted by the World-Devourer.
Silver Surfer #1, Jun.1982

Master and servant
Transformed into a
silver-skinned being with
space-time powers and
a cosmic-powered
surfboard, the Surfer
served Galactus for
several decades.
Annihilation Silver Surfer #3,
Aug.2006

The coming of Galactus

When the Silver Surfer first arrived at Earth's
location ahead of his master, the herald
was confronted instead by a field of debris.
The planet had been concealed by Uatu,
the sector's Watcher, who had broken his
vow of noninterference in an attempt to
protect Earth. This ruse only momentarily
slowed the Surfer, however, and he duly
summoned Galactus, who arrived and
began preparing for his feeding.

As Uatu tried to dissuade the World-
Devourer from carrying out his terrible task,
and Earth-based heroes the Fantastic Four
used all the means at their disposal to defeat
the giant, the Surfer found himself in the
apartment of Alicia Masters, the blind
girlfriend of the Fantastic Four's Thing.
Her kindness and compassion persuaded
him to turn against his master, while Uatu
dispatched the Human Torch to Taa II to
retrieve the only weapon that could harm
Galactus—the Ultimate Nullifier.

Confronted by this device, Galactus agreed
to leave Earth in return for the Nullifier, while,
for his defiance, the Surfer was deprived
of his space-time powers and confined to
the planet by an invisible barrier. With that,
Galactus departed, leaving the Surfer a
prisoner of Earth; but the Devourer of Worlds
and his former herald would encounter each
other on many subsequent occasions.

Four against Galactus
Against the odds and aided by the Silver Surfer, the Fantastic Four were able to stop the World-Devourer from consuming Earth.
Marvel Masterworks: Fantastic Four #5, Oct. 1993 (reprinting *Fantastic Four #49*, Apr. 1966)

"For the first time ... since the dawn of memory ... my will has been thwarted!**"**

Galactus

Whence soars the Surfer

After a series of Earthbound trials and adventures and a period as a team member of the Defenders, the Surfer eventually pierced the barrier Galactus had placed around Earth with the help of the Fantastic Four. The Silver Surfer made peace with Galactus after rescuing his current herald, Nova, from the clutches of the Skrulls. He then returned to Zenn-La, only to find that Shalla-Bal was now the planet's leader, and there was no place for him there. Realizing that his destiny lay among the stars, the Silver Surfer left behind his former life for good.

Thereafter, the Surfer became embroiled in a series of conflicts, including a flare-up between the Kree and the Skrulls and a conflagration between the Elders of the Universe and Galactus. The Surfer met and began a relationship with Mantis, alias the Celestial Madonna, and then became embroiled in Thanos's machinations as the Titan acquired the Infinity Gems. Later still, during the war against Annihilus, he became Galactus's herald once more to help stop the Annihilation Wave.

Fire power
After gaining fire-generating powers, Earth's Frankie Raye was transformed into Galactus's herald, Nova.
Silver Surfer #1, Jul. 1987

The Silver Surfer had been prompted to join forces with Galactus after they were enslaved by the ruler of the Negative Zone. The World-Devourer had been captured by Tenebrous and Aegis, ancient cosmic entities who had been recruited to Annihilus's cause by Thanos. Long ago, at the dawn of the universe, these Proemial Gods had been defeated by Galactus, who had imprisoned them in the Kyln. But when the prison was destroyed as the Annihilation Wave broke through from the Negative Zone, Tenebrous and Aegis allied with Annihilus, helping bind Galactus and the Surfer and turn them into cosmic weapons.

"Galactus was given his due. The Devourer is no longer of consequence."

Tenebrous

Power grab
With the six Infinity Gems in his possession, Thanos could exert all manner of cosmic power on Drax the Destroyer and the Silver Surfer. *Silver Surfer* #44, Dec. 1990

Proemial problems
Galactus thought he had removed the threat of Aegis and Tenebrous by imprisoning them in the Kyln, but millennia later, they defeated him in service to Annihilus. *Annihilation* #1, Oct. 2006

Forces to be reckoned with

After being freed by Drax the Destroyer, the furious World-Devourer unleashed what became known as the Galactus Event: a massive energy blast, heralded by the Silver Surfer, which obliterated much of the Annihilation Wave, turning the tide of the war. Not long after, Galactus and the Silver Surfer were among those who defended the universe from an assault by the forces of the Cancerverse, forming a defensive wall against the invaders with other cosmic entities, including both Tenebrous and Aegis.

The cosmic bond between Galactus and the Silver Surfer seemingly transcends time and space. Indeed, such has been the extent of the Silver Surfer's travels that he was one of the first beings to encounter the Abyssal God, Knull. Sucked though a black hole and deposited billions of years in the past, the Surfer found himself on the Symbiote throneworld of Klyntar, where Knull infected him with his insidious darkness. Despite this, with the assistance of Ego the Living Planet, the Surfer escaped Knull's clutches and made his way back to the present. On the journey there, he was able to use the regenerative power conferred on him by Ego to return life to many of the worlds he had led Galactus to eat, atoning for his sins. Moreover, once back in the present, he was able to locate and free the Enigma Force, Knull's opposite, allowing it to bond with a host and stop the King in Black's rampage.

Holding the line
Galactus and the Silver Surfer were joined by cosmic entities and even former foes Tenebrous and Aegis in the battle against the invasive Cancerverse. *Thanos Imperative* #2, Sep. 2010

"Darkness is the beginning. Darkness is the truth."

Knull

Billion-year battle
Flung billions of years into the past, the Silver Surfer faced Knull, managing to wound the Abyssal God with a blast of the Power Cosmic.
Silver Surfer: Black #2, Sep. 2019

Galactus, too, became a literal Lifebringer for a time. Following the reconstitution of the Multiverse in the wake of the Beyonders' attempt to destroy it, a proactive team of Earth heroes, the Ultimates, decided to tackle the problem of Galactus once and for all. They forced him inside the incubator that had originally birthed him, transforming him into the Lifebringer, a being who restored worlds rather than destroyed them. Fittingly, the first planet that Galactus returned to life was Archeopia, the world he had first decimated.

As the Lifebringer, Galactus sought to defend Eternity, the embodiment of the Multiverse, from the First Firmament, the earliest universe ever to exist. He joined forces with the Infinaut, Ego the Living Planet, and other cosmic beings to form the Eternity Watch. Inevitably, Galactus reverted to his original purpose as the World-Devourer: a cosmic constant, a perennial check and balance in a chaotic and war-torn cosmos. ◼

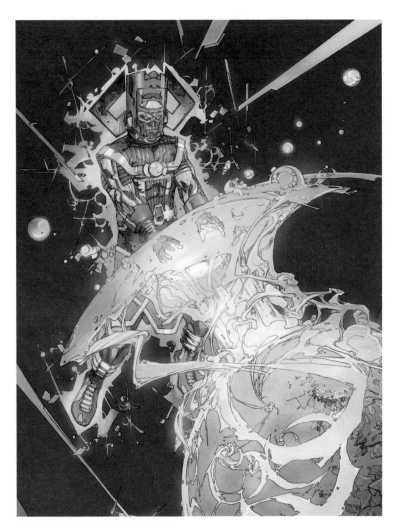

Restoration process
Transformed into a Lifebringer, Galactus restored Archeopia, the first planet he destroyed when he was the World-Devourer.
Ultimates #2, Feb. 2016

The heralds of Galactus

While the Silver Surfer is the best known of Galactus's heralds, the World-Devourer has created many others besides. His first, the Fallen One, was powered by dark energy but proved troublesome and as a result was imprisoned in the Kyln. Galactus met with more success when he imbued Norrin Radd with the Power Cosmic, transforming him into the Silver Surfer—at least until the Surfer betrayed him. Galactus went on to select the captain of a Xandarian starship, Gabriel Lan, as his next herald, who was named Air-Walker. When Lan was killed, his first officer, Pyreus Kril, inherited the role as Firelord (pictured above).

Other heralds followed, among them a ruthless dictator from the planet Birj, Tyros, who was transformed into Terrax the Tamer; Earthwoman Frankie Raye who became Nova; a brutal executioner named Morg; and a member of the Ethereal (a race of energy beings) named Lambda-Zero, who became the fanatical Stardust. At one point, Galactus even took the Asgardian Destroyer armor as his herald, and later the Asgardian God of Thunder himself, Thor.

Moonrise Kingdoms

Though the 17 Kree who were transported to Earth's moon as part of the Skrulls' test of fealty were returned to their homeworld, the shining city they built—and the atmosphere surrounding it—remained. For a million years, this Blue Area lay silent, abandoned save for a sole Watcher, Uatu, assigned to keep a lonely vigil observing the Earth.

The Blue Area of the Moon's eventual discovery by humankind heralded its transformation into a focal point for successive cosmic events and conflicts, culminating in a war that brought the cycle of strife among the Skrulls, the Kree, and the Cotati full circle. The Fantastic Four were the first humans to explore the Blue Area, along with Russian scientist Ivan Kragoff, aka the Red Ghost, who sought to claim the moon for his motherland. After being bathed in cosmic rays, as the Fantastic Four had once been, Kragoff landed his rocket on the moon at the same time as the American adventurers. When the two sides came into conflict, Uatu announced his presence, bringing hostilities to a halt. Explaining his species' self-appointed mission to observe but never interfere, he stated that, nevertheless, he could not allow a wide-scale war between Russia and the United States to take place in his domain and that only the Fantastic Four and the Red Ghost (and his super-ape assistants) would be permitted to fight.

After the Fantastic Four triumphed, Uatu declared now that mankind had reached the moon, he would withdraw to a more distant vantage point to continue his observations. Though he would occasionally intercede in events—as when Galactus attacked Earth—he would largely, as befitted his title, merely watch—even as his Blue Area citadel became the arena for a cycle of violence.

Urban decay
By the time the Blue Area was discovered by the Fantastic Four and others, the fabulous city built by the Kree had fallen into ruin.
Empyre: Avengers #0, Aug. 2020

He who watches
Billions of years ago, after their attempts to advance a species resulted in its destruction, the Watchers vowed to passively observe the universe's races—until Uatu broke that promise.
Last Hero Standing #1, Aug. 2005

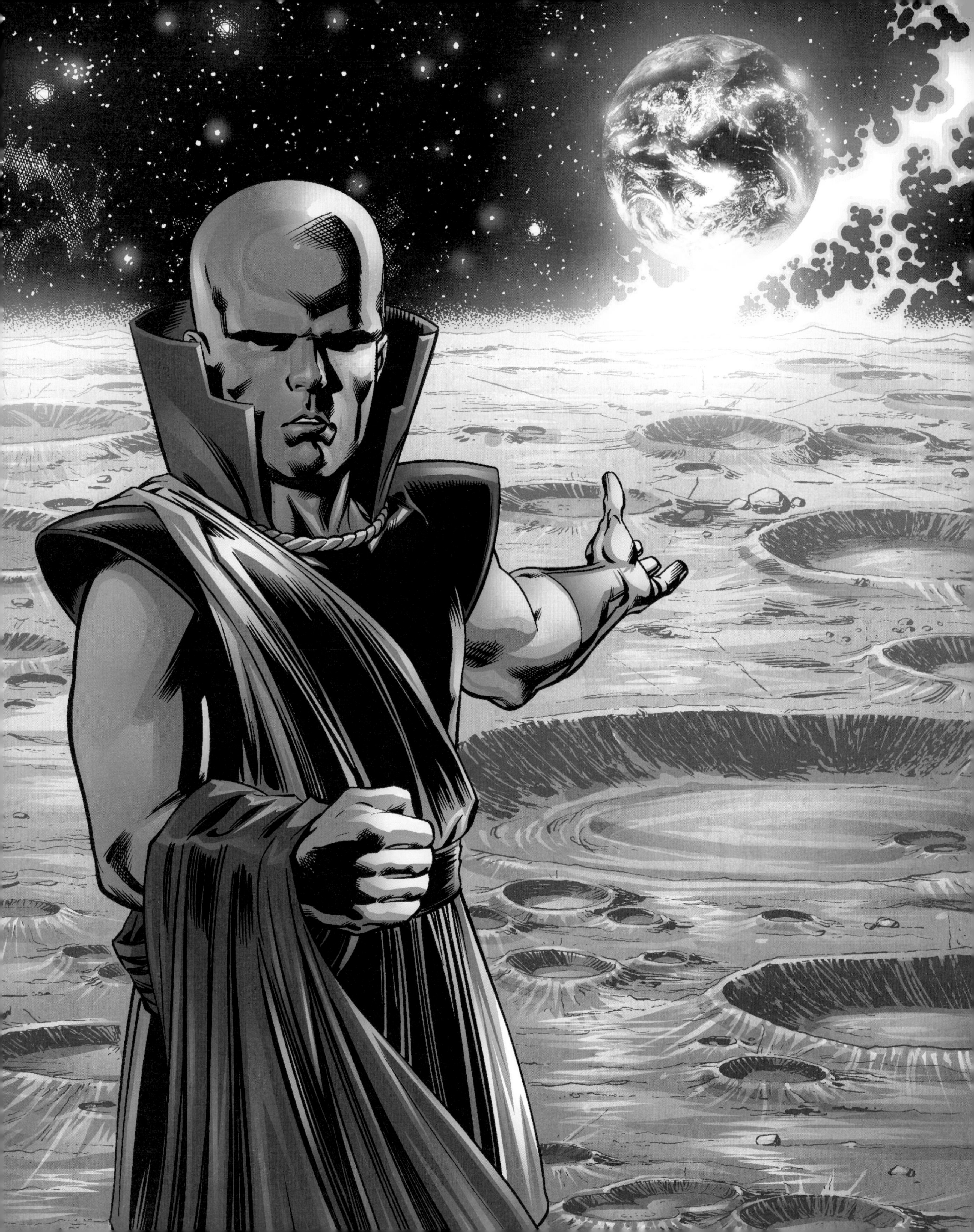

X marks the spot

The Fantastic Four's tussle with the Red Ghost was a foretaste of the fate in store for the Blue Area. Following the Phoenix's destruction of the D'bari System's sun, Jean Grey—the cosmic entity's host— and the rest of the X-Men were summoned by Majestrix Lilandra of the Shi'ar Imperium, who demanded that Jean be handed over to pay for her crimes. When Professor Charles Xavier instead challenged Lilandra to a duel, the Blue Area was selected as the arena for a battle between the X-Men and the Shi'ar Imperial Guard, with two representatives of the Kree and the Skrulls—who also feared the Phoenix—looking on.

During the fracas, Wolverine at one point unwittingly found himself in the domicile of the Watcher, where he was propelled from the Earth's primordial past to its fiery future, before being ejected. After then being attacked by Raksor, the Skrull observer, Wolverine realized that both Raksor and the Kree representative, Bel-Dann, were not merely observing the battle; they were, in fact, participating. Eventually the X-Men were defeated, and with the Phoenix Force beginning to assume control of her once again, Jean Grey took her own life—though in time it would be revealed this was a duplicate, and the real Jean survived on Earth.

As for Raksor and Bel-Dann, these mortal enemies were tasked by their superiors with fighting on in the Blue Area as avatars of the Kree-Skrull conflict, before Uatu declared their long war over and dispatched them back to their respective empires.

> "The Phoenix is a cosmic power. It can neither be contained nor controlled— especially by a human vessel."
>
> **Jean Grey**

Breathable blue
Transported to the Blue Area by the Shi'ar, the X-Men were briefed on the region by team member Beast, who explained the breathable atmosphere.
Uncanny X-Men #137, Sep. 1980

Force to be reckoned with
The nexus of all psionic energy, and one of the oldest entities in the cosmos, the Phoenix Force has chosen a succession of hosts, most notoriously Jean Grey.
Avengers vs. X-Men #4, Jul. 2012

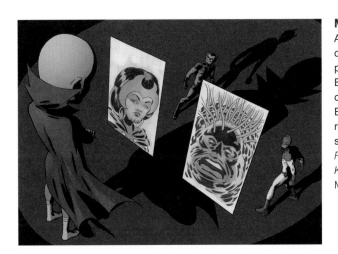

My enemy, my ally
As the respective champions of their people, Raksor and Bel-Dann battled ceaselessly in the Blue Area, before realizing they should join forces.
Road to Empyre: The Kree/Skrull War #1, May 2020

The Phoenix Force would later play a role in another major conflagration in the Blue Area, but there were other clashes before then. A group of fanatical Kree calling themselves the Lunatic Legion used the Blue Area as a base to stage an attack on Earth, installing the Supreme Intelligence on the Moon. After Iron Man, Warbird (Carol Danvers), Captain America, Quicksilver, and the Scarlet Witch each fought the Legion separately, the Avengers took the fight to the Kree in the Blue Area, destroying their modified Omni-Wave Projector, which threatened to horribly mutate all humanity. Afterward, S.H.I.E.L.D. and Starcore took the opportunity to study the Blue Area—and to keep an eye on the Supreme Intelligence.

Lunatic fringe
Galen-Kor led his Lunatic Legion from their Blue Area base in an effort to transform humanity into genetically identical Kree, before being defeated by the Avengers.
Avengers #7, Aug. 1998

Attilan on Earth

The product of Kree experimentation long ago, Earth's Inhumans kept themselves apart from humanity in their hidden city, Attilan. Originally an island in the Atlantic Ocean, Attilan was colonized by the Inhumans following their exploration of the Eurasian continent. In time, the Inhuman geneticist Randac devised a method of mutation using the Terrigen Mists—heralding a new age of technological advancement for the race. Attilan grew into a fabulous city and consequently piqued the interest of the outside world. By the time the Inhuman Blackagar Boltagon, aka Black Bolt, became ruler, it was apparent Attilan was not safe where it was.

Scouting a new location, Black Bolt encountered the Eternal Ikaris, who took him to the Eternals' city, Olympia. Understanding the need to hide from prying human eyes, Eternal leader Zuras helped Black Bolt find a new refuge. Choosing a site in the Himalayas, they combined their mental energy to excavate the foundations for what would become the Great Refuge. Back in Attilan, Black Bolt set about planning to relocate the entire island using giant gravimetric machines.

The Great Refuge was eventually discovered by the Fantastic Four, prompting Maximus, Black Bolt's deranged brother, to generate a negative zone around the city, cutting it off from the outside world.

Beyond the battles

As a nexus for cosmic events, the Blue Area was more than just a base for battles. When the Universal Inhumans—members of five extraterrestrial species who, like Earth's Inhumans, had been evolved by the Kree—came to reunite with their brethren, it was the Blue Area their Universal City landed on. Later, the Blue Area was the site of an unthinkable crime, as S.H.I.E.L.D.'s Nick Fury shot and killed Uatu, taking one of his all-seeing eyes to stop the villainous Doctor Midas from gaining ultimate power. As a result, Fury assumed the Watcher's mantle and abilities, taking his place as the Unseen.

Yet warfare continued to figure in the Blue Area of the Moon's destiny. Just prior to Fury's murder of the Watcher, the Blue Area became a battleground in the escalating conflict between the X-Men and the Avengers over custody of Hope Summers. The young mutant was set to become the host of the returning Phoenix Force. To try and join with the Phoenix before it reached Earth, Hope convinced Wolverine to take her to the Blue Area, little realizing that he had informed the Avengers of their plan. No sooner had Earth's Mightiest Heroes arrived, however, than the X-Men also appeared, swiftly followed by the Phoenix Force itself. In the ensuing melee, the Phoenix was shattered by Iron Man, with pieces of it finding homes in five mutants: Namor, Cyclops, Emma Frost, Colossus, and Magik.

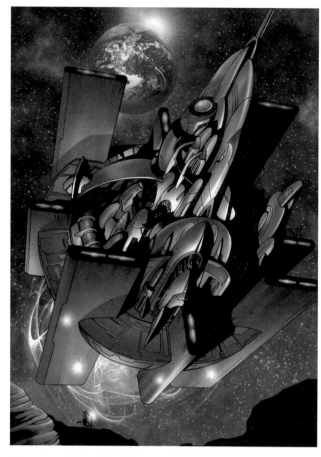

Inhumans from the stars
Arriving at the Blue Area in their city-ship, the Universal Inhumans comprised Kree-altered members of five alien species.
Fantastic Four #577, May 2010

Curse of watching
World War II warrior, Cold War super-spy, head of S.H.I.E.L.D.: after seeing so much front-line action, Nick Fury was sentenced to merely observe events as the Unseen.
Original Sin #8, Nov. 2014

Uncivil war
Always uneasy allies, the Avengers and the X-Men came to blows over the fate of Hope Summers—believed by many to be the savior of mutantkind.
Avengers vs. X-Men #5, Aug. 2012

Phoenix Five
Split among five mutants, the Phoenix Force gave its hosts delusions of grandeur and saw them plan to save Earth.
Avengers vs. X-Men #5, Aug. 2012

In search of a quiet place to think, Cyclops returned to the Blue Area shortly after, where he considered how the Phoenix Force had corrupted Jean Grey and wondered whether the same fate awaited him. His use of the Blue Area as a place of meditation prefigured the later founding there of an outpost of the newly established mutant nation-state of Krakoa. A Krakoan flower planted by Nightcrawler grew into a portal, allowing mutants from Krakoa instantaneous travel to a serene habitat they called the Summer House.

"We are more than you now. More than human … more than mutant."

Cyclops of the Phoenix Five

Summer moon
Occupied by Cyclops, his family, and allies, the Summer House was a biome adjacent to the Blue Area that also served as a staging post for missions.
X-Men #7, Apr. 2020

Child of three worlds
Raised on Earth, Teddy Altman was the son of Kree Captain Mar-vell and Skrull Princess Anelle.
Incoming #1, Feb. 2020

Receiving an SOS from the Blue Area, the Avengers were astonished to find not only that the region had been transformed into a verdant garden but also that there to greet them was their former member-cum-Cotati vessel, Jacques Duquesne, aka Swordsman. He introduced the team to his and Mantis's son, Sequoia—the new Celestial Messiah, prophesied savior of the universe. Quoi, as his friends called him, intended to create a paradise for the Cotati, not just on the moon but everywhere, but it seemed that the united Kree and Skrulls were en route to destroy the Cotati garden.

Battle rejoined

True to form, warfare soon returned to the Blue Area, and this time it involved the three species that were instrumental in the region's genesis: the Skrulls, the Kree, and the Cotati. Far out in space, on the border of the Skrull Empire, the Kree-Skrull hybrid Teddy Altman, aka the Young Avenger Hulkling, was crowned Emperor Dorrek VIII, ruler of the new Kree-Skrull Alliance. The two empires had been united in the face of a threat to both of them—one that had taken root in the Sol System. Meanwhile, on Earth, Bel-Dann was found murdered, while Raksor, who had since become a friend and ally of his old enemy, soon followed suit, torn apart from the inside by, of all things, a tree.

New messiah
Brought up by the Cotati, Sequoia believed that all animal life was untrustworthy—as the Skrulls and Kree had been—and must be purged.
Empyre: Avengers #0, Aug. 2020

Green area of the Moon
When the Avengers arrived at the Blue Area of the Moon, they discovered that it had been turned into a green area, with vegetation growing over the ruins.
Empyre: Avengers #0, Aug. 2020

Invasive species
With the Avengers distracted on the moon, Quoi and the Cotati launched an invasion of Earth, turning the planet's plant life against its people.
Empyre: Avengers #2, Sep. 2020

Naturally, the Avengers sided with the Cotati, and when neither they nor the Fantastic Four, who had boarded Emperor Dorrek's flagship, could convince the Kree-Skrull fleet to desist, all hell broke loose. Unfortunately, the Avengers had picked the wrong side; as the battle raged, it became clear that Quoi's true agenda was to wipe out all animal life in the universe and establish a new Cotati Empyre—with Earth as its first conquest. The ensuing battle against the Cotati raged across not just the Blue Area but also across the face of the Earth. Earth's heroes and military joined with the Kree and the Skrulls to fight on multiple fronts. The struggle to stop the Cotati's Death Blossom from gaining control of all plant life almost resulted in the sun being destroyed, but in the end, the treelike invaders were defeated.

Witnessed by the Unseen, the surviving Kree, Skrulls, and Cotati, together with Earth's heroes, gathered in the Blue Area to lay to rest their ancient conflict. The Cotati were transported to a new home in uncharted space, while Emperor Dorrek declared that no longer would there be Kree and Skrull Empires but one united Alliance. As the remaining participants departed the Blue Area, the Unseen was stunned by a sudden reappearance: Uatu had returned, promising a reckoning. ◼

Watcher's warning
Seemingly killed by Nick Fury, Uatu returned when he learned that Watcher technology was being misused.
Empyre: Fallout Fantastic Four #1, Nov. 2020

Moon base Attilan

When it was discovered that the Inhumans were slowly dying due to Earth's pollution, Black Bolt and the Fantastic Four's Reed Richards devised a way of using anti-gravity motors to lift Attilan to a new home: the Blue Area of the Moon.

Since then, Attilan has moved several times, but one of the most consequential relocations came following Black Bolt's rescue from the clutches of the Skrulls, who had intended to use his sonic abilities as a weapon. Determining that the Inhumans' only chance of survival lay in an alliance with the race that had created them—the Kree—Black Bolt ordered Attilan to be lifted into space, where he used his voice as a means of propulsion. Attilan eventually settled above the Kree homeworld of Hala.

Following the War of Kings, the Inhumans left the Kree, returning Attilan to the Blue Area of the Moon. The city's days were numbered, however, and Attilan was relocated to New York, where it hovered above the city. Destroyed during Thanos's invasion of Earth, the remains of Attilan were rebuilt and renamed New Attilan, while the Inhuman Royal Family established a base on the moon. Named New Arctilan (pictured), it was situated in an atmospheric pocket called the Gray Area of the Moon.

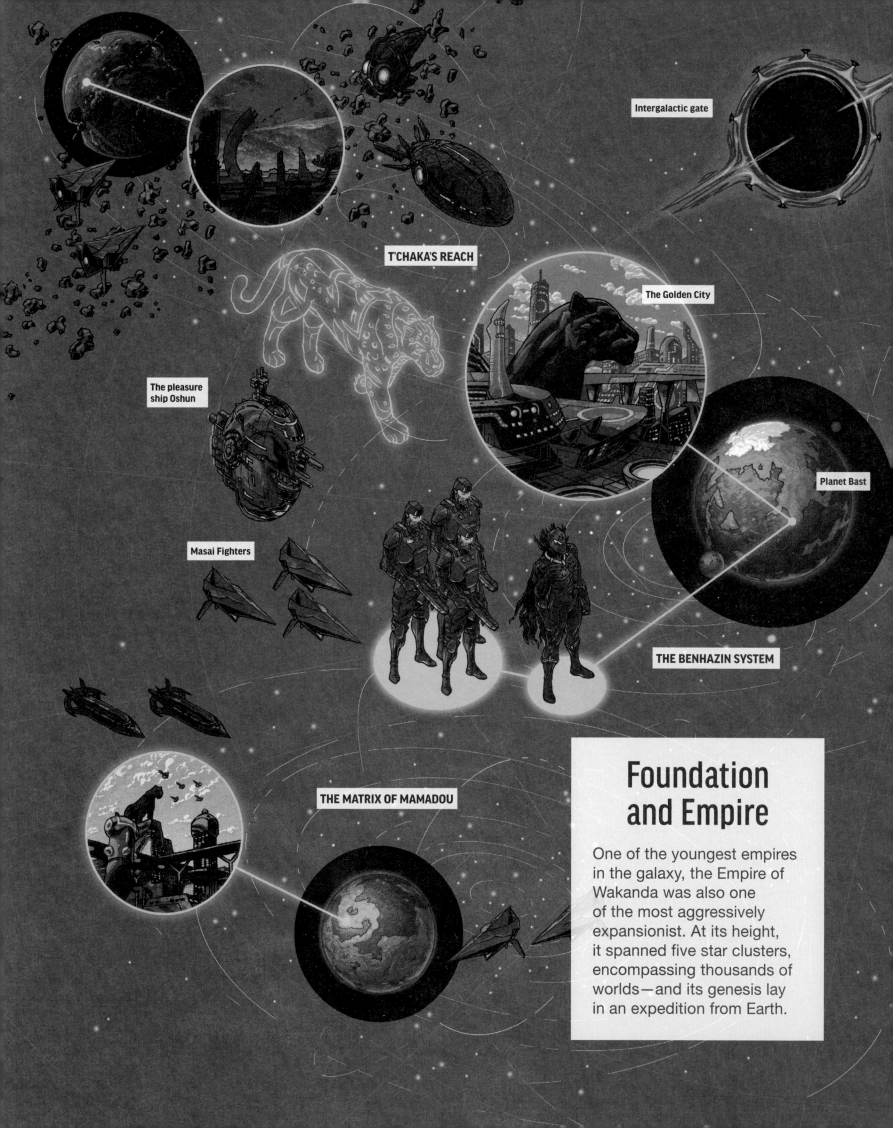

Intergalactic gate

T'CHAKA'S REACH

The Golden City

The pleasure
ship Oshun

Masai Fighters

Planet Bast

THE BENHAZIN SYSTEM

THE MATRIX OF MAMADOU

Foundation
and Empire

One of the youngest empires
in the galaxy, the Empire of
Wakanda was also one
of the most aggressively
expansionist. At its height,
it spanned five star clusters,
encompassing thousands of
worlds—and its genesis lay
in an expedition from Earth.

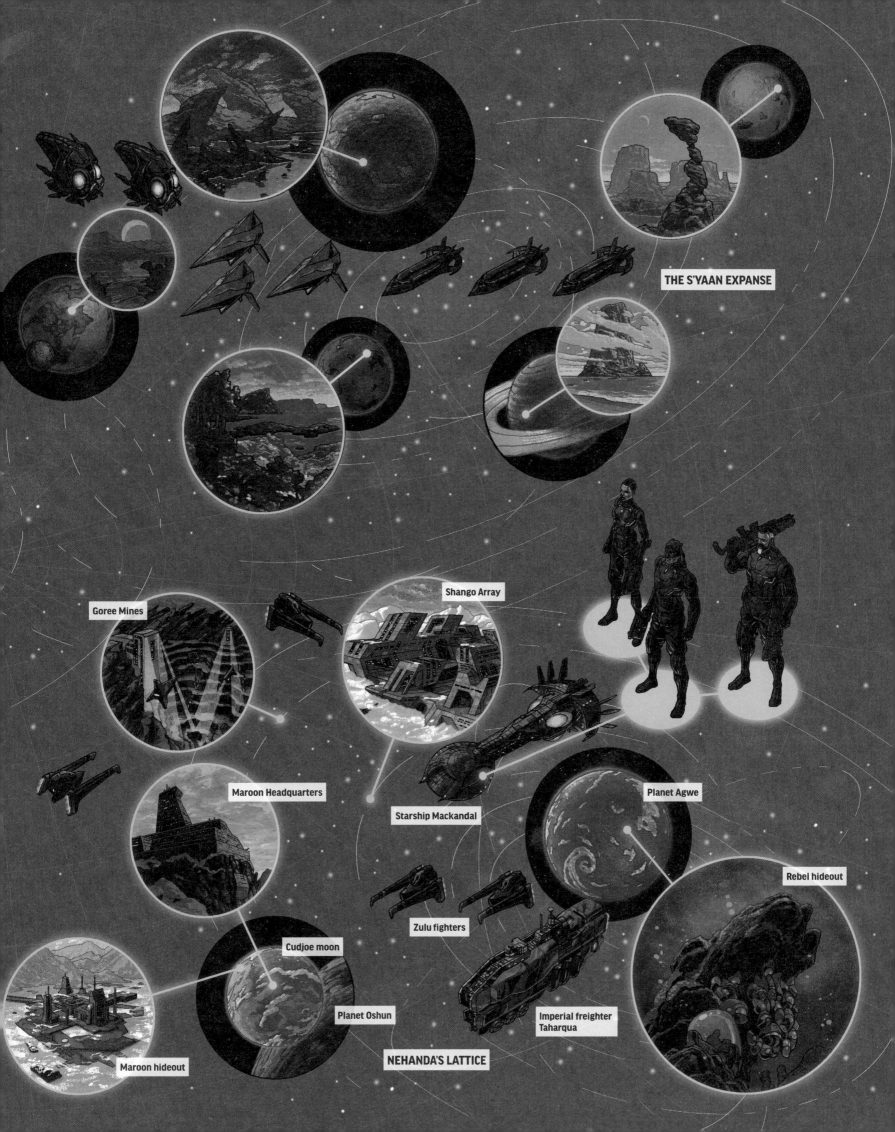

THE S'YAAN EXPANSE

Goree Mines

Shango Array

Maroon Headquarters

Starship Mackandal

Planet Agwe

Rebel hideout

Zulu fighters

Cudjoe moon

Imperial freighter
Taharqua

Planet Oshun

Maroon hideout

NEHANDA'S LATTICE

The mission was ordered by T'Challa, the Black Panther, ruler of the African nation of Wakanda. Like his mother, N'Yami, before him, T'Challa understood the importance of locating the source of the Mena Ngai, aka the Great Mound, the store of Vibranium that had helped transform his country into an advanced technological utopia. After all, if Wakanda did not secure it, its enemies surely would. His mother's astronomical investigations had pointed to a region far beyond the Milky Way, and following the trail of N'Yami's research, T'Challa determined that the source of the meteor that had carried the Vibranium to Wakanda was the Vega System.

T'Challa ordered his Alpha Flight outer space team to investigate; when they did not return, he and the teleporter Manifold took a starship there themselves. What T'Challa did not know until he arrived at his destination was that the Alpha Flight team had traveled through a wormhole that had sent them 2,000 years into the past. By the time T'Challa arrived, a vast empire had been established— the Intergalactic Empire of Wakanda.

"My fellow Wakandans, we need our Alpha Flight to investigate."

T'Challa

Flight to the stars
Originally a team of Canadian Super Heroes, Alpha Flight evolved into Earth's defense force before being co-opted by T'Challa in his search for the source of Vibranium.
Black Panther #12, Jul. 2019

Heart of empire
Named after a Wakandan goddess, Bast was the seat of the Intergalactic Empire of Wakanda—a planet of splendor and wealth, but one built by slavery.
Black Panther #1, Jul. 2018

Imperial designs

The Alpha Flight team sent by T'Challa had settled in the Benhazin System, which was rich in Vibranium. Initially peaceful, as befitted their Wakandan heritage, the settlers kept to themselves on the planet Bast. But a series of attacks and invasions from other systems convinced the Wakandans that self-defense would not be enough to keep them safe. They began making their own preventive strikes, which, as they developed deep space travel and ranged farther, became preventive occupations, eventually leading to preventive conquests.

The first galaxy to be conquered was the closest, T'Chaka's Reach. This system was inhabited by an offshoot of the Rigellian Empire, from who the Wakandans had gained an extensive knowledge of the stars. Other galaxies and their inhabitants followed; from the Teku-Maza, the Wakandans took literature and music; from the Shadow People, a knowledge of governance and hierarchy; and so on. One after another, civilizations fell before the Wakandans, their peoples either assimilated into the emerging Wakandan Empire or consigned to a life of slavery in Vibranium mines. Dubbed the Nameless, their memories were taken from them by their vicious warders, the Askari. Instead of being deleted, however, these memories were stored in the Imperial Archive to be mined, researched, plundered, and appropriated for the Empire's interests. The Archive was the font of the Wakandan Empire's power.

As the Imperial Wakandans impacted and changed their region of space, they also changed themselves. They took the names of illustrious forbears and even developed gene therapies that allowed them to extend their lives. More than that, however, one sect embraced transcorporealism, transmitting their essences from flesh to machine. Scorned by most Wakandans, the Between, as they were known, boasted mutated Vibranium bodies that allowed their limbs to be reformed into tools.

"**Assets are the exclusive property of Emperor N'Jadaka!**"
The Askari

Golden rule
On Earth, the capital of Wakanda, Birnin Zana, was also known as the Golden City—a name adopted by the Intergalactic Empire of Wakanda for its capital on Bast.
Black Panther #7, Feb. 2019

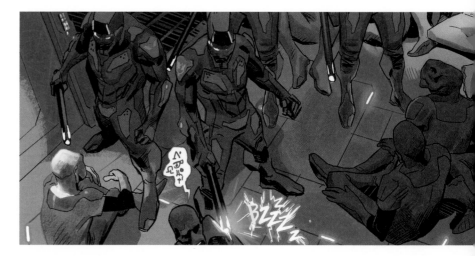

Imperial troops
Composed of multiple species from across the Wakandan Empire, the hated Askari were slave wardens, police, and military rolled into one.
Black Panther #1, Jul. 2018

N'Jadaka's reach

Leading the Wakandans in their galactic conquests was their commander, N'Jadaka. A ruthless warrior, he spearheaded the razing of entire star systems and imposed order where there was none. Before long, the Wakandan Empire numbered five galaxies: T'Chaka's Reach; the Benhazin System; the S'Yaan Expanse—the second galaxy to be conquered, it possessed a surfeit of lush planets that led to an Imperial population boom; Nehanda's Lattice—home to the Teku-Maza; and the Matrix of Mamadou, where the Kronan, Shadow People, and a colony of Klyntar lived.

Eventually, N'Jadaka became so popular with the people that the king, fearing he would be usurped, maneuvered N'Jadaka into a deathtrap. Dispatched to what was supposedly a small Between outpost, N'Jadaka and his men were overwhelmed by an army of the machine-people. Retreating to a cave, N'Jadaka found salvation in an unlikely form: a Klyntar, who he bonded with and singlehandedly defeated the Between. Pledging himself to the Symbiote, he returned to Bast and killed the king, taking the throne himself as emperor.

Attack on Cudjoe
Hidden on a moon in the Zanj Region, Cudjoe was the Maroons' main base—until it was destroyed by Askari raiders. *Black Panther* #3, Oct. 2018

Far from being able to enjoy his new position, however, N'Jadaka instead found himself dealing with a rebellion. A group of freed slaves and disillusioned Imperials, the Maroons, established a hideout known as Moonbase Cudjoe, in the Zanj Region in the remote galaxy of Nehanda's Lattice. The rebels were led by Captain N'Yami of the Teku-Maza, who, like other Nameless slaves, had been born away from her homeworld of Agwé and had had her memories wiped. Believing that a way of reversing the memory-stealing process lay on Agwé, N'Yami had returned to her ancestral home and led a revolution, freeing her people. Thereafter, she had risen through the Maroons' ranks to become commander.

> "The time of my ascension is at hand."
> N'Jadaka

A god among men
Powered by his Klyntar Symbiote, N'Jadaka believed he would ascend to godhood once he had killed Bast. *Black Panther* #6, Jan. 2019

T'Challa's way

Under N'Yami's command, the Maroons had carried out a series of daring raids, but these were, in truth, little more than hit-and-runs. That was until a raid on the Vibranium mining colony Gorée bore unexpected fruit. When a detachment of Maroons—led by seasoned fighters Nakia and M'Baku—launched an assault on the colony, freeing the slaves there, one of the liberated turned out to be a highly capable warrior. Taken aboard the Maroons' ship the *Mackandal*, he was introduced to Captain N'Yami. The Nameless slave had no recollection of his former life, and so N'Yami awarded him the handle of a man who was born a king and who died a hero, who banished the usurper Klaw, who thrashed the demon Mephisto—T'Challa.

Little did the liberated slave know that he was, indeed, the true T'Challa. When he had first arrived on Bast from Earth, he had been welcomed by Emperor N'Jadaka and hailed as a prophesied savior by the people. After undertaking a trial of combat to prove his identity, T'Challa had been taken on a tour of the Empire, where he had beheld wonders galore and happy citizens. It was only later that he had learned the truth of how the Empire had been built—that his own quest for Vibranium had birthed an intergalactic crime. Shortly after, he was betrayed by the Emperor, who had T'Challa's memories stripped from him, forcing him into the ranks of the Nameless.

Finally freed from servitude by the Maroons, T'Challa quickly demonstrated his prowess as a warrior, operating two steps ahead of any opponent. On one mission, he flew a fighter craft against the heavily fortified Shango Array, enabling the procurement of the powerful M'kraan Shard.

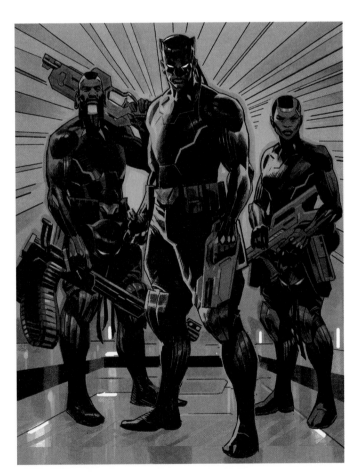

Maroon warriors
Like all denizens of the Empire, T'Challa's fellow Maroons M'Baku and Nakia took their names from famed Wakandans.
Black Panther #1, Jul. 2018

Aquatic ancestors
Revered by their descendants the
Teku-Maza, the giant Jengu once ruled
the aquatic world of Agwé and were the
repositories of the planet's memories.
Black Panther #9, Apr. 2019

> **"The ancient Jengu is the symbol of the Teku-Maza resistance."**
> T'Challa

After communing with the Jengu, T'Challa's memories
were restored. With Manifold also freed from the Empire's
clutches, a plan was hatched. Utilizing Manifold's
teleporting abilities, Agwé would first be evacuated,
then turned into a deadly trap for the Emperor and his
forces by using raw Vibranium and the M'kraan Shard to
detonate Agwé's core. Unfortunately, N'Jadaka arrived
earlier than expected. A fierce fight erupted between
the Maroons and the Imperial forces before Agwé was
detonated, seemingly killing N'Jadaka.

Showdown on Agwé

News of his exploits in the Zanj Region reached Emperor
N'Jadaka, who was mightily displeased, having thought
he was rid of T'Challa. Some solace for N'Jadaka came
with the death of N'Yami. The Maroons' captain was
lost when a rebel raid was disastrously disrupted by
Imperial forces bolstered by Manifold—who had also
had his memories stolen but had sided with the Empire.

Subsequently, the Maroons, now led by M'Baku,
spent five years stranded on an icy rock in Nehanda's
Lattice. It was only when T'Challa accepted his destiny
as "the one who put the knife where it belongs" that
the rebellion began to gain the advantage. On Agwé,
T'Challa learned that the Teku-Maza were descended
from giant aquatic beasts, Jengu, which they revered.
The Teku-Maza built a great civilization beneath the
waves, but the Empire enslaved them and hunted
the Jengu to extinction. Only one Jengu remained.
Hiding herself away, she had rejoined the Teku-Maza
when they rebelled, becoming a repository of the
memories that had been taken from them.

Switching sides
Manifold had once been an aide to
T'Challa, one of Nick Fury's Secret
Warriors, and an Avenger.
Black Panther #9, Apr. 2019

A hero's welcome
When T'Challa returned to Wakanda
Prime, he was greeted by cheering
crowds and welcomed by his sister, Shuri,
and his lover, the mutant hero Storm.
Black Panther #15, Oct. 2019

Return to Wakanda

With that battle won, a galactic bridge was established with
the Sol System, allowing T'Challa to return home to Wakanda
Prime. Once there, however, he realized that he would
have to return to the Empire and finish what he had started:
restore the memories of all the millions of Nameless slaves.

Meanwhile, unbeknownst to T'Challa, N'Jadaka had survived,
his Klyntar Symbiote allowing him not only to escape the blast
but to follow T'Challa to Wakanda. Taking control of T'Challa's
ally, Changamire, and forming an allegiance with the rebels Tetu
and Zenzi, he possessed the body of one of Wakanda's greatest
adversaries: his namesake, the original N'Jadaka, Erik Killmonger.
Returning to Imperial space, he began to turn the tide against
the Maroons and prepared to invade Wakanda Prime.

To meet the threat, T'Challa's sister Shuri, and Storm of the
X-Men, positioned a Wakandan starship armada on the far side
of the galactic gate. However, when N'Jadaka summoned an
overwhelming force of Massai ships, T'Challa's forces were
compelled to turn back through the portal. To cover their
retreat, Nakia transformed her vessel, the *Mackandal-3*, into a
giant gun, destroying the Imperial ships but blowing herself up
in the process. Elsewhere, on the Djalia, the plane of Wakandan
memory, T'Challa called on the power of his ancestors—all the
Black Panthers who came before him—to restore the memories
of the Nameless. In so doing, he unleashed a wave of bloody
revolts across the Imperial forces.

One body, two souls
Allying with Wakanda's foes Tetu and Zenzi,
N'Jadaka took control of Erik Killmonger's body,
but the dead man's soul sought dominance.
Black Panther #19, Feb. 2020

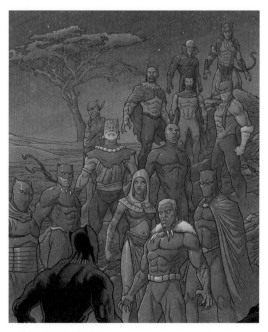

Spiritual guidance
In the face of the Empire's threat, T'Challa traveled to
the Djalia, the plane of collective Wakandan memory,
to seek advice. *Black Panther* #19, Feb. 2020

Warriors' gate
T'Challa believed he had control of the gate between the Empire and Wakanda, but he was proved wrong when Askari troops began pouring through.
Black Panther #17, Dec. 2019

"No, N'Jadaka. You are not Wakanda. You are a slave driver.**"**
T'Challa

The Empire retaliates

With his grip on his Empire weakening, N'Jadaka committed his forces to an all-out assault on Wakanda Prime. There to meet him on the other side of the gate were not only T'Challa and Storm but myriad other heroes as well, including Spider-Man (Miles Morales), Luke Cage, Misty Knight, the Falcon, and Doctor Voodoo, all of whom had been called upon by T'Challa to bring an end to N'Jadaka's corrupt reign.

As N'Jadaka's Imperial troops poured through the portal, Wakanda's defenders did their best to repel them. Storm and Spectrum (Monica Rambeau) rained down energy blasts and lightning bolts on the invading vessels, while Cloak enveloped the Askari troops in darkness and War Machine neutered their ordnance. But as N'Jadaka dispatched Symbiote soldiers into the fray, and the Imperials kept on coming through the gate, it became clear that this was a battle Wakanda could not win.

Wakanda forever
To help defend Wakanda, T'Challa summoned honorary Wakandans like War Machine, Misty Knight, and Luke Cage.
Black Panther #24, May 2021

N'Jadaka himself declared as much when he faced T'Challa on the battlefield. However, the despot had miscalculated, for the Wakandan king had an ace up his sleeve. T'Challa summoned the Originators, mythical beasts such as the serpentine Simbi and apelike Vanyan, who had called Wakanda home long before even the Orisha. With the Originators fighting for glory and honor, the scales were finally tipped in T'Challa's favor. ▨

Originators unleashed
Banished from the country for millennia, the Originators—Wakanda's first inhabitants—were called forth by T'Challa to help defeat the Empire.
Black Panther #24, May 2021

Bast and the Orisha Gate

The throneworld of the Intergalactic Empire of Wakanda, the planet Bast was named after one of the oldest of the Wakandan deities, or Orisha. This was not merely in tribute to Bast, however. On the planet was the Orisha Gate, a portal that allowed Emperor N'Jadaka to travel to the chamber of the Wakandan gods and commune directly with the goddess. The Orisha had looked kindly on the Empire, but with T'Challa and the Maroons threatening all he had built, N'Jadaka determined that he himself must become a god.

Aided by his Klyntar Symbiote, N'Jadaka fought and slew Bast, taking her power—or so he reckoned. In fact, Bast survived and possessed N'Jadaka's daughter, Zenzi, and began to work against him. She returned Manifold's memories to him and defected with him to the Maroons; helped to facilitate the restoration of T'Challa's memories when he communed with the Jengu on Agwé; and used her vast powers against the Imperial forces during the battle above the planet. Irascible and impetuous she may have been, but Bast proved a formidable ally for T'Challa in his efforts to overthrow the Empire.

This Savage World

Far out in the Fornax Cluster of galaxies lies the Tayo Star System. The fourth planet from Tayo is Sakaar, the only inhabited world of the eight planets orbiting the central star. Itself circled by two moons, originally Sakaar was a geographically diverse planet, boasting tropical jungles, vast deserts, frozen wildernesses, lakes, and oceans.

Sakaar was populated by an array of non-sentient species, along with four main sentient races: Imperials—pink-skinned humanoids who became Sakaar's rulers; Natives—an insectoid species that once dominated the planet; Shadow People—giant, gray-skinned nomads who lived in the Great Desert; and the Spikes—gelatinous shape-shifters and body snatchers who were banished to one of Sakaar's moons following a terrible war. Which, if any, of these four species was indigenous was a subject of much debate among them.

Sakaar's destiny was forever altered when a cosmic vortex suddenly opened above the planet. Its appearance was accompanied by a blast of energy that shattered one of the planet's moons, causing huge earthquakes and tidal waves that scoured its surface. Sakaar's denizens were unable to determine the origin of what they came to call the Great Portal, but it was theorized that its appearance must be related to the arrival of the extraterrestrial Spikes, an event that had also plunged the planet into the long-running Spike War.

A hole in space
Existing above Sakaar, the Great Portal was a wormhole that randomly connected with different sectors of the cosmos.
Incredible Hulk #92, Apr. 2006

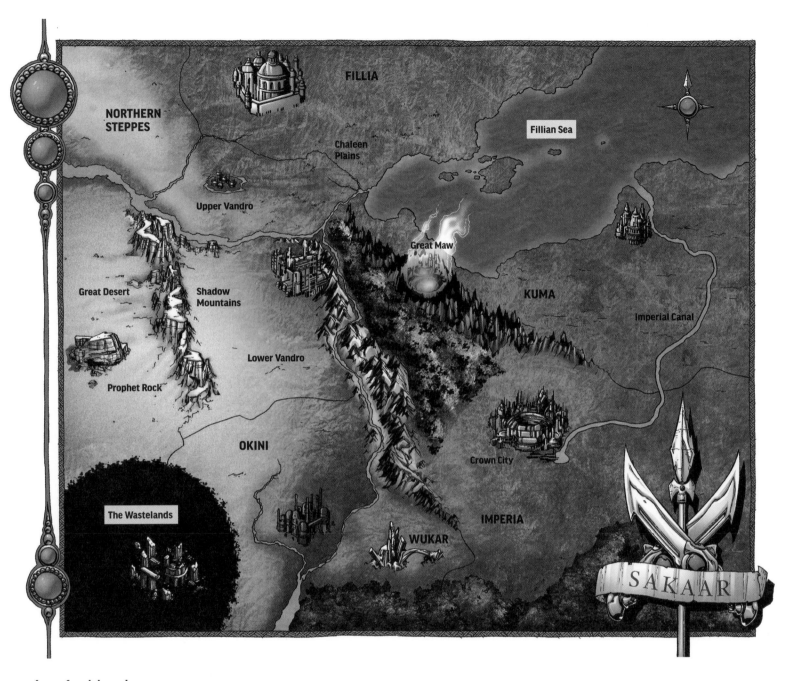

An unforgiving place
From the Great Desert and the Wastelands in the
west and south to the Great Maw and Crown City
in the north and east, Sakaar was rife with danger.
Planet Hulk: Gladiator Guidebook #1, Sep. 2006

The Great Portal periodically disappeared and reappeared after its initial manifestation, each time depositing extraterrestrial technology and species from every corner of the galaxy. It also had the effect of disrupting any technology that passed through it and sapping the physical strength of anyone who similarly exited it. This was something that would have a great bearing on the future of Sakaar when, one fateful day, the Incredible Hulk was ejected from the Portal.

The raging, Gamma-irradiated alter ego of Earth scientist Bruce Banner, the Hulk had been exiled from his home planet by the Illuminati—Reed Richards, Tony Stark, and other "big brains"—who feared his increasingly destructive rampages. Maneuvered onto a shuttle by S.H.I.E.L.D., Hulk was blasted into space, his destination a lush planet with no intelligent life, where it was thought he could live out his days in peace. Instead, the shuttle fell through a wormhole and crashed on the savage world of Sakaar.

Savage city
With the Imperial Palace at its center, and the Great Arena providing an outlet for frustration and unrest, Crown City was the seat of Imperial power on Sakaar.
Planet Hulk: Gladiator Guidebook #1, Sep. 2006

Gladiators ready

Emerging from his shuttle, the Hulk was confronted by the Governor of the Wukar Province, who decreed that as all detritus that exited the Great Portal was Imperial property, both the Hulk and his ship now belonged to the Lord Emperor of Sakaar, Angmo-Asan II, alias the ruthless Red King. Naturally, the Hulk disagreed, throwing the shuttle at the governor's forces, but in his weakened state, he was easily felled and transported to Crown City, the walled Imperial capital.

Awakening in a slave market, the Hulk was sold and sent to fight in the Great Arena for the entertainment of the assembled throng and the emperor. Fighting beside a group of Natives, the Jade Giant single-handedly slew the fearsome Great Devil Corker, prompting the Native Miek to comment that the Red King would surely pardon them—that was, until the Hulk attempted to murder the Red King. He was prevented from doing so first by the emperor's bodyguard, Caiera of the Shadow People, then by the Red King himself, who donned battle armor and faced the Hulk in the arena. The fight left both combatants with scars on their faces, and the Hulk was on the verge of killing the emperor before Caiera stepped in again.

Theater of war
Clearly visible across the capital, the Great Arena was a vital tool in the Red King's subjugation of Sakaar—a means of pacifying subjects and disposing of enemies.
Incredible Hulk #94, Jun. 2006

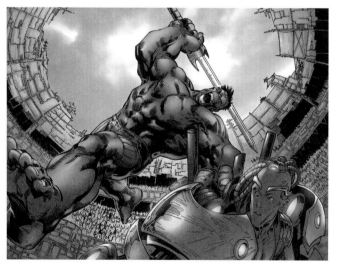

The sword and the scar
Despite being weakened by the Great Portal, the Hulk bested the Emperor in the Arena, leaving him scarred.
Incredible Hulk #92, Apr. 2006

As word began to spread among Sakaar's downtrodden subjects about a slave whose face had been slashed by the emperor, but who had slashed back, Hulk and Miek were sent to the Great Maw, the lethal gladiator training school. After being fitted with obedience disks to control them, they and 20 other slaves and criminals were ordered to fight … or die. By the time the brutal brawl was over, just seven were left standing: Hulk; Miek; the rocklike Korg, a Kronan; No-Name of the Brood; Hiroim of the Shadow People; Lavin Skee, formerly of the Imperial Guard; and Elloe, an Imperial whose father had defied the Red King. Later, in a holding cell, all seven agreed that in order to survive, they would need to fight together. They became the Warbound.

Training days
Run by former gladiator Primus Vand, the Great Maw was Sakaar's harshest gladiator school, built around a pit harboring a lava monster against which warriors could test their mettle.
Incredible Hulk #92, Apr. 2006

"Let us be Warbound. In life and death. The oath that cannot be broken."
Hiroim of the Shadow People

Celebrity Hulk
Having been trained in the Maw and won two rounds in the Great Arena, Hulk and his Warbound achieved a level of notoriety.
Incredible Hulk #95, Jul. 2006

Legend of the Green Scar

As they triumphed in a series of battles and contests, the Hulk—or Green Scar, as the people called him— and his Warbound grew in fame, to the extent that a group of democratic insurgents tried to recruit them. They were rebuffed by the Hulk, as was Caiera when she attempted to buy him. Finally, in the Great Arena, the Hulk and the Warbound faced their most formidable opponent yet: the Silver Surfer.

The Surfer had been intrigued by the Great Portal and had let himself be pulled through it—only to find when he arrived on Sakaar that it had weakened him. Fitted with a Control Disk, his will was bent in service of the Imperials and he was reborn as the Silver Savage. When the Hulk encountered the Surfer in the Arena, he greeted him as a friend, only to find himself on the receiving end of a mighty blow from the Surfer's mace. The Warbound and the Surfer fought fiercely, until the Hulk drove a spear into the Surfer's chest, destroying his Control Disk.

Victorious, the Warbound demanded their freedom. Instead, the emperor insisted on one last test of loyalty: that the Warbound kill a group of his enemies, including Elloe. When they refused, the Red King triggered their Control Disks, frying them—until the Surfer intervened, disabling every Control Disk in the Arena and freeing every slave. Smashing their way out of the stadium, the Hulk and the Warbound escaped, bade farewell to the Surfer, and began a new life of freedom.

Savage Surfer
The Silver Surfer's Control Disk subsumed his will, turning him into the Silver Savage and forcing him to fight his friend.
Incredible Hulk #95, Jul. 2006

Slave to a slave
Once a slave herself before she was freed by the Red King, Caiera oversaw the enslavement of the Hulk, until eventually fighting beside him.
Incredible Hulk #98, Nov. 2006

Escape to victory
His Control Disk disabled, Korg smashed a hole in the wall of the Arena, allowing the Warbound and some slaves to escape.
Incredible Hulk #95, Jul. 2006

Invasion of the body snatchers
Used as weapons by the Red King, the alien-insectoid Spikes faced off against the Hulk's forces.
Incredible Hulk #99, Dec. 2006

Enemy of the empire

Pursued by Caiera and the Imperial forces, the Hulk and the escaped gladiators made their way across Sakaar, razing an Imperial village and freeing the Native slaves kept there. As the legend of the Green Scar continued to grow, so did his army, either from willing recruits who sought him out, or the slaves he freed. When the ragtag group reached the Steppes—a no-man's-land that had been turned into a wasteland by the Spike War—the Hulk thought he had found a home. However, with a revolt underway in Crown City, the rest of the Warbound convinced him to turn around and take the fight to the emperor instead.

En route, the Hulk was confronted by Caiera, who, knowing that the Red King would slaughter millions to get to the Green Scar, tried to kill him first. Their duel was interrupted by a missile sent by the emperor—one that was full of Spike spores that began infecting and changing

all and sundry into Spikes. When the Red King then cut off the infected village with a ring of fire, Caiera joined the Hulk in the fight against the Spikes, before allying with him permanently when the emperor bombed the village itself, killing all of its denizens.

As they progressed toward Crown City, the rebels were assailed by waves of Spikes that infected everything in their path. Fearing that the rebellion would falter, Hiroim took the Hulk to the Elders of the Shadow People. The Elders revealed that it was they who had created the Great Portal, using the engines of the ship that had brought them to Sakaar from their homeworld. They had done this so that it would bring them the Hulk, who they believed was the prophesied Sakaarson—the hero who would free Sakaar. Looking deep within his heart, however, they determined that someone so full of hate could not be the Sakaarson—but that did not deter the Hulk from taking their ship and using it in his fight against the Imperials.

> "All right. Next stop … Crown City."
> **Hulk**

Made of stone
The Hulk's forces were in danger of being overrun by the Spikes and the Imperial vessels—until Hulk and Caiera arrived aboard the Shadow People's stone starship.
Incredible Hulk #101, Feb. 2006

Spike alliance
In the Spikes' stronghold, the Hulk came face-to-face with their leaders, who told him of their history and wish to return to the stars.
Incredible Hulk #101, Feb. 2006

between the Imperials, the Natives, and the other races was not so easily soothed. Intent on making their new king remember his true nature, Miek and No-Name found the shuttle that had brought the Hulk to Sakaar and showed him the message from Reed Richards and the Illuminati to remind him of what had been done to him. Even this did not deter the Hulk from rebuilding Crown City, keeping his promise to the Spikes, nor relishing the fact that Caiera had gotten pregnant.

> "We can help you…
> if you help us."
> **The Spikes**

The Green King

The Hulk made a pact with the leaders of the Spikes that they would join the assault on Crown City in return for passage off Sakaar. Once more, the Jade Giant faced off with the Red King in his battle armor, but as defeat neared for the Emperor, he unveiled a fall-back plan—with the push of a button, he cracked the planet's tectonic plates. Fortunately, the Hulk was able to pull them back together, and after throwing the emperor to the mercy of the vicious robotic Wildebots, he was crowned the Green King of Sakaar.

Taking Caiera as his queen, the Hulk established a new treaty with the Shadow People and tried to bring peace to Crown City and Sakaar. Not everyone was minded to go along with this, however. The bad blood

City rebuild
After the Emperor's defeat, Hulk and the Warbound turned their strength to reconstructing Crown City.
Incredible Hulk #104, May 2006

**Dreams turn
to dust**
Caught in the blast
of the exploding warp
core of Hulk's shuttle,
Caiera died, her body
crumbling to dust
in the Hulk's arms.
Incredible Hulk #105,
Jun. 2006

The shuttle was installed as a monument to the
Hulk's arrival on Sakaar, but no sooner had it been
moved into position than a warning siren sounded—
the ship's warp core had been compromised. The Hulk
managed to throw the shuttle into the sky, but the
explosion still destroyed Crown City, killing Caiera and
cracking Sakaar's tectonic plates. The Green Scar had
become the world-breaker. With the planet in ruins,
Hulk and the Warbound took the Shadow People's ship
and left Sakaar, heading for Earth … and revenge.

Toward World War Hulk
Devastated at the loss of Caiera and the decimation of
Sakaar, Hulk and the Warbound boarded the stone starship,
seeking revenge on those they deemed responsible.
Incredible Hulk #105, Jun. 2006

Skaar, son of Hulk

Unbeknownst to the Hulk, as Caiera
disintegrated from the exploding
shuttle, a cocoon fell from her body
into the cracking ground. With the
Shadow People's accelerated
growth genes, the child quickly
emerged from molten lava into a
chaotic world plunged into savagery.

The son of Hulk and Caiera
had inherited not just his father's
strength but his mother's Old
Power, allowing him to wield the
energy of the planet. Even so,
Skaar, as he called himself,
struggled against the threat of the
Imperial barbarian Axeman Bone
and his dragons, though he found
a number of allies, including the
Red King, reborn as a cyborg.

When the Silver Surfer returned to
Sakaar with a warning that Galactus
was nearing the planet, Skaar fitted
him with an Obedience Disk and
added him to the army he was
leading against Axeman Bone.
Sure enough, Galactus arrived and
devoured Sakaar—though not
before Skaar was sucked through
a wormhole and deposited on Earth,
where a new chapter in his life began.

This was not the end for Sakaar
itself, however. The planet was
restored by the Time Stone, one
of the Infinity Gems, allowing Earth
genius Amadeus Cho to travel there
and retrace the journey made by the
Hulk—from who he had gained his
own Gamma powers.

The Living Planet

Of all the worlds in the universe, perhaps the strangest is Ego—a planet controlled by a single consciousness. Dwelling in the Black Galaxy—a living bio-verse bordering the Rigellian Empire—Ego has, on occasion, ventured out into the wider cosmos, and, just as often, the denizens of that cosmos have invaded the Living Planet's domain, much to his displeasure.

Ego was originally Egros, a scientist on a planet in the Black Galaxy. Eons ago, the cosmic entity the Stranger visited Egros's homeworld and began conducting an experiment, causing the star around which the planet orbited to go nova. Together, Egros and another scientist, Chimu, came up with a way of saving the planet's people: Project Worldcore. The entire population was placed in suspended animation and projected into the center of the planet, with the aim that they would be able to return to the surface once the sun had cooled again. In the event, the star exploded sooner than expected, and Egros was unable to reach the planet's core. He was bonded not only with his world but also with the two billion men and women at its center, becoming Ego, the Living Planet.

Two become one
When the star of his homeworld went nova, Egros and the planet were bathed in radiation, merging together.
Thor #228, Oct. 1974

A powerful planet
Ego possessed destructive psionic abilities and could replenish his powers by accessing stars or other energy sources.
Ultimates 2 #8,
Aug. 2017

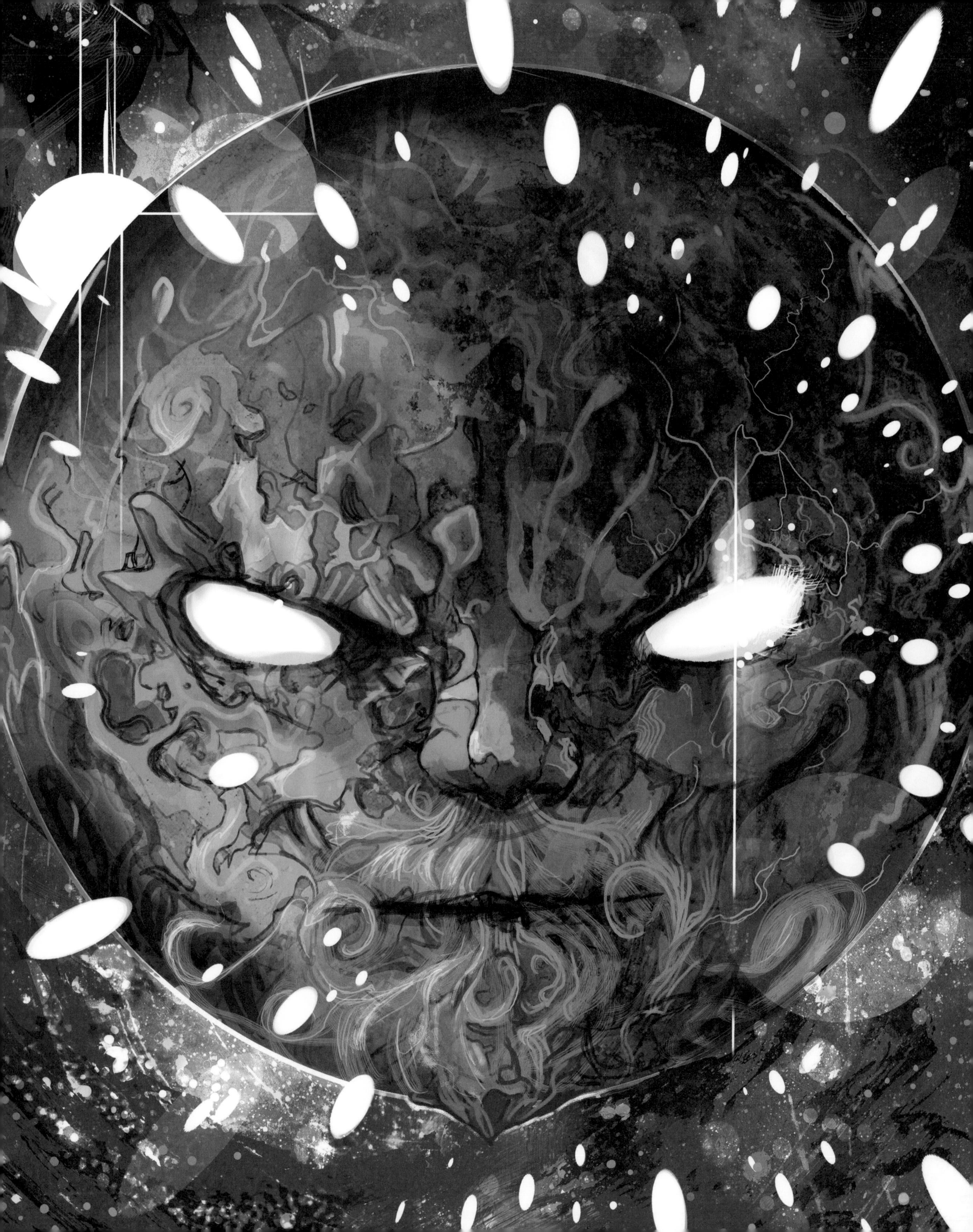

For a million years, Ego held in check his guilt at what had happened to his planet and its people, but eventually it drove him mad. A foretaste of that insanity came when Ego manifested a desire to conquer. For some time, interlopers from the neighboring Rigel Constellation had been attempting to breach the Black Galaxy, alerting Ego to their existence and prompting him to begin his own incursions into their space. Originating on the planet Rigel-3, the Rigellians were an aggressively expansionist species who established a method whereby roaming Colonizers staked claims to planets. One such Colonizer, Tana Nile, attempted to lay claim to Earth, but her claim was rejected by her superiors when Thor, the God of Thunder, agreed to side with the Rigellians against Ego.

Thor was flown into the Black Galaxy aboard a ship piloted by a Rigellian Recorder—who would make a record of what they witnessed. The Black Galaxy turned out to be a fantastically fecund and bizarre bio-verse,

Colonizer in chief
The High Commissioner was in charge of imperial colonization, coordinating Colonizers such as Tana Nile in their efforts to expand the Rigellian Empire.
Thor #162, Mar. 1969

"I am Ego, the largest, most powerful intelligence in all of infinity! You are like dust unto my feet!"
Ego, the Living Planet

A robot to remember
Despite being an AI, the Rigellian Recorder that accompanied Thor to the Black Galaxy was hailed by the Thunder God as an ally and hero.
Thor #133, Oct. 1966

with Ego at its center. Recognizing Thor's power, the Living Planet challenged the God of Thunder to a duel, theorizing that if Thor could be defeated, Ego would be able to conquer the entire universe. Instead, despite confounding Thor with a sequence of assaults, Ego was the one who met with defeat and swore to never again attack Rigel or any other galaxy and promptly sealed off his bio-verse.

"For the first time in countless millennia I have been bested! Never again shall I suffer such humiliation!!"

Ego, the Living Planet

A world apart …?
Ego lamented his defeat at the hands of the Thunder God, pledging that henceforth he would forever be a world apart … a pledge he was destined to break.
Thor #133, Oct. 1966

The Black Galaxy

Located on the edge of the known universe and composed entirely of organic matter, Ego's birthplace— the mysterious and dreaded Black Galaxy—was also the site of a once-in-an-eon event.

Sometime after Ego departed the unique bio-verse, its true purpose was revealed when Thor, Hercules, the High Evolutionary, and the Celestial hunter Stellaris were drawn into an experiment devised by the Celestials. Many millennia ago, the space gods created the Black Galaxy as a breeding place to spawn a new Celestial but needed singular elements to realize their ambitions.

Harvesting genetic material from Hercules, the High Evolutionary, and Thor's mortal host Eric Masterson, the space gods awaited the spark to ignite conception. That came in the unexpected form of Stellaris, avenging the death of her world at the hands of the callous Celestials by destroying their project in a huge explosion. The blast, however, proved to be the very catalyst required for birth. As it was being born, the new Celestial released Hercules and Masterson and then absorbed the nurturing bio-verse in its entirety, bringing about the death of the Black Galaxy.

Weaponized comets
During his titanic struggle with Ego, Galactus diverted comets from their cosmic paths, flinging them toward the Living Planet, turning the tide of battle in the World-Devourer's favor.
Thor #161, Feb. 1969

Enter Galactus

Ego's self-imposed exile did not last. When Galactus arrived at the Black Galaxy having torn through the Rigel System, Ego lashed out with bolts of force to deter the World-Devourer. The attack merely spurred on Galactus, bringing him face-to-face with Ego. Meanwhile, Tana Nile visited Thor and entreated upon him to help the Rigellians against Galactus, propelling the Thunder God into the fray. Accompanied once again by the Recorder, Thor reached the Black Galaxy only to be caught in the waves of destructive energy emanating from the battle between Ego and Galactus.

Thor and the Recorder were rescued by a group of Wanderers—survivors of planets previously consumed by Galactus. The Thunder God joined Ego in his battle against Galactus, forcing the World-Devourer to retreat; as a reward, Ego grew a verdant jungle and invited the Wanderers to live there forever. Sadly, their stay turned out to be far from permanent. When Tana Nile blasted free a section of Ego in order to use it to terraform a planet named Blackworld, not only did she create a dangerous being named Ego Prime, but she also drove Ego insane. The Living Planet consumed the Wanderers, and then, after defeating Galactus when the Devourer of Worlds again tried to feed on him, swore that he would conquer the entire universe.

Ego mania
In the face of an insane and even more powerful Ego, Galactus piloted a vessel toward the Living Planet, carrying with him Thor, Firelord, and Hercules.
Thor #227, Sept. 1974

Tana Nile's tale
One of Rigel's most fanatical Colonizers, Tana rebelled against her race's colonial ways and became an outcast.
Thor #131, Aug. 1966

Warriors three
While fellow demigods Thor and Hercules were longtime allies, they were unfamiliar with Firelord, but the Xandarian was formidable in the fight against Ego.
Thor #227, Sep. 1974

With Ego on the rampage, Galactus and his herald Firelord formed an alliance with Thor and the demigod Hercules in the fight against the raging world. After a titanic struggle, Galactus attached a propulsion unit to Ego's south polar axis, shooting the Living Planet deep into space. This was but a temporary solution, however. Not long after, seeking revenge, Ego used the engine to propel himself to Earth. His threat to destroy the planet was thwarted by the Fantastic Four, who tampered with the propulsion unit. When Ego triggered it, intending to smash into the Earth, he was instead thrown toward the sun, crumbling in its immense gravity.

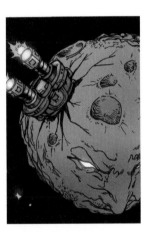

Immortal engine
The clever plan to drive Ego into space with an engine backfired when the Living Planet used it for a scheme of his own.
Ultimates 2 #8, Aug. 2017

Shot into the sun
Ego's faulty engine sent him away from Earth and towards the sun, where he succumbed to its searing heat and crushing gravity.
Fantastic Four #235, Oct. 1981

Alter Ego

While the Stranger's role in Ego's genesis was recognized, what was not widely known was that a second world-entity had also been created: Ego's brother, Alter Ego. When the Stranger had helped to create Ego, he had used instruments and formulae provided by another cosmic entity—the Collector. These were supplied on the condition that the Stranger create a second living planet—one destined for the Collector's museum. For his part, the Stranger hoped to one day pit Ego and Alter Ego against one another and see whether freedom or captivity bred the stronger will.

Millennia later, the Stranger set his experiment in motion. He told Ego that he had a brother, setting the pair on a collision course that would see Alter Ego reduced to the size of a moon. He fell into orbit around his brother, becoming a kind of devil's advocate. When a battle erupted on Ego's surface between bandits the Ravagers, a group of Asgardians, and space marauders the Raiders, Alter Ego angrily exhorted his brother to eject all concerned into the void—including the refugees they were fighting over. Ego, however, let the refugees stay—a measure, perhaps, of how having the company of his brother had finally brought him a little peace.

Pulling himself together

Though Ego was torn asunder, the sun also triggered a photosynthetic form of revitalization within him, and the Living Planet was able to pull together his gaseous matter before bringing his biomass back to life.

Thereafter, for a time Ego served as a meeting place for the Elders of the Universe—a group of ancient cosmic entities, including the Stranger, the Collector, and the Grandmaster—and later hosted the Xandarian Worldmind, who transformed him into Nu-Xandar, a base for the Nova Corps. More often than not, though, true to his combative nature, he tended to clash with entities whose paths he crossed, whether that be the Silver Surfer, the Korbinite Beta Ray Bill, or any number of other space-faring beings. That was until he was approached by Galactus once again—for this was not the same World-Devourer that Ego had fought before. Galactus had become the Lifebringer, a being who restored worlds rather than destroyed them.

Ego tripping
Having reconstituted himself, Ego used the propulsion engine to search for energy sources in order to restore his strength.
Rom #69, Aug. 1985

Appointment with Elders
Acting as both a venue and a participant, Ego met with the Elders of the Universe— among them the Grandmaster and the Collector—to plot the downfall of Galactus.
Silver Surfer #4, Oct. 1987

Worldmind over matter
After Xandar was decimated by the Annihilation Wave, the Xandarian Worldmind inhabited Ego for a time while it restored the Nova Corps.
Nova #21, Mar. 2009

Now, Galactus was in desperate need of Ego's help. The embodiment of the present Multiverse, Eternity, had been enslaved by the embodiment of the original universe, the First Firmament—who was said to be the creator of even the Celestials. Seeking allies to help free Eternity, Galactus breached Ego's crust and descended deep within him until he reached his core: his brain. There, the two met as they never had before—in their original forms as fellow scientists Egros and Galan. The pair put the past behind them, with Galactus helping Ego evolve into a new Ego Prime. Consequently, Ego could join the Eternity Watch—a group of cosmic beings assembled by Galactus to combat the First Firmament and his allies the Dark Celestials and Logos. With Ego's assistance, the Eternity War was won, allowing the Living Planet to return to his natural state. ■

Brothers to the core
At Ego's core, the Lifebringer and the Living Planet spoke of their former lives as Galan and Egros, clasping hands as brothers.
Ultimates 2 #8, Aug. 2017

"In the face of the end of everything—in the face of oblivion—we cling on, we two. Always reaching—desperately, helplessly—for that last hope of survival … Always fighting. Always alive."
Galactus, the Lifebringer

Head space
His mission with Galactus and the Eternity Watch over, Ego allowed his planetary self to float free in space once again.
Ultimates 2 #100, Oct. 2017

Ethereal Realms

As far away as a distant star, yet as close as home, numerous celestial realms are linked intrinsically to the planet Earth, tethered in place by the faith and belief of ordinary women and men. Immortal beings and mythical creatures inhabit these intangible places. They are the abodes of gods and monsters. There is Otherworld, an idolized version of the British Isles that has given birth to the powerful and ever-watchful Captain Britain Corps; and the Seven Capital Cities of Heaven from which martial arts heroes like the Immortal Iron Fist draw their spiritual strength. Then there are the godly domains, majestic citadels like Asgard and Olympus, where the gods of ancient times continue to be challenged in ways that light up the stars, their struggles rocking the foundations of reality and reverberating back down to Earth.

Mythical Mirror

The extradimensional kingdom of Otherworld is shaped by the collective subconscious of the peoples of the British Isles. Traditionally a land of fairies, elves, and other mythical beasts, the recent influx of new inhabitants has seen it come to reflect the complex nature of modern times.

Forest of a Thousand Sorrows

Last Watchtower of Del Di'Lorr

Dryador Rift

Floating Kingdom
of Roma Regina

Merlyn's Tower

Starlight Citadel

Darkmoor

Citadel of the
Manchester Gods

Castle Camelot
and The Rift

Castle le Fay

Stonehenge

Goblin territory

In ancient days, as the peoples of the British Isles gradually developed strong cultural identities, their varied and disparate beliefs conjured into reality a mythical realm that would become known as Otherworld. A relatively flat landmass suspended in a sea of stars, Otherworld's geography mirrored that of the physical islands, with places of power and special significance—such as Stonehenge and Hadrian's Wall—serving as gateways between the tangible world and ethereal kingdom.

The Tuatha de Danaan and the Fomorians, two races descended directly from the primordial Earth Mother Gaea, were Otherworld's first inhabitants. They were soon joined by a host of other mythical creatures: elves, trolls, leprechauns, and many more. All were born of the human imagination and sustained in Otherworld by the power of subconscious thought.

Otherworld was formed close to a dimensional interface that allowed for travel between the various realities of the Multiverse and, because of this connection, the kingdom became a prize coveted by many. Necrom, the sorcerer supreme of an alternative reality, was the first to attempt to tame Otherworld's energies and thus empower himself. Traveling with his mystic apprentices, Feron and Merlyn, Necrom traveled to Earth-616 where he drew on the cosmic power of the Phoenix Force to create a tower throughout every realm of the Multiverse, including Otherworld. The tower was a linchpin—designed to knit the divergent alternative realities together and create a singularity where there was currently a multiplicity of dimensions. The resulting eruption of primal energy would transform Necrom into a god.

When they finally realized Necrom's evil intent, Feron and Merlyn both turned on their former master. Feron attacked the mage, driving him away, while Merlyn leapt into the energy matrix in a desperate effort to contain its volatile energies. As a result, he was swept uncontrollably across the Multiverse. It took an age, but Merlyn eventually mastered the matrix energy and returned to Otherworld, where he established the Starlight Citadel near the cosmic tower's Otherworld counterpart.

> "I mastered the energy matrix and established (a presence) on Otherworld."
>
> Merlyn

Mage of mystery
Merlyn declared himself the ultimate defender of the Multiverse, but he kept his full agenda to himself.
X-Men: Die by the Sword #3, Jan. 2008

Science and sorcery
Suspended above King Arthur's Isle of Avalon, the Starlight Citadel was a city of science in a legendary realm of magic.
X of Swords: Creation #1, Nov. 2020

Silver Citadel

Like a silver needle swirling on a fine, cosmic thread, the Starlight Citadel floated in a geosynchronous position above Otherworld's Isle of Avalon. From this new base, Merlyn operated as a self-appointed Omniversal Guardian, on the lookout for Necrom's possible return and other existential threats to the Multiverse.

During Earth's Middle Ages, Merlyn took a particular interest in the affairs of Great Britain, anointing champions like King Arthur and the Black Knight to fight against malign forces, including his own sorceress half sister Morgan le Fay. Referring to himself as "Merlin" and appearing to be little more than an aged practitioner of magic, Merlyn weaved himself into King Arthur's story. The events of those times became so embedded in the collective memory—became such a rich part of the British cultural tapestry—that they further confirmed Otherworld as a realm where the mythical and legendary were real. After a traitorous act brought the house of Camelot to ruin, the dead King Arthur and many of his courtiers were resurrected in Otherworld by Merlyn. Castle Camelot was rebuilt close to the chasm known as the Great Rift, and, thanks to Otherworld's unique temporal qualities, King Arthur and his knights remained active and vital until modern times.

Armies of darkness
Otherworld's mythical creatures, such as ogres, dragons, and trolls, were often dragooned into the armies of would-be conquerors.
Uncanny X-Force #22, Apr. 2012

Camelot was the first of many attempts by Merlyn to establish a force for good in the Multiverse. In the modern age, he enlisted an agent—James Braddock—and sent him to Earth-616 to sire a champion. Braddock and his wife, Elizabeth, produced three children: Jamie and twins Brian and Betsy. Although both Jamie and Betsy were mutants, possessing latent psi-abilities, it was Brian who was destined to become Merlyn's hero. While still a physics student, Brian became embroiled in a terrorist assault on a nuclear research facility. Grievously wounded, he used the last of his strength to flee into the night. Stumbling into an ancient stone circle, he found himself in the ethereal presence of Merlyn and his daughter, Roma. The twin spirits urged Brian to decide between two icons of power: the Sword of Might and the Amulet of Right. Opting for the latter, Brian was transformed into Captain Britain.

Brian went on to have an illustrious career as the UK's premier Super Hero. Eventually, he learned that he was but one of many, an entire Captain Britain Corps that Merlyn had stationed throughout the sundry Earths of the Multiverse. While some of these Captain Britains were unique individuals, most were alternative-reality doppelgängers of Brian, with similar links to Otherworld. In this manner, the Captain Britain Corps was a reflection of Brian as an individual in much the same way that Otherworld was a reflection of the British Isles as a whole.

City on the hill
Medieval Camelot was rebuilt in Otherworld where it endured for centuries despite being besieged countless times.
Excalibur #1, Dec. 2019

Her Majestrix

While each member of the Captain Britain Corps had their own alternative-reality Earth to protect, the Starlight Citadel served as a base for ceremonial gatherings and administrative affairs. Overseeing the day-to-day running of the Corps—and thus the smooth maintenance of the Multiverse—was Opal Luna Saturnyne. Given the rank of Omniversal Majestrix by Merlyn, Saturnyne was as overbearing and as imperious as her title might suggest. The ultimate politician, she was always seeking ways to further her own agenda and enhance her power.

Given his mercurial nature, Merlyn was frequently absent from Otherworld, off somewhere in the Multiverse furthering his complex schemes. During these times, Roma served as Omniversal Guardian in place of her father. On one such occasion, she was deposed by a malign artificial intelligence called Mastermind, which spread a techno-organic virus throughout Otherworld, transforming the pastoral countryside into a polluted landscape of mechanized factories. The Captain Britain Corps was decimated by Mastermind's cyborg forces. Consequently, it fell to Brian Braddock to rally the survivors, including Captain UK from Earth-238 and the human-dragon hybrid Sir Benedict of the Falls, and take the fight back to the enemy. Brandishing the Sword of Might, which was finally revealed as King Arthur's fabled blade Excalibur, Brian bested Mastermind in personal combat and helped restore Otherworld's bucolic splendor. For a time, he ruled as sovereign but resumed his heroic duties upon Merlyn's eventual return.

Two masters
Roma promoted Captain Britain (Brian Braddock) as the leader of the Captain Britain Corps while Saturnyne embroiled him in her political schemes. *Captain Britain Omnibus,* Jul. 2009 (variant cover)

> **"I created the Corps to patrol the Multiverse."**
> Merlyn

Call to arms
Saturnyne gathered together the entire Captain Britain Corps only in the direst of circumstances, such as when Otherworld was threatened by reality-shaper Mad Jim Jaspers. *X-Men: Die by the Sword* #3, Jan. 2008

Marching machines
Even an army of trolls was not strong enough to stop the mechanized cities of the Manchester Gods as they strode relentlessly southward.
Journey into Mystery #639, Aug. 2012

Industrial revolution

In some ways, Mastermind's industrialization of Otherworld served as a prelude for what was to come. The realm suddenly found itself under assault from a fresh force that King Arthur and the rulers of Avalon found unfathomable. Huge ambulatory cities spontaneously appeared in the north, marching south toward Camelot on girderlike appendages. These were the Manchester Gods, unknown deities that had arrived to stake their claim on Otherworld.

Two centuries earlier, with Great Britain leading the way in the industrial age, the Manchester Gods had sprung into being, conjured up by the hopes and dreams of a new urban population. These giant modern deities had failed to establish a foothold in Otherworld but, with Surtur from the Asgardian pantheon providing a suitably energetic power source, their vast city-states were finally on the move. King Arthur feared for the future of Otherworld, but as Mister Wilson—the Manchester Gods' spokesperson—explained, this was as much a battle of ideas as it was a clash of arms. "They say Britain is fundamentally rural, we say that Britain is fundamentally urban," Wilson declared.

Repelling the Manchester Gods was no easy task, made harder by the fact that many ordinary citizens of Otherworld moved to the cities in search of fresh opportunities. In the end, with neither side gaining an advantage, a truce was brokered by the Asgardian God of Mischief, Loki. The Manchester Gods would remain in their northern strongholds, while King Arthur and his knights would still have full jurisdiction in Avalon's southern counties.

Industrial dispute
Mister Wilson represented the Manchester Gods in peace negotiations with the Asgardian Loki and the powers of Otherworld.
Journey into Mystery #640, Aug. 2012

Sole survivor

During a universal crisis that saw the destruction of the entire Multiverse and its subsequent reformation, the Captain Britain Corps was wiped out almost completely. As part of a grand existential experiment, the extradimensional Beyonders, who had previously created Earth's Savage Land, plotted to bring about the end of all reality. Their cosmic manipulations resulted in a cascade of so-called incursions—countless alternative realities obliterated within an instant as they collided violently with each other.

To prevent interference in their plans, the Beyonders attacked the Captain Britain Corps, leaving Brian Braddock of Earth-616 as the sole survivor. Imbued with the secrets of the Starlight Citadel by Saturnyne, he was cast out of Otherworld and back to his home reality in the desperate hope that he might somehow survive the unfolding cataclysm.

Ultimately, the Beyonders were defeated by a coalition of Earth's Super Heroes, and a new version of the Multiverse was created to replace that which had been destroyed. The Captain Britain Corps remained a casualty, however. In its absence, Otherworld was thrown further into chaos. Seeking to consolidate her remaining power, Saturnyne closed off the Starlight Citadel and this precipitated open conflict in Avalon and elsewhere. Merlyn and Roma turned against one another, dividing their kingdom into two rival dominions: the Holy Republic of Fae and the Floating Kingdom of Roma Regina. In Camelot, King Arthur mysteriously disappeared and, in his absence, Morgan le Fay assumed the throne as queen regent and declared war on Saturnyne. Uncertain times had come to Otherworld and, just as in the real world, the tumultuous events reignited old rivalries and widened existing schisms.

The war for Otherworld took an unexpected turn when Apocalypse entered the fray. The immortal mutant coveted Otherworld's magic, and he attempted to create a teleport gateway from the mutant homeland of Krakoa that would give him direct access to the mystical realm and all its power. Furthermore, given Otherworld's unique position as a conduit to other realities in the Multiverse, Apocalypse planned to use it as a stepping stone in order to reach the distant realm of Amenth. There, the immortal hoped to liberate the mutants of Arakko, who had been lost to that bleak dimension many centuries earlier.

Undefeated
Brian Braddock was the last hero standing when the Beyonders decimated the Captain Britain Corps as a prelude to universal destruction.
New Avengers #30, Apr. 2015

Trial by combat

Apocalypse recruited Betsy Braddock and other mutant heroes—including former X-Men Rogue and Gambit—into a new Excalibur squad and convinced them to join his cause. With the Krakoan gateway to Otherworld mystically barricaded by Morgan le Fay, Betsy asked her brother, Brian, to use his powers to transport her to Otherworld to investigate matters. Offended by the attempted encroachment of mutants into her domain, Morgan took control of Brian. She transformed him into her thrall and ordered him to slay his sister. Brian fought to shrug off Morgan's possession and, in doing so, was able to magically conjure up the Amulet of Right. Transferring his power into the icon, he urged Betsy to take it. In that moment, the heroic mantle was passed from brother to sister, and Betsy became the new Captain Britain. She escaped from Morgan le Fay but later returned with her new teammates to successfully empower the Krakoan gateway. Recognizing how formidable her foes were, Morgan le Fay agreed to Apocalypse's proposal that the conflict be settled in an age-old fashion—a trial by combat.

War witch
Already at war with her rival for power, Saturnyne, sorceress Morgan le Fay promised to defend Avalon from mutant incursions.
Excalibur #1, Dec. 2019

Otherworldly conduits

Over the centuries, portals to the realm of Otherworld emerged spontaneously across the entirety of the British Isles, generally in places of cultural or historical significance such as Buckingham Palace and Stonehenge. A lesser-known location was a nondescript ring of standing stones in the hills of desolate Darkmoor. This was where Merlyn and Roma first appeared to a wounded Brian Braddock and urged him to become their champion, Captain Britain.

In addition to the larger portals, various hidden sidhe mounds also linked directly to the mystical realm. On rare occasions, countryside travelers might unwittingly stumble through one of these to find themselves in the fairytale-like surroundings of Otherworld.

With the establishment of the Manchester Gods in Otherworld, a new tranche of portals opened up across the British Isles. These fresh gateways reflected the political and social changes ushered in by the Industrial Revolution and included places like the grave of Karl Marx in Highgate Cemetery. A particularly significant portal was located on the former site of the Stockton and Darlington Railway, Britain's first commercial passenger train line.

> "To the death, then. For the Kingdom of Avalon."
> **Morgan le Fay**

Morgan commanded the mind-controlled Brian into the arena while Apocalypse chose the newly christened Captain Britain as his champion. The twins met each other in battle but, unwilling to slay her brother, Betsy set aside her sword. Brian, though, refused to surrender. In the resulting tussle, Betsy unintentionally killed him with his own weapon. Betsy was declared victorious, and Apocalypse subsequently installed the twins' older brother, Jamie, on Morgan le Fay's vacated throne. At Betsy's insistence, the new King of Avalon used his reality-warping powers to resurrect Brian. The twins subsequently returned to Earth, where Brian struggled to come to terms with the recent events in Otherworld.

Heroic cauldron
Not even a fiery dragon could intimidate Betsy Braddock as she claimed her family legacy to become Captain Britain.
Excalibur #4, Feb. 2020

Crossed swords

Shortly after Apocalypse's intervention in Otherworld, the sanctity of the realm was violated yet again when a demonic horde emerged from the Dryador Rift and began an inexorable march toward the Starlight Citadel. At the head of the invading army were the Four Horsemen—Apocalypse's ageless children— who had been dispatched to fight the marauding demons of Amenth eons earlier. They were now back after their long self-exile and seemingly as hungry for conquest as the enemy they had fought so hard to defeat.

Along with their mother, Genesis, and mutants from the land of Arakko, the Four Horsemen had held back the Amenthi demons for centuries. However, the tide of battle turned when Genesis was tricked into taking up the golden helm of the demon's leader, Annihilation, and was subsequently possessed by the creature's malign spirit. Her will broken completely, Genesis became Annihilation's latest host form and pledged the mutants of Arakko to the Amenthi cause.

Apocalypse was lured to Otherworld on the promise of a family reunion but was attacked by his children. All-out war between the forces of Arakko and the mutants of Krakoa seemed inevitable—a conflict that would almost certainly obliterate Otherworld. It was at this moment that Saturnyne finally showed her hand. Ever the schemer, she proposed a tournament between the two sides: the Swordbearers of Arakko versus the Swordbearers of Krakoa. The Braddock twins were among those chosen to represent Krakoa. Betsy was armed with the Starlight Sword, a blade conjured into being by Saturnyne, while Brian wielded the Sword of Might. Apocalypse and some former X-Men, all armed with blades of immense power, made up the rest of the team.

Hard fought, the tournament proved inconclusive until Apocalypse faced Genesis in the final bout. He overcame his wife in combat but was unable to stop her from summoning the entire Amenthi horde to Otherworld. With battles erupting all around him, Apocalypse snatched up the helm of Annihilation. Rather than succumb to its dark influence, however,

The last watchtower
All that stood between Otherworld's kingdom of Dryador and the hostile forces of Amenth was the fortified watchtower of Del Di'Lorr.
X of Swords: Creation #1, Nov. 2020

Dogs of war
The Four Horsemen of Apocalypse sent their army into battle, overrunning Del Di'Lorr, annexing Dryador, and threatening all of Otherworld.
X of Swords: Creation #1, Nov. 2020

Betrayal
Apocalypse arrived in Otherworld expecting a family reunion. Instead he was attacked by his daughter, War, and stabbed in the back by his grandson, the Summoner.
X of Swords: Creation #1, Nov. 2020

"You can call me Captain Britain."
Betsy Braddock

he tamed Annihilation, bending the creature to his own indomitable will and forcing it to call an end to the hostilities. With the immediate battle over, Apocalypse agreed to accompany his wife back to Amenth as part of a peace accord brokered by Saturnyne. Similarly, the island of Arakko would return to Earth where it would be reunited with Krakoa.

Having secured the peace, Saturnyne finally achieved her ambition and was declared Omniversal Guardian of Otherworld. Her grip on power was not absolute, however, as Betsy Braddock promised to be a continual thorn in her side, a check on her authoritarian ambitions. During the Tournament of Swords, Betsy had been struck a mystical blow and shattered into countless slivers of glass. Saturnyne restored Betsy's true form but also used the magical glass to create an entirely new Captain Britain Corps. She had hoped these freshly forged champions would be blindly obedient, but because Betsy was their template, many were counterparts of her—sharing the same fierce will and independent spirit. They were alternative reality reflections of a particularly gifted hero, a Captain Britain equipped to handle the complexities of the modern era. ■

The battle joined
Molded from shards of mystical glass, a new Captain Britain Corps rained down on the Amenthi army.
X of Swords: Destruction #1, Jan. 2021

Heavenly Perfection

Seven serene cities sit on seven separate planes of existence, each one a paradise unto itself. Gliding through eternity in seemingly endless orbits, the cities embody heavenly perfection. Tranquility comes at a cost, however, and one of the Seven Capital Cities of Heaven was built on a foundation of lies and deceit.

With spiritual and cultural links to specific regions of the globe, seven divine realms came into being eons ago, each in its own pocket universe: K'un-Lun, K'un-Zi, Tiger Island, Peng Lai, the Kingdom of Spiders, Z'Gambo, and the Under City. All were separated physically from the Earthly plane yet still connected to it mystically. Home to hardy immortals, these legendary Seven Capital Cities of Heaven were talked about in hushed and reverent tones. They were understood to be celestial utopia, believed to be filled with carefree citizens and governed by benevolent rulers.

The seven realms were not without danger, however, and each of the cities was occasionally bedeviled by monstrous demons or jealous warlords. To defend themselves, each city anointed a champion—an expert martial artist who could draw on their chi, or life-force, to perform incredible feats of strength and agility. Collectively, the heroes were known as the Immortal Weapons and their duties were passed down through countless generations. Every 88 years, the cities merged with each other to form the Heart of Heaven, a mystical arena where the Immortal Weapons faced each other in the Tournament of the Heavenly Cities, a contest designed to hone their fighting skills to perfection.

"It is here (in the Tournament of the Heavenly Cities) that we, the lords of the Seven Capital Cities of Heaven, convene and celebrate that which is our most holy duty."

Crane Mother

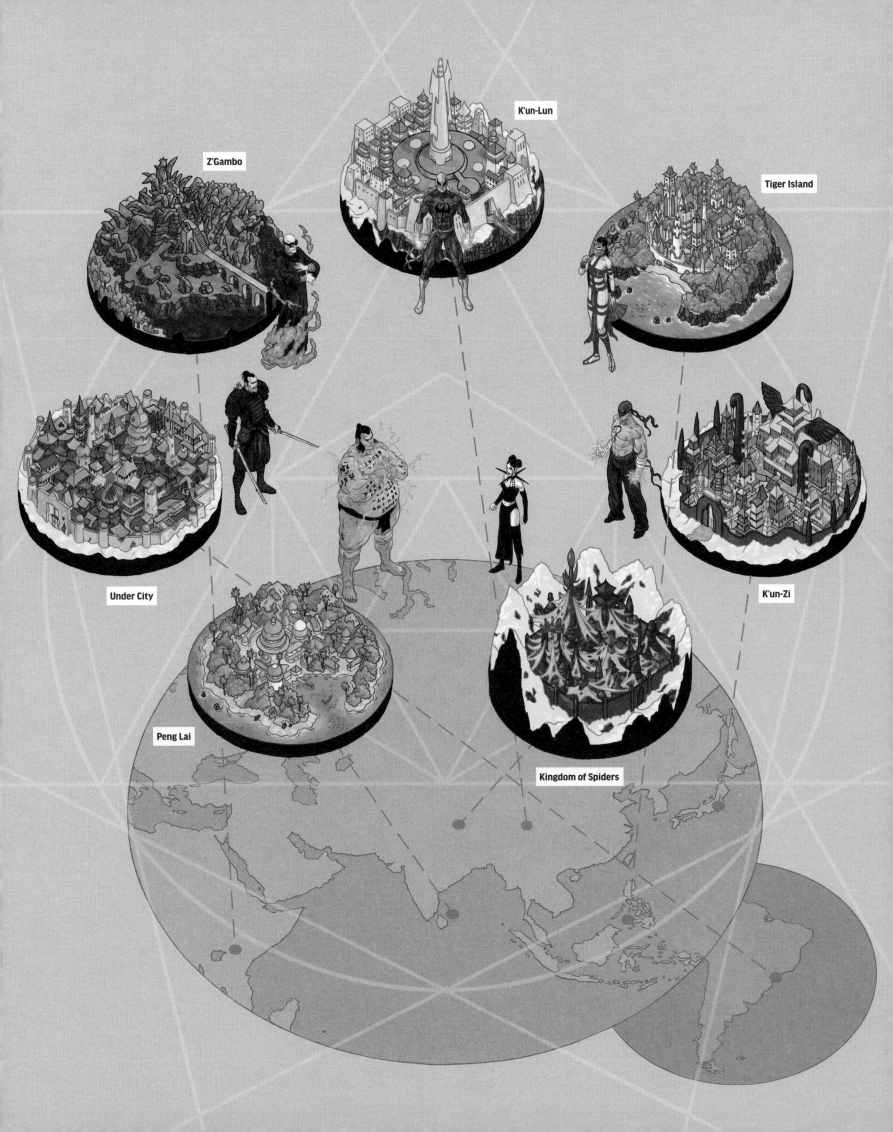

Z'Gambo

K'un-Lun

Tiger Island

Under City

Peng Lai

Kingdom of Spiders

K'un-Zi

Heaven sent
Once every 10 years, the city of K'un-Lun appeared in the snowcapped mountains, bringing enlightenment and danger in equal measure.
Avengers #13, Mar. 2019

were exceedingly rare. K'un-Lun was ruled by the Dragon-Kings, a clique of ancient mystics who adhered to outdated traditions and actively discouraged change for fear of losing influence and wealth.

Caged monsters

K'un-Lun was particularly vulnerable to attack from marauding monsters and demons, losing many of its citizens to savage attacks. A solution to the city's plight presented itself when a party of warriors, sent to map the geography of Earth, stumbled upon a portal in a mountaintop region of East Asia. The magical gateway led to a bleak and empty realm, a land that produced grief and existential anguish in those unfortunate enough to wander aimlessly into it. Some mockingly referred to this new domain as the Eighth City, while others described it more succinctly as hell. Nevertheless, it proved to be the salvation of K'un-Lun. The ruling Dragon-Kings realized that the amorphous demons who breeched their walls could be contained within the Eighth City. They petitioned the other Seven Cities for aid, and the Immortal Weapons were soon on the streets of K'un-Lun, fighting to capture and contain the monsters.

Like combatants circling each other in a training arena, the cities cycled through the heavens on slow trajectories. Sometimes they intersected with the material plane and appeared on Earth for brief periods of time. K'un-Lun, foremost among the cities, materialized in the Himalayan peaks once every 10 years. In theory, citizens could leave the city on such occasions to forge new lives in the outside world. Similarly, the door was supposedly open for seekers of wisdom to enter K'un-Lun and hopefully achieve spiritual enlightenment. However, in reality, such exchanges

Mystical marketplace
Many of K'un-Lun's fishermen and farmers would sell their produce at the market. The city's rare manifestations allowed for welcome trade with the outside world.
Immortal Iron Fist #24, May 2009

Gatekeepers
Pooling their magical strength, the Immortal Weapons created a mystical gate to barricade the entrance to a demon-filled hell.
Immortal Iron Fist #22, Mar. 2009

"To seal the gate … I had to close it from the inside, damning myself to life in this hell—far below the steel spires of K'un-Lun."
Iron Fist (Quan Yaozu)

Leading the war against the demons was K'un-Lun's own champion, Iron Fist Quan Yaozu. Like those who had served before him, Quan Yaozu had defeated the magical dragon Shou-Lao the Undying in combat and had absorbed the creature's powerful chi. Yaozu could now channel the dragon's strength and deliver blows of explosive force. His fists smoldering with this power, Yaozu cut a fiery path through the invading monsters and helped secure victory for the Immortal Weapons.

With the creatures defeated, the greatest sorcerers of the Seven Cities came together to ensure their eternal banishment. The mages weaved an enchantment that meant only a quorum of Immortal Weapons could successfully open up the portal to the Eighth City. Yaozu and his fellow champions traveled to Earth, empowered the spell with their combined chi, and then forced the monsters through the gateway and into the abyss. Unfortunately, there were so many detainees, that the sheer weight of numbers threatened to force open the gate unless something drastic was done. Seeing no other available option, Yaozu entered the Eighth City to guard the portal from the other side— bravely assuming a burden he would have to endure throughout the rest of time.

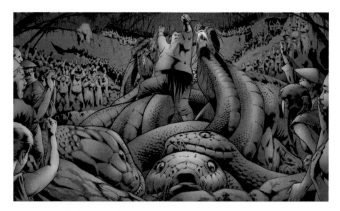

The Fat Cobra strikes
Upon defeating the snake-dragon Xiang Yao, Fat Cobra became Peng Lai's most recent Immortal Weapon.
Immortal Weapons #1, Sep. 2009

Self-sacrifice
Quan Yaozu pledged his life to the protection of K'un-Lun, holding back a horde of demons for an eternity as the unflinching Iron Fist.
Immortal Iron Fist #25, Jun. 2009

New age

With the demons trapped, the Seven Cities continued on their perpetual journeys through the cosmos. In K'un-Lun, the Dragon-Kings reigned with absolute power just as they had always done. To help them maintain order, they dispatched hardened criminals to the Eighth City to languish alongside the monsters. As the years progressed, the duties of the Immortal Iron Fist were borne by many unique individuals, some of who took the opportunity every 10 years to explore the material world and develop reputations on Earth as legendary heroes. In the early part of the 20th century, an outsider named Orson Randall inherited the title. After his parents' experimental airship crashed in K'un-Lun, he was adopted as a member of the city and trained in the martial arts by Lei-Kung the Thunderer.

During World War I, Orson left his mystical home to fight for the allies alongside other early Super Heroes like the Phantom Eagle and the Union Jack. The conflict scarred him, however, and when he was summoned back home to participate in the latest Tournament of the Heavenly Cities, he refused to fight. His fellow Immortal Weapons were ordered to strip him of his power and, in the ensuing confrontation, Orson inadvertently killed Crane, the champion from the city of K'un-Zi. Declared a wanted man, he fled back to Earth and spent the subsequent decades evading mystical agents from the Seven Cities.

While on Earth, Orson adopted a young orphan. He named him Wendell Rand and taught him all he knew about the martial arts. The boy was enthralled by his guardian's tales of exotic K'un-Lun and longed to one day visit the city. Orson, however, forbade discussion of such matters. In the end, after a particularly heated argument, young Wendell ran away. When K'un-Lun next materialized among the mountains, the boy successfully slipped into the mystical city.

> "When they summoned me home, I returned, but I was more of an outworlder than ever."
>
> **Iron Fist (Orson Randall)**

Dragon slayer
Where his father failed before him, Danny Rand bested Shou-Lao and obtained the power of the Iron Fist.
Immortal Iron Fist #1, Jan. 2007

Seeking wisdom
Wendell Rand almost died in his search for spiritual enlightenment. When he was at his lowest ebb, K'un-Lun appeared before him and he entered the realm of the immortals.
Immortal Iron Fist #8, Oct. 2007

Family legacy

Like his adoptive father before him, Wendell became a student of Lei-Kung. He impressed the rulers of K'un-Lun with his fighting prowess and was selected over Lei-Kung's own son, Davos, to become the latest Iron Fist. However, when the moment arrived for him to face the dragon Shou-Lao, he panicked and fled back to Earth in disgrace.

Years later, now head of an international corporation, Wendell attempted to return to the mystical city with his wife, Heather, and their nine-year-old boy, Danny. Unfortunately, Wendell was unable to find K'un-Lun's exact location among the snowcapped mountains, and both parents died while fruitlessly searching for the city's gates. Danny was lucky enough to survive, however, and was rescued by the people of K'un-Lun. He was inducted into Lei-Kung's school and trained to meet the challenge of Shou-Lao. When ready, he braved the dragon's lair and defeated it in combat. He pressed his chest against the creature's burning heart and absorbed its mystical chi, the process leaving behind a dragon-shaped tattoo on his flesh. As Iron First, Danny was K'un-Lun's anointed champion. He was also the inheritor of a significant legacy—the third member of a family whose destiny had been changed irrevocably by the mystical allure of K'un-Lun.

Force of nature
The Iron Fist granted Danny Rand the ability to channel his life-force into achieving harmony with his surroundings.
Immortal Iron Fist #27, Aug. 2009

Train to nowhere

The Crane Mother, ruler of the city of K'un-Zi, seethed with anger when her champion warrior was accidentally killed by Iron First Orson Randall. Seeking vengeance on Iron Fist's home city of K'un-Lun, she entered into an alliance with the mysterious Mr. Xao and the terrorist organization, Hydra. She helped the villains develop an experimental new technology—a maglev train.

Mr. Xao and his cohorts traveled to the mountaintop region where K'un-Lun intersected with the material world and began to lay track for the new train much to the amusement and the bemusement of the local population. Many of them wondered out loud what had possessed these crazy outsiders to build a train that seemingly went nowhere. In reality, the vehicle was a weapon—a literal bullet train. It was packed with explosives, and when activated, its electromagnetic field generators pierced the dimensional void that led to the city of K'un-Lun. Impact would have destroyed the venerable city, but Iron Fist Danny Rand was able to summon enough strength to destroy the train with a single, smoldering punch.

Martial arts taskmaster
Stern Lei-Kung, aka the Thunderer, trained K'un-Lun's champions at the behest of its ruler, the hooded Yu-Ti.
Immortal Iron Fist #6, Jul. 2007

The tournament

Danny Rand was always an outsider in K'un-Lun. His questioning nature frequently set him at odds with those in authority and, in time, he abandoned the city for the outside world. Ostensibly this was to learn more about the death of his parents, but in reality it was about finding a purpose beyond his assigned role as K'un-Lun's living weapon. After claiming ownership of the powerful Rand Corporation, Danny joined Luke Cage as a Hero for Hire and forged a reputation on the streets of Manhattan as an advocate for the weak and dispossessed. Thanks to various magical means,

Danny returned to K'un-Lun on occasion but never stayed long. Finally, when the cosmic clock signified it was time, he was recalled to participate in the latest Tournament of the Heavenly Cities. In the arena, he was pitted against Tiger's Beautiful Daughter from Tiger Island, Fat Cobra from Peng Lai, Bride of Nine Spiders from the Kingdom of Spiders, Prince of Orphans from Z'Gambo, Dog Brother #1 from Under City, and Davos, who had been recruited as K'un-Zi's new Immortal Weapon—Steel Serpent.

It seemed that in Danny's absence, eternal K'un-Lun had changed very little. In reality, though, the city teetered on the precipice of change. The venal Yu-Ti, who had ruled for many decades as the August Personage in Jade, had grown lazy and no longer bothered to hide his corruption. For centuries, K'un-Lun's women had been marginalized, forbidden to engage in many areas of life, including politics and the martial arts. Now they were at the vanguard of a new movement. A serving girl—nameless because she had been born illegitimately—formed the Army of Thunder. This force received secret training from the serving girl's adoptive father, Lei-Kung, and waited for the right moment to make its move. When Danny saw the righteousness of the cause for himself and learned that the serving girl was actually Orson Randall's daughter, he signed up. Danny persuaded his fellow Immortal Weapons to side with him, and Yu-Ti—and the corruption he represented—was consigned to the history books.

Lightning strike
In the first round of the tournament, Fat Cobra delivered the explosive Cudgel of Misfortune to knock Iron Fist out of the arena.
Immortal Iron Fist #9, Nov. 2007

"We became trapped
(in the Eighth City) ...
and have spent what
seems an eternity fighting
monsters and demons."

Iron Fist (Danny Rand)

Lei-Kung then became the new ruler of K'un-Lun and, as such, uncovered the full, awful truth about the Dragon-Lords' reign. It soon emerged that the old rulers had consigned not only criminals to the void of the Eighth City but also rivals to those in authority. Upon hearing this news, Danny rallied his fellow Immortal Weapons for a rescue mission. Using mystical methods, they traveled to Earth and then, drawing on the enchantment created centuries earlier, combined their chi to enter the Eighth City. Unfortunately, the experience was disorienting and, upon their arrival, the Immortal Weapons were captured by the mysterious Changming.

The Immortal Weapons were forced to participate in bouts of bloody combat in the tyrant's arena. During one of the staged gladiatorial matches, they pooled their resources and managed to break free. The plan was to open up the mystic gateway and escape back to Earth with the innocents who had been trapped in the hellish realm for so long. However, everything changed when Changming revealed himself to be Quan Yaozu, the Iron Fist of ages past. For an incalculable amount of time, Yaozu had stoically defended the gate against the monstrous demons, but as he witnessed more and more innocent souls arriving in the Eighth City, his heart had hardened. He came to hate his once-beloved city and its corruption, and he began to plot revenge. Now, as the Immortal Weapons opened up the portal from the Eighth City, he planned to seize the moment and lead an army of conquest upon K'un-Lun. Yaozu's forces poured through the gateway, the Immortal Weapons barely able to contain them. Eventually, with the two sides too evenly matched, they agreed on a truce. All the human prisoners of the Eighth City would be allowed to return home and perhaps, with this act of reconciliation, K'un-Lun would be able to move on from its past. ∎

Weapons ready
The Immortal Weapons Fat Cobra, Bride of Nine Spiders, Prince of Orphans, Dog Brother #1, and Tiger's Beautiful Daughter fell in behind Iron Fist to defend K'un-Lun.
Immortal Iron Fist #13, May 2008

War and peace
The Immortal Weapons battled Quan Yaozu's demonic army until a truce was called and peace restored.
Immortal Iron Fist #26, Jul. 2009

Family Feuds

A shining city floating in the void, Olympus was a place of uncommon and captivating beauty, replete with lush gardens and lavish temples. It was an architectural wonder, and, perhaps unsurprisingly, it was home to a race of beings whose jealousies and rivalries were as monumental as their surroundings.

When humankind began its slow rise toward sentience, its collective consciousness influenced the mystical energies prevalent in Earth's atmosphere and helped give birth to many godly pantheons. Shaped by the will of humanity, these divine beings were sustained by the love and devotion of their followers. One of the first gods to emerge from the ether was the sky father Uranus. Together with the primordial Earth-Mother Gaea, he parented the Titans, a race of godlike beings who established the glorious city of Olympus in a small, pocket universe immediately adjacent to Earth.

In addition to the Titans, the realm was home to other mythical creatures, such as gigantes, centaurs, cyclopes, gorgons, and satyrs. When Uranus banished the cyclopes, Gaea sought revenge and sent their children against him. In the ensuing struggle, the youngest Titan, Cronus, killed his father. With his last breath, Uranus prophesied that Cronus would likewise be dethroned by one of his own progeny. Seeking to escape this awful fate, Cronus proceeded to imprison each of his offspring in the dank underworld of Hades. However, before Cronus had an opportunity to banish his sixth child, his pregnant wife, Rhea, fled through a dimensional portal to Earth, arriving near Greece's Mount Olympus. She gave birth to a boy, Zeus, who was raised among lowly shepherds and dreamed of one day claiming the majestic splendor of Olympus as his own. Upon reaching adulthood, he freed his siblings Demeter, Hera, Neptune, Pluto, and Vesta from Hades. Then he led them in a war against their own father, a brutal conflict that lasted for a decade and became known as the Titanomachy.

After achieving victory and imprisoning Cronus and the Titans in Hades, Zeus established himself in Olympus as the supreme ruler of the gods, taking Hera as his wife and queen. Pluto was assigned to rule over the underworld and guard its prisoners. Meanwhile, Zeus busied himself with Earthly matters, instructing Neptune to defend the seas, Demeter to watch over the land, and Vesta to protect the people.

Pathway of Infinity

Arena of Ares (circle of combat)

Pit of Hades

Garden of Athena

Hall of Hephaestus (forges below)

Pantheon Hall

Hall of Athena (archives)

Dimensional bridge to Earth of Greek heroes

Hall of Zeus

Hall of Ares

Hall of Apollo

Lightning strike
Zeus declared war against Cronus with a blistering lightning storm, careless of the human lives endangered by his actions.
Assault on New Olympus #1, Jan. 2010

In time, Zeus and Olympus were threatened by Typhon, the so-called Last of the Titans. Having evaded capture during the Titanomachy, Typhon lay siege to Olympus. Manifesting as a monstrous creature with many serpentine limbs and heads, he forced the gods to flee to Earth. Eventually, bristling at Typhon's effrontery, Zeus lured his enemy to the mortal realm and dropped Mount Etna upon his multiple-headed form. Peace restored, and with Typhon seemingly trapped for all eternity, Zeus triumphantly took the gods back to Olympus. In the years that followed, Zeus and his fellow Olympians luxuriated in their unchallenged hegemony, populating their realm with divine offspring.

Zeus fathered children to mortals and immortals alike and, while Hera generally tolerated her husband's infidelities, she became incensed when Zeus sired his personal champion via the Mycenaean princess Alcmene, rather than his own wife. Alcmene tried to appease the goddess by naming the child Herakles— or "Glory to Hera"—but this was a futile gesture. The queen of Olympus viewed the child's very existence as a personal insult, and she continued to seethe with anger even after Zeus tried to make amends by wedding Herakles to Hera's favorite daughter, Hebe, goddess of youth.

Myths and legends

As a result of his parentage, Herakles possessed a fundamental connection to the Earth and found himself frequently drawn back to the world of his birth. Even the unquestioning love and unwavering devotion of Hebe was not enough to keep him in Olympus on a permanent basis. During his many sojourns in the mortal realm, he developed a legendary reputation— building a myth that would endure throughout the ages.

Toppled Titan
Typhon unleashed his wrath on Olympus until Zeus put an end to his temper tantrum in an equally bombastic manner.
Incredible Hercules #141, Apr. 2010

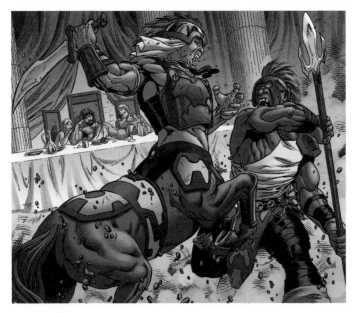

Empty revels
Even his beautiful wife, Hebe, and jousting centaurs were not enough to hold Herakles's attention for long in Olympus.
Assault on New Olympus #1, Jan. 2010

Herakles joined Jason's crew of heroic Argonauts and later undertook a series of challenges to prove his worthiness to his father, Zeus. These Twelve Labors, which included the taming of the Nemean Lion and the killing of the man-eating Birds of Lake Stymphalis, cemented his reputation as a hero. While generally selfless, Herakles was also prone to fits of rage. Friends, such as the Greek hero Theseus, believed that Hera must have cursed Herakles with a terrible and uncontrollable bloodlust. The truth was far more prosaic, however. The demigod was merely young and had not yet learned to control his darker impulses. Eventually, seeking to distance himself from the volatile Hera and his own misdeeds, he modified his name from the Greek Herakles to the Roman Hercules.

In time, as new faiths proliferated around the world, the power of the Olympian gods waned. Zeus eventually took the fateful decision to withdraw from the Earthly sphere. For the next few centuries, the Olympians were largely content to remain in their splendid city, observing mortal events unfold before them but never venturing forth to interfere. They spent their time in empty revels and reminisced about past glories. With little else to do, the

"The majesty of Olympus … there is no place else so marvelous, so wondrous and resplendent in all of existence than the cradle of the immortals."
Hercules

gods frequently squabbled among themselves, each seeking to court favor with Zeus. Athena, goddess of war and wisdom, would clash with Aphrodite, the goddess of love; while the war-god Ares would jealously plot against his half brother, Hercules. The Olympian gods were a family, and, as with every family, tensions bubbled just beneath the surface. What made the gods different, though, was that they would harbor resentments for centuries and their anger could move mountains.

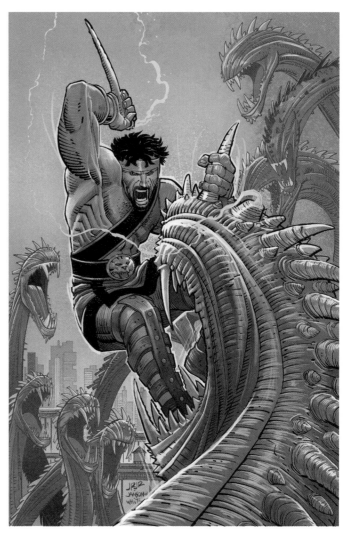

Hero Hercules
On Earth, Hercules found the adventure he craved, such as taming monsters like the many-headed hydra.
Herc #1, Jun. 2011 (variant cover)

Prince of power

Of course, some of the Olympian gods ignored Zeus's edict and continued to secretly interfere in mortal affairs, most notably Ares and Pluto. The latter frequently sought to supplant his brother as king of the gods. On one occasion, Pluto tried to escape his responsibilities as master of the underworld by tricking a gullible Hercules into taking his place. The demigod had recently befriended the Asgardian Thor, however, and the God of Thunder swiftly came to Hercules's rescue. Shortly after that incident, the Enchantress mesmerized Hercules and used him as a living weapon against Thor and his fellow Avengers. The Super Hero team soon freed Hercules from his thrall, but, enraged at his son's unauthorized excursion to Earth, Zeus banished him from Olympus.

In time, Hercules became a full member of the Avengers, his phenomenal strength proving to be a particular boon during a period when powerhouses like Iron Man and Thor had stepped back from active duty. Time and again, Hercules was instrumental in helping the heroes triumph over some seemingly undefeatable foe. However, his own overconfidence proved to be his ultimate undoing. When the Masters of Evil temporarily seized control of Avengers Mansion, Hercules was warned against tackling them on his own. He dismissed such concerns with characteristic aplomb, however,

Chains of office
Pluto grew bored with his underworld duties and frequently conspired to replace Zeus as ruler of the gods. When the opportunity arose, he put his brother on trial for his life.
Incredible Hercules #129, Jul. 2009

only to find himself overwhelmed by the numerous villains. On hearing the news that his son had been beaten into a coma, Zeus grew enraged. He blamed the Avengers for the incident and, encouraged by belligerent Ares, gave orders for the Super Heroes to be rounded up and sent to Hades. The Avengers broke free of Pluto's hellish domain, though, and successfully fought back against the gods of Olympus. Eventually, they agreed on a truce and Hercules revived. He was initially confused—still traumatized by the vicious assault—and he struck out at his heroic teammates. In the end, as his faculties slowly returned, Hercules admitted that it was his own arrogance that had led to his downfall. Even Zeus confessed to hubris, reaffirming his belief that the Olympians should stay out of mortal affairs.

Earth's Mightiest
Hercules served as an Avenger, even forming his own strike force to battle his fellow Olympians when they tried to rewrite reality.
Incredible Hercules #139, Feb. 2010

> "There is no escape (from Hades), Avengers ... you will be mine."
> **Pluto**

Dragon slayers
Beneath the Olympus Group headquarters, teen genius Amadeus Cho and Hercules combined brains and brawn to defeat a robotic dragon. *Incredible Hercules* #140, Mar. 2010

Family business

In time, though, Zeus relented. With powerful beings proliferating on Earth, and with the universe becoming evermore connected, the Olympian realized the futility of his people's splendid isolation. In a rare about-turn, Zeus created an Earth-based business consortium called the Olympus Group. This served as a means to study and better understand humanity—and, of course, the ever-practical king of the gods was not averse to the huge profits that would be engendered in the process.

Hercules became as frequent a visitor to Earth as he had been in ancient times. During an incident in which Earth's Super Heroes joined forces to expel an enraged Hulk from New York's Manhattan, Hercules befriended Amadeus Cho, a remarkable teen with a genius-level intellect. The pair became traveling companions and enjoyed many adventures together. Unfortunately, Hera's hatred for her stepson flared to new intensity, and Hercules and Cho frequently found themselves targeted by the vengeful queen of the gods. When the Asgardians passed beyond the realm of the living during one of their periodic Ragnarok cycles, an evil Shinto god, Amatsu-Mikaboshi, seized the opportunity to conquer the remaining godly pantheons. He first led his demonic forces in an attack on Olympus, leaving the city in a ruinous state. Zeus was thought slain in the conflict but was actually dispatched to Pluto's Hades. Ever the opportunist, the lord of the underworld put his brother on trial for his seemingly disastrous stewardship of the Olympian gods. Found guilty, Zeus drank from the river Lethe and was transformed into a child.

Following the battle with Amatsu-Mikaboshi's demonic forces, the surviving Olympian gods abandoned their derelict city and relocated to Earth. Hera inherited her husband's holdings in the Olympus Group and proceeded to develop a mysterious new product dubbed Continuum®.

Advertised as the perfect solution to the challenges of modern-day life, the device was actually a quantum-empowered computer network. When activated, it would create an idealized version of reality in which humanity still worshiped the gods with unquestioning devotion. The current version of history would be obliterated in the process and, in the Continuum®, Hera would reign unchallenged forever. At the Olympus Group, Hebe served as Hera's administrative assistant. When she learned the full truth of her mother's plans, she revealed all to Hercules. Rallying a team of Avengers that included Spider-Man and Wolverine, the demigod led an assault on Hera's company HQ on Wall Street. The heroes met stiff resistance, organized by Typhon, who, having escaped captivity some years earlier, was now Hera's lover. That didn't prevent him from betraying her, however, and he brutally murdered both Hera and Zeus in an attempt to usurp the power of Continuum®. Giving free rein to his righteous anger, Hercules defeated Typhon in single combat. He managed to turn off Continuum® and save reality from extinction but became trapped in a "bubble" universe while doing so.

Amadeus Cho eventually retrieved Hercules from his interdimensional jail cell. Drawing on his technical and scientific expertise, Cho had embarked on a series of labors of his own, amassing vast quantities of divine energy from a variety of different sources. He used this gathered omnipotence to free his friend and then passed on the great power to Hercules. Stronger than ever before, the demigod went on to prevent Amatsu-Mikaboshi's planned conquest of the godly realms. In the aftermath of victory, Hercules burned out his remaining omnipotence by returning the city of Olympus to its former glory and resurrecting all the gods who had died in the recent conflicts.

Restoration
Watched by a Super Hero crowd, Hercules used his new god power to restore his people's city atop Mount Olympus. *Chaos War* #5, Mar. 2011

Olympus aflame
Hercules led fellow Avengers Hawkeye, Hulk, Vision, Scarlet Witch, Voyager, and Rocket to his home to find it in ruins and his family dead.
Avengers No Road Home #1, Apr. 2019

Darkness falls

Although their surroundings were as serene as they had ever been, the Olympian family was not at peace for very long. Nyx, the Mother of Night, awakened from centuries of slumber to attack the city of the gods. With the aid of her eldritch offspring, Hypnos, Dolos, Apate, and Oizys, Nyx savagely murdered Zeus and his brethren.

Eons earlier, Nyx had been a member of the original Olympian pantheon—the essence of primordial darkness in tangible form. However, as the nighttime became increasingly associated with humanity's fears, she was ostracized by her divine brothers and sisters. In response, Nyx started a family of her own, giving birth to her dark offspring. She then isolated herself even further from

the wider group. As the Olympians' contempt for Nyx grew—and their belief in their own supremacy strengthened—conflict became inevitable. When war finally broke out, Nyx and her children were easily defeated. To further weaken the Mother of Night, Zeus split her soul into three gemlike Night Shards, which he then proceeded to scatter throughout time and space. Finally, he cast Nyx and her brood into a realm of complete darkness, ensuring their eternal slumber with a spell that sealed them in for as long as the sun shone upon the Earth.

Unfortunately, in modern times, the Earth was briefly removed from the solar system by the extraterrestrial Grandmaster and this allowed Nyx to break free of her cloying confinement. Her first move was to attack Olympus, and she then set about tracking down the lost Night Shards with the intent of using their power to remake reality in her own dark image. Alerted to the threat by the cosmic hero Voyager, Hercules formed a small band of Avengers to oppose the villain. The team ultimately triumphed over the goddess through an act of pure faith, their wholehearted belief in a vibrant and colorful universe proving powerful enough to wipe away Nyx and her vision of unending night.

> **"Now I claim your throne, mighty Zeus ... let fall the night."**
> **Nyx, Mother of Night**

Dark domain
Mother of Night Nyx spent countless eons caged in a realm of perpetual darkness.
Avengers No Road Home #4, May 2019

Otherworldly wrath
The resurrected Zeus was consumed by a righteous anger that lit up the stars and caused him to attack planets.
Guardians of the Galaxy #11, Apr. 2021

Following their victory, the Avengers worried for Hercules's future now that his fellow gods were dead. The demigod was far more optimistic, however, believing that the Olympian gods were such a fundamental force of nature that they would eventually be resurrected somewhere in the universe. He was proven right, of course, but when Zeus and the others were finally reborn, it was in an entirely new form. Seemingly consumed by an uncontrollable rage, they embarked on a campaign of universal conquest and it took the combined might of Hercules and Star-Lord's Guardians of the Galaxy to trap them in a bleak dimension with no sunlight and thus nothing to power their divine wrath.

The Olympians were the original sky gods, and they spent countless years looking down from the city of Olympus, seemingly above the petty travails of ordinary mortals. They were secure in the knowledge of their superiority, but their idolized personas and beautiful surroundings ultimately failed to mask the truth. They were a race born from conflict—from a war with their own parents—and conflict was fuel for the fire of their eternal existence. ■

War gods
The Olympian gods Artemis, Hera, Athena, Zeus, Hermes, Hephaestus, and Apollo, were reborn in a dangerous new form, promising to deliver an eternity of war.
Guardians of the Galaxy #10, Mar. 2021

New Olympus

Following their untimely death at the hands of Nyx, Zeus and the gods of Olympus were eventually reborn. When they came back from the beyond, however, they were radically different. The formerly benevolent figures were now hungry for war, claiming the universe had resurrected them to be the harbingers of a darker, much more violent epoch. "These are the times that wake the gods and drive them mad," was how Athena summed up the situation. Along with a new version of the gods came a new kind of city. No longer tied to a specific location in time and space, Olympus now rotated in and out of reality at the capricious will of Zeus. In this manner, the gods attacked numerous planets—including remote Kree and Skrull outposts—leaving nothing in their wake but smoking ruins.

Olympus had once been a city of warm marble; now it was a city of cold steel, with golden automatons created by the metalsmith Hephaestus patrolling its sterile boulevards. The old Olympus brought to mind joyous laughter and celebrations; the new Olympus provoked anguished screams and unholy terror.

The Tree of Life

The Ten Realms of Asgard are bound together by the roots and branches of the World Tree, Yggdrasil. This mystical ash tree provides the cosmic axis that links the disparate kingdoms, connecting them on a fundamental level. The realms are home to powerful gods, mercurial angels, monstrous demons, and, perhaps most significantly, courageous mortals.

Of all the Ten Realms, Earth—or Midgard, as the Asgardians would have it—seemingly stands apart. Largely populated by mortal beings, it is unlike the other kingdoms knotted together by the branches of the World Tree, Yggdrasil. The likes of Asgard, Muspelheim, and Jotunheim are home to hardy immortals, beings who have endured for countless centuries and whose epic struggles have lit up the heavens and spawned legends that have been recounted by many generations. By contrast, the peoples of Earth have generally lived fleeting lives—their stories short but sweet. In the grand scheme of things, mortals are here today and gone tomorrow. Nevertheless, Earth sits at the center of mighty Yggdrasil. Nestled in the World Tree's branches—held, as it were, in Yggdrasil's secure embrace—Earth has been a crucial part of the Asgardian cosmology since the beginning.

> "(Yggdrasil is) the tree that is everything. That has its roots and branches in all that is. There are ten realms ... and the tree winds through them all."
>
> **All-Father Odin**

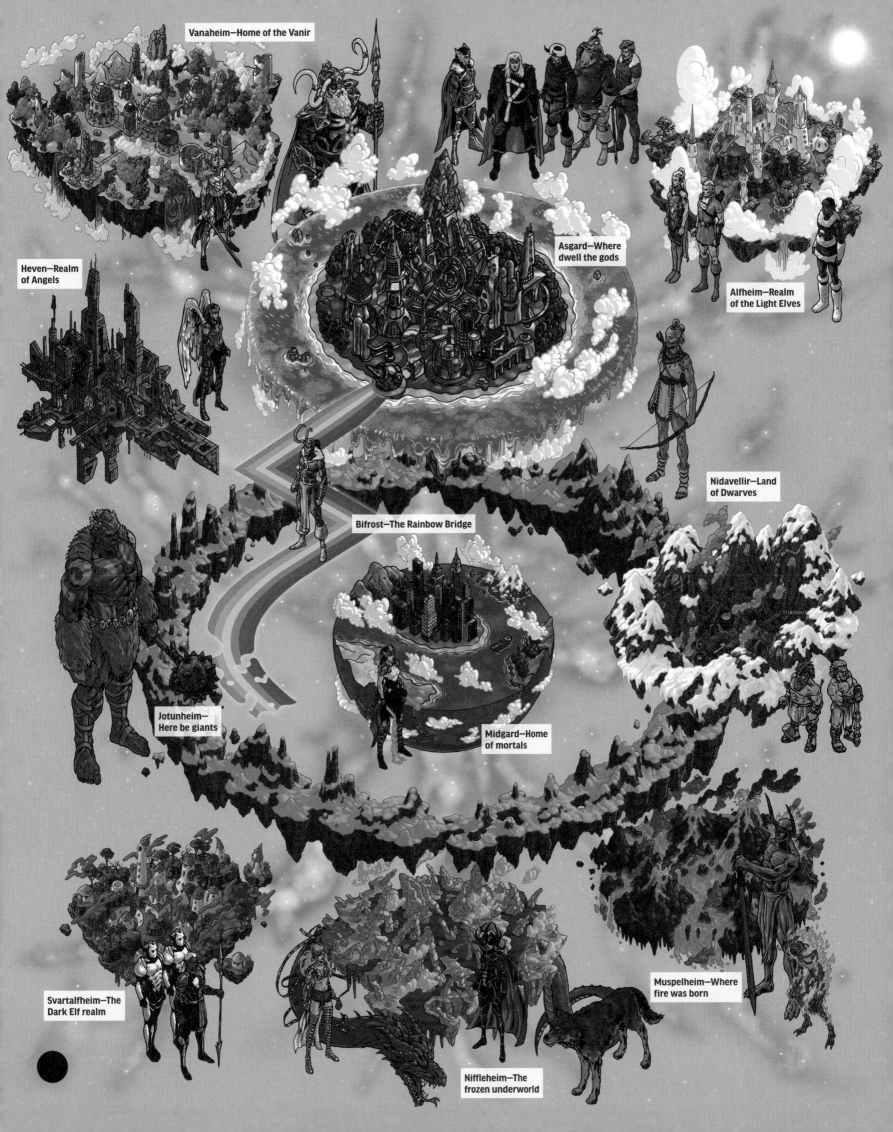

Vanaheim—Home of the Vanir

Asgard—Where dwell the gods

Heven—Realm of Angels

Alfheim—Realm of the Light Elves

Nidavellir—Land of Dwarves

Bifrost—The Rainbow Bridge

Jotunheim—Here be giants

Midgard—Home of mortals

Svartalfheim—The Dark Elf realm

Niffleheim—The frozen underworld

Muspelheim—Where fire was born

Over the rainbow
With the Bifrost linking Asgard to its sister kingdoms,
Odin was able to oversee the entirety of the Ten Realms.
Avengers: Earth's Mightiest Heroes #6, Mar. 2005

Eons ago, the faith of early humans caused the godlike Aesir to spark spontaneously into life. One of Earth's first divine pantheons, the Aesir were formidable clansmen and women, fiery warriors who staked a claim to the world's cold northern climes. However, as new divine races were born, the Aesir found themselves increasingly hemmed in. Seeking to escape the limitations of Earth, they accessed Yggdrasil and used its magical branches to travel to an adjacent dimension that they dubbed Asgard. Under the stewardship of the chieftain Bor, Son of Buri, Asgard became known as the Golden Realm and its people were henceforth referred to as Asgardians. The capital city, which shared the same name as the kingdom, was blindingly beautiful—a splendid crown that glistened atop a granitelike landmass amid a sea of stars. As might be expected of a city dedicated to the history and exploits of a martial race, Asgard was filled with many reminders of the heroic past. The Monument to the Unknown Warrior dominated the skyline and the Warriors' Walk led to the majestic Museum of Weaponry. A physical representation of Yggdrasil burst from the ground and dominated a central garden-plaza.

Thanks to their domain's metaphorical position at the apex of the World Tree, the Asgardians could use the aptly named Rainbow Bridge, Bifrost, to travel to the other Nine Realms. In this way, and perhaps taking their position at the top of the tree quite literally, they sought to impose a universal peace on the frequently cantankerous kingdoms, forging lasting alliances with the Dwarves of Nidavellir and the Light Elves of Alfheim, and waging war on the likes of the Frost Giants of Jotunheim and the Dark Elves of Svartalfheim.

In time, Bor was succeeded by his eldest son, Cul. Living up to his reputation as the God of Fear, the new All-Father of Asgard was a brutal tyrant. Instead of ruling from Asgard's capital city as his father had done, he chose Midgard as his throneworld. The Earth was still freshly formed and largely uninhabited. In fact, it had yet to be properly named and was referred to as Aesheim by Cul and his warriors.

Cul's brothers, Ve, Vili, and Odin, opposed his rule, outraged that he used his godly powers to induce fear in the emergent mortals of Aesheim. After Odin sought guidance from the spirit of Yggdrasil, the brothers ousted Cul from power, imprisoning him at the bottom of the Pacific Ocean. They then razed the God of Fear's fortress to the ground, salted the earth, and renamed Aesheim Midgard so that no god would ever be tempted to subjugate mortal beings ever again.

Fascinated by Midgard's remarkably resilient and hugely imaginative denizens, Odin ignored his own royal decree to leave the realm in peace and returned there repeatedly. He saw a potential in early humanity that he felt was worth preserving. Approximately one million years ago, he joined with other extraordinary individuals like Iron Fist Fan Fei, and Firehair, an early human mutant who wielded the cosmic power of the Phoenix Force, to form a prehistoric Avengers team. Together, these nascent heroes defended the Earth from predatory outsiders and established a legacy that would echo down the centuries.

Seeking wisdom
Odin asked Yggdrasil for guidance in thwarting Cul's ambitions. The wisdom he received came at the cost of his right eye. *Thor #7, Dec 2011*

> "I was able to make Midgard what I would."
> **All-Father Odin**

Awesome All-Father
Secure in his position as All-Father, Odin's power grew exponentially, so much so that it often seemed he could bend the very cosmos to his will. *Thor #21, Dec. 2012*

Odin's reign

As Asgard's new All-Father, Odin continued Bor's work of taming the Ten Realms. The tribes of distant Vanaheim—steeped in the ways of ancient magic—resented the Asgardians' self-serving mission, however, and the two realms were bitter rivals for the longest time. When Odin sought to impose Asgard's will on Vanaheim, the two realms went to war. Vanaheim was hopelessly outnumbered, prompting Freyr, the Vanir chieftain, to elicit aid from Surtur, the demonic ruler of Muspelheim. The two armies clashed repeatedly on the field of battle and with Freyr's troops empowered by the demon's infernal magic, neither side achieved a significant advantage. The conflict ultimately ended with a peace treaty and the marriage of Odin to Freyr's daughter, Freyja. The couple's union symbolized the partnership of the twin realms, and a temple to their shared love was erected in Vanaheim to stand as a lasting testament to the new era of peace and understanding.

A short time after the alliance with Vanaheim was established, Asgard was engulfed in yet another conflict. Odin's actions had made him countless enemies throughout the Ten Realms, none more so than the Frost Giants of icy Jotunheim. King of the Jotuns, Laufey, approached the Angels of Heven to help devise a strategy to break Asgard's hegemony. An ancient ally of Vanaheim, Heven was ruled by the volatile Queen of Angels, who enthusiastically accepted Laufey's commission and gleefully set about forming alliances among the disaffected of the Ten Realms. Her scheme complete, and the Ten Realms teetering on the brink of unprecedented conflict, the Queen revealed all to Odin—promising to call off the dogs of war if he agreed to hand over vast amounts of treasure. Enraged at this attempted blackmail, Odin renounced Heven's Queen and ordered his armies into battle. The war was the most brutal ever witnessed. Ultimately, the Asgardians were forced to retreat back to their realm, with Odin and Freyja rallying the defenders against a host of invading angels.

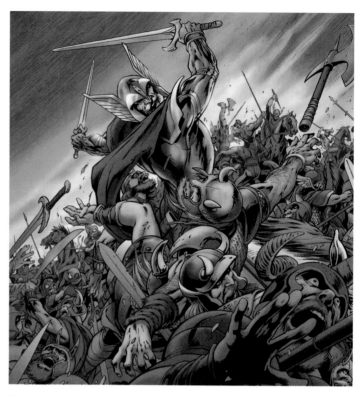

Cry war!
The rivalry between Asgard and Vanaheim exploded into open conflict, with Odin leading his armies against the unruly realm. *Thor* #18, Oct. 2012

Love will out
The Asgardian Odin's love for the Vanir Princess Freyja helped secure peace between their kingdoms. *Thor* #18, Oct. 2012

"So Odin, in the depths of his fury, tore the Tenth Realm loose from the others."

All-Mother Freyja

Heven's above
In Heven, sunlight glistened from towers of topaz and gold, and gentle creatures glided through the incense-filled skies.
Guardians of the Galaxy #7, Dec. 2013

Death and rebirth

Peace settled over the remaining Nine Realms, but Odin was unable to enjoy his costly victory. To his dismay, the All-Father discovered that the Asgardians were locked in a 2,000-year cycle of death and rebirth. They were seemingly condemned to live out their preordained lives and then be wiped away during the catastrophic events of Ragnarok, the Twilight of the Gods. After each fresh apocalypse, which would see Asgard succumb to fire, floods, and ruinous battles, the gods would be resurrected in slightly different forms and the whole process start over.

About 2,000 years ago, following the most recent version of Ragnarok, Odin vowed to break the cycle and free the gods of Asgard from their predetermined destiny. Odin the All-Father observed that of all the inhabitants of the Nine Realms, it was only the mortals of Midgard who emerged from Ragnarok unscathed. Coupling this knowledge with his belief that it was the transitory nature of humankind that made it uniquely adaptable, Odin set in motion a plan to tether Asgard's fate even more tightly to that of Midgard. As the first step in his grand scheme, he traveled to Earth and, while there, sired a new heir—Thor, God of Thunder.

As this final battle built to a crescendo, the Queen of Angels breached the lines and seemingly murdered Odin and Freyja's firstborn daughter, Aldrif. Odin and Freyja's retaliation was swift and certain. Odin cut Heven from the branches of Yggdrasil and cast the realm into a bleak dimension. Freyja then used her magical powers to ensure that, upon their death, each Angel would be consigned to Hel, condemned to serve as thralls for the Death Goddess Hela. Odin's curse upon the Angels was so powerful, his repudiation of them so final, that even the memory of them was erased from history. Thus Ten Realms became Nine.

Banished to beyond
Angered at the Angels, Odin cast Heven into the void. His curse was so forceful that the Angels used the residual energy to power their world for centuries.
Original Sin #5.1, Sep. 2014

Midgard matters

In the years that followed, Odin always claimed that Thor's mother was Gaea, the living consciousness of the Earth itself. However, recent revelations have cast doubt on that assertion, with the spirit of the long-dead Firehair suggesting she was Thor's maternal parent. Regardless of the truth of his parentage, Thor's connection to Midgard made him unique among the Asgardian pantheon, possessing a capacity for self-awareness unseen in his divine sisters and brothers.

Still grieving over the loss of Aldrif, Freyja was happy to raise Thor as if he were her own child. In time, the royal family of Asgard expanded even further when Odin and Freyja accepted Loki, the uncharacteristically diminutive and physically unimpressive child of Laufey, into their home. Following yet another violent uprising by the Frost Giants, in which Odin was forced to kill Laufey, Loki was adopted by the Asgardians. He was raised as a prince of the realm, supposedly equal in status to Thor. Unfortunately, Loki was as much a misfit in the Golden Realm as he had been in Jotunheim. Over time, he grew to resent his adoptive brother, jealous of the attention lavished on Thor for his courage and fighting prowess. Loki became the self-styled God of Mischief, sometimes acting against Thor, sometimes working with him—but always feeling every bit the outsider.

In recognition of Thor's abilities, Odin gifted his son the mighty war hammer known as Mjolnir. The weapon, which Odin had carried himself during his days adventuring on Midgard with the Prehistoric Avengers, was the work of Eitri, Brokk, and Buri—the legendary Dwarf blacksmiths of Nidavellir. Made from unbreakable Uru metal, Mjolnir was among the trio's greatest creations. While Odin had found the hammer somewhat unwieldy, Thor did not. Mjolnir's concussive music—the rhythmic beat of hammer blow after hammer blow—accompanied the young God of Thunder as he forged a formidable reputation throughout the Nine Realms.

War child
After the conflict between Asgard and Jotunheim, the orphaned Loki was found and taken back to the Golden Realm. *Thor* #12, Jan. 2009

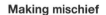

"Make me a weapon, dwarves. Or the next time the trolls invade your realm you can fight them yourselves."

Odin

Making mischief
As youths, Loki and Thor enjoyed many misadventures, but their fellowship became strained by Loki's increasing jealousy.
Heroic Age: Prince of Power #4, Oct. 2010

Mighty metalsmiths
The dwarf blacksmiths Eitri, Brokk, and Buri used the heat of a star
to fashion unyielding Uru metal into the legendary hammer Mjolnir.
Thor #80, Aug. 2004

Breaking free

In modern times, as Odin witnessed Thor's confidence turn to
arrogance, he banished his son to Midgard. Thor looked on this
as punishment, but the move was actually the final stage in the
All-Father's grand plan to foster his son's independent spirit.
Thor's time on Earth—where he was generally perceived as
just another costumed Super Hero—changed him dramatically.
Thor learned humility while living as the disabled Dr. Donald Blake,
and his friendships with his fellow Avengers and his romance with
nurse Jane Foster confirmed his status as the most mortal of
immortals. On Earth, Thor learned to truly live in the moment.
The gods of Asgard concerned themselves with monumental
events, while the mortals of Midgard focused on more mundane
matters—and seemed happier because of it.

Thor's sojourn on Earth prepared him for what was inevitable.
When Ragnarok came around once again—after Loki freed the
savage Fenris Wolf and Surtur wielded his fiery Twilight Sword
to topple the towers of Asgard—Thor refused to accept the
certainty of defeat. His unique perspective, gained through his
association with Earth, allowed him to perceive what others could
not and, after communing with Yggdrasil, he was horrified to learn
that the cycle of death and rebirth was controlled by a band of
self-styled "gods to the gods." Those Who Sit Above in Shadow had
spent eons consuming the copious mystical energies released by
each Ragnarok event. Confronting the shrouded deities directly,
Thor broke their hold over his people by destroying the tapestry of
the Three Fates. Ragnarok wiped away the Asgardians just as it
had in the past and their rebirth was a certainty, but, thanks to
Thor's actions, they would be free to chart their own future course.

Puppet masters
Those Who Sit Above in Shadow
manipulated the Asgardian pantheon
for centuries until Thor exposed them.
Thor #84, Nov. 2004

The final conflict
The long-prophesied Ragnarok finally arrived and the Asgardians were swept away by a coalition of monsters and demons.
Thor #1, Sep. 2007

Restoration

When the Asgardians returned from the void, they found themselves in unlikely surroundings. The gods were resurrected on Earth and rebuilt their capital city on a plot of land outside the sleepy American town of Broxton, Oklahoma, which Thor had purchased for a truckload of Rhine gold. When complete, the new version of Asgard was raised into the sky where it became something of a local tourist attraction.

Unfortunately, the Asgardians were not welcomed by all, and governments around the world feared that the emergence of such a powerful force in America's heartland would destabilize the global balance of power. Even after Asgard was recognized as a fully independent nation with full diplomatic rights and responsibilities, there were still many who conspired against the realm. Ultimately, the city was destroyed by the Machiavellian Norman Osborn and his team of Dark Avengers.

Down to Earth
Thor established a new city on Earth, hoping the Asgardians would benefit from being closer to Midgard's mortals.
Thor #601, Jun. 2009

"Ragnarok. I can see ... the old dream. Now I know ... now I remember. This has happened before."
Thor (Odinson)

Of all the reborn gods, it was only Odin who refused to make his home on Midgard. For a time, he remained in self-imposed exile among the decrepit ruins of the original city of Asgard. Alone on that bleak other-dimensional outcrop, he became preoccupied with past glories and failures, and he cursed the fates that his people had fallen so far. His mood was made even darker when he witnessed the mortal Tony Stark use his repulsor technology to remake the Asgardian's Earthly abode, transforming Asgard into Asgardia—a city that was a fusion of ancient magic and modern mechanics.

Wood burner
When Yggdrasil burst into flame, it was seen as a portent of doom, with Surtur declaring war. *Thor* #18, Oct. 2012

Old scores

When Odin's brother, Cul, was awakened from his long slumber beneath the waves of the Pacific Ocean by the villain Sin, the All-Father enjoyed a brief reconciliation with his former subjects. They worked together to meet the growing threat and, after victory was secured, Odin retired back to old Asgard, vowing to keep his errant brother imprisoned there for all time. His final act before departing was to anoint Freyja, Gaea, and Idunn as the collective All-Mother of Asgardia, asking them to rule more wisely over the kingdom than he had done.

Asgardia was looked upon as particularly vulnerable by many malign actors. Seeking to undermine the Asgardians' already wavering authority over the Nine Realms, Surtur entered into an alliance with Gullveig, Freyja's sister and current ruler of Vanaheim. Just as he had done with her father, the fire demon stoked the flames of Gullveig's resentment, urging her to break from the Asgardians and establish Vanaheim as a wholly self-sufficient realm. Thus the age-old civil war between the two tribes was reignited. With Thor and the forces of Asgardia distracted by the belligerent Vanir, the infernal ruler of Muspelheim made his move on the rest of the Nine Realms. Having recently helped the Manchester Gods establish a foothold in the mystical kingdom of Otherworld, Surtur now demanded a tithe in return for his assistance.

The fire demon accepted some of the Manchester Gods' ambulatory cities as suitable payment in kind.

High and mighty
High-tech Asgardia replaced Asgard before being relocated into outer space. *Thor* #21, Dec. 2012

The Battle of New York

In ancient times, Surtur was trapped in his fiery realm of Muspelheim by the Asgardian brothers Ve, Vili, and Odin. The fire demon plotted revenge for centuries, eventually breaking free and reforging his giant Twilight Sword. To usher in Ragnarok—the prophesied end times for the gods—Surtur needed to light his blade with the Eternal Flame that burned brightly in Asgard. Reaching the flame was no easy matter, however, as powerful spells barred Surtur's entry into the Golden Realm.

Seeking to circumvent these defenses, Surtur invaded New York City with an army of fire demons. From there, he planned to access the foot of the Bifrost and then march all the way up the fabled Rainbow Bridge to Asgard. Alerted to the threat, Odin marshaled the Einherjar warriors of Valhalla and dispatched them to Midgard to defend the streets of New York City.

The Asgardians were joined by members from the US military, standing shoulder-to-shoulder with troops from the renowned 82nd Airborne Division—the so-called "Screaming Eagles." The fire demons were pushed back and Surtur's apocalypse forestalled ... at least for the time being.

Faerie land
Svartalfheim was a bleak realm of faerie magic that spawned the malignant evil of Malekith and the dark elves.
Thor: At the Gates of Valhalla #1, Jul. 2018

"Queen of Angels! Why am I not surprised to see you here among the scum of the realms?"

All-Mother Freyja

He then used the fortress-like citadels to lay siege to the Nine Realms, his assault so powerful that it caused the version of Yggdrasil that grew in Asgardia to burst into flames. With Asgardia's warriors overwhelmed, Thor had no choice but to petition the Goddess of Death for assistance. With Hela's fallen legions his to command, Thor struck back at Surtur's army, managing, at least, to hold the line. Meanwhile, the Manchester Gods were persuaded by Loki, who had previously had dealings with the freshly created pantheon, to depower their cities. The act cost the Manchester Gods their very existence, but their sacrifice was enough to weaken Surtur and enable Thor to win the day.

Return of Heven

Peace returned to the Nine Realms, but there was little respite for the God of Thunder. After experiencing a vision of a mysterious 10th realm and a sister he never knew, Thor demanded answers from the All-Mother. Freyja admitted to the existence of Heven and granted Thor access to the dimension that housed the banished realm. While there, Thor discovered that Aldrif yet lived. She had survived the Queen of Angels's attack and had been raised in secret by a royal handmaiden. Consequently, Thor's sister grew up believing she was an Angel called Angela, sharing a hatred of all things Asgardian with her winged sisters.

The Asgardian royal family was finally reunited, but it was far from a happy event. There had been too many lies told—too many secrets kept—that mistrust lingered for some time. Only after Angela saved Freyja and Odin's new daughter, Laussa, from Surtur's machinations and Heven was reaffirmed as the Tenth Realm did relations begin to slowly improve. The Queen of Angels never stopped plotting revenge, however, and she was recruited by Malekith to serve in his Dark Council. The ruler of the Dark Elves of Svartalfheim had learned from the folly of other would-be conquerors and had been conspiring against his enemies in secret.

First strike
When Malekith launched his War of the Realms, one of the first worlds to fall was Nidavellir. *Thor: At the Gates of Valhalla* #1, Jul. 2018

Twin worlds
After serving as Thor, Jane Foster became Valkyrie, personifying the best qualities of Asgard and Earth.
Jane Foster: Valkyrie #10, Aug. 2020

Together, they went on to defeat Malekith and free the realms. In the aftermath of the War of the Realms, Odinson was hailed as the new All-Father, and he subsequently used his sovereign powers to restore the original city of Asgard to its rightful place in the heavens. Once again, the Golden Realm floated in the interdimensional void, sitting symbolically at the top of stout Yggdrasil.

It was no coincidence that the outcome of the war had been determined on Earth, no happenstance that the Odinson had been inspired to pick up his mantle because of Jane's courageous example. It was now obvious to all that the Asgardians looked to the people of Earth for hope in much the same way mortals had sought guidance from the gods in ancient times. No longer possessing the powers of Thor, Jane became the last remaining Valkyrie, a hero who embodied the shared values and tumultuous history of Asgard and Midgard. ▪

Only when his alliance was strong enough, when he had united the likes of Surtur's daughter Sindr and a resurrected Laufey, did he launch a full-scale assault on the Ten Realms, swiftly conquering them all, save Midgard.

Prior to Malekith's declaration of war and following an encounter with Gorr, the so-called God Butcher, Thor Odinson had come to doubt the legitimacy of the Asgardians' divine mission. This made him unworthy to serve as God of Thunder. Left unattended, Mjolnir called out telepathically to Odinson's former love, Jane Foster. Upon lifting the hammer, Jane was instantly transformed into Thor, Goddess of Thunder. Every bit her predecessor's equal, Jane fought valiantly to defend Earth and Asgardia. Unfortunately, when both Asgardia and Mjolnir were destroyed following an attack by Mangog, Jane lost her godly powers. Along with All-Mother Freyja and the Asgardians, she escaped to New York City just as Malekith launched an assault on Midgard. All seemed lost, but Foster, empowered by an alternative-reality version of Mjolnir, helped rally Earth's defenders. Her courage inspired Odinson to return to the heroic fold.

Homecoming
Using the inherited powers of the All-Father, Thor restored Asgard to the heavens and rebuilt the Rainbow Bridge.
Thor #1, Mar. 2020

Other Dimensions

Adjacent to the Earthly plane, yet separate from it, there exists a multitude of different dimensions, each one suspended like a single pearl on a chain that stretches into infinity. Few people ever glimpse these worlds but to enter them is to step through the barriers of one reality and emerge into a new universe. Among the dimensions closest to Earth are the Mystic Realms—chaotic dominions governed by the unpredictable laws of magic and explored by the likes of Sorcerer Supreme Doctor Stephen Strange. From here, nightmarish apparitions plot humanity's downfall and conspire to subsume the Earth within their realms. Beyond are the infernal kingdoms ruled by devils like Mephisto and Belasco, who care little for showy acts of conquest but take great delight in tormenting innocent souls. Perhaps the fullest expression of the vast nature of this Multiverse are the countless alternative-reality Earths and divergent timelines, where anything can occur.

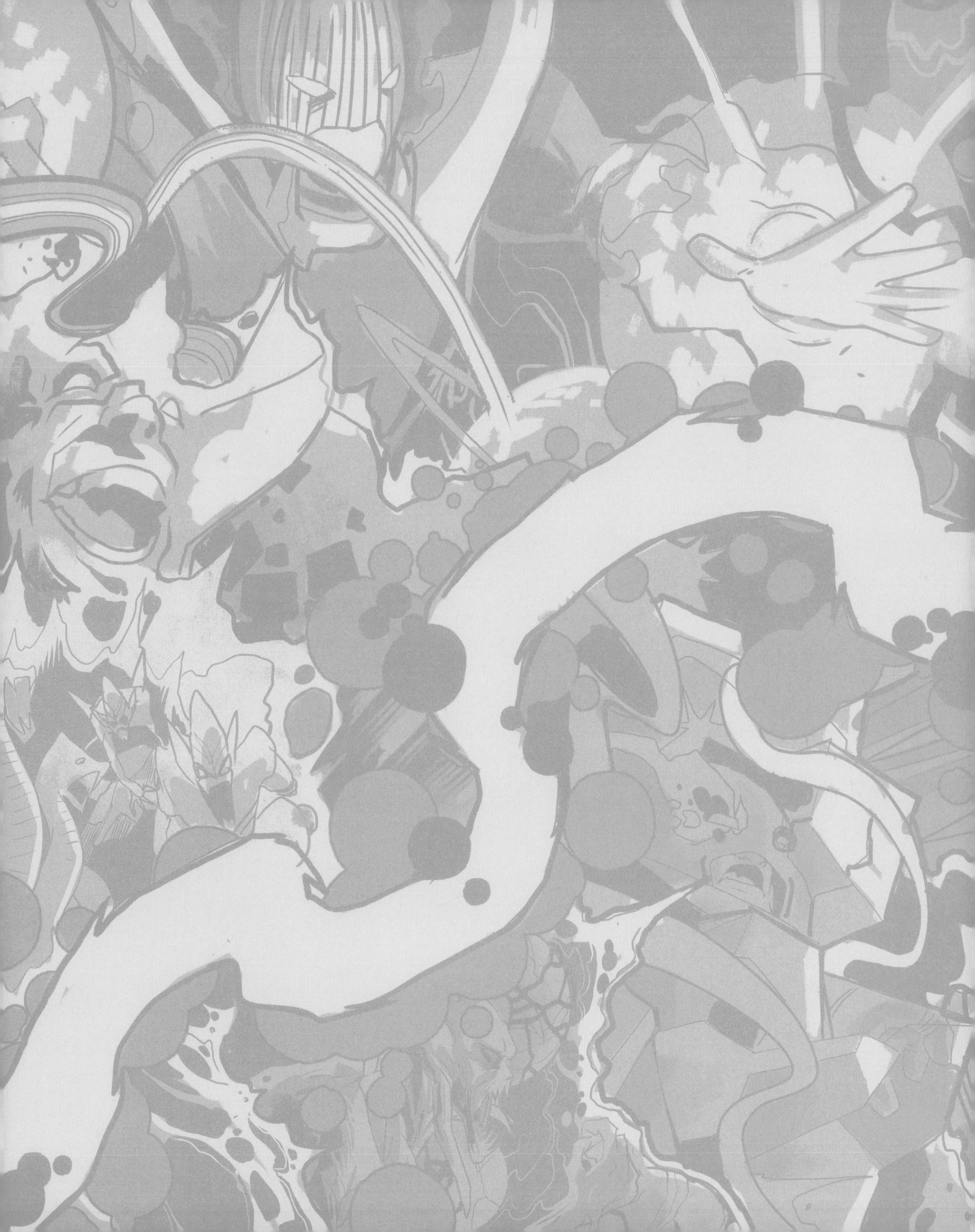

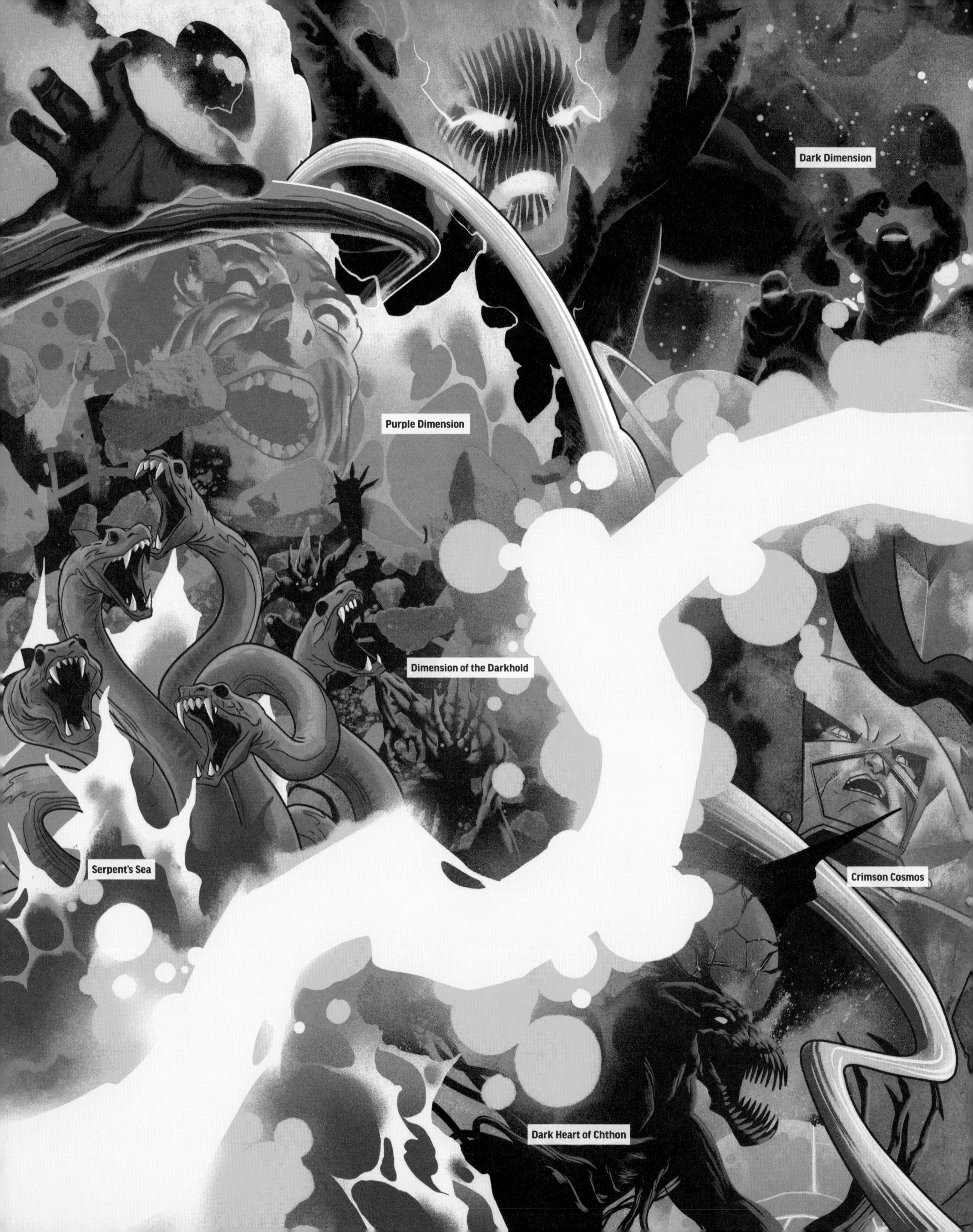
Dark Dimension
Purple Dimension
Dimension of the Darkhold
Serpent's Sea
Crimson Cosmos
Dark Heart of Chthon

Reality's Kaleidoscope

Clouded from the perceptions of ordinary people, there exists a myriad of Mystic Realms, volatile dimensions where the power of magic trumps the laws of physics. The dominions of dark gods and demons, these metaphysical spheres roil and shift and have the potential to warp the mind of the unsuspecting traveler.

Training in the mystic arts not only helped Doctor Stephen Strange regain the partial use of his damaged hands, but it also opened his eyes to a hitherto unsuspected multitude of Mystic Realms—otherworldly dimensions governed by the chaotic precepts of magic, rather than the strict prescriptions of science. First as a Master of the Mystic Arts and then as Earth's Sorcerer Supreme, Doctor Strange made frequent sojourns into these colorful regions, either to meet an emergent demonic threat or on some urgent quest to gain important arcane wisdom.

Since time immemorial, all Earthly magicians have drawn their power from the Mystic Realms and, ultimately, the Well Beyond the Worlds that is the fabled font of all magical energy. Unlike his fellow mystical journeymen, however, Doctor Strange was as much at home surveying the mysteries of the Mystic Realms as he was strolling along the crowded streets of Greenwich Village in New York City. For the most part, he reached the magical planes via astral projection, casting his ghostlike spirit into the ether, while his physical body remained safely behind in his Sanctum Sanctorum on Earth. Sometimes, however, he was forced to enter the Mystic Realms physically, and each time, it took all of his skill as a sorcerer to stop himself from becoming overwhelmed by the hallucinatory nature of the experience. In the Mystic Realms, up was frequently down, time unpredictable, and individuals were in danger of constant sensory overload.

Next-door realms
Only skilled magicians like Doctor Strange were able to pass from one plane of existence to the next.
Infinity Abyss #2, Aug. 2002

The inner planes

Many of the Mystic Realms formed eons ago when the first heroic deity, Atum, expelled the malign Elder Gods and their demon spawn from the primordial Earth. The monstrous creatures scattered across inter-dimensional space, populating the worlds and realms they found there. In time, the individual spheres coalesced into distinct planes of existence. Those realms that still retained some fundamental connection to the Earth formed the Inner Planes, while the more chaotic and esoteric dimensions drifted further afield. Furthest out from the physical world, close to the borderlands of reality itself, sprang the Well Beyond the Worlds.

Passing between the individual realms of a single plane of existence was a relatively straightforward exercise, but magical barriers generally prevented movement between the different planes—protecting the mortal sphere from roaming hordes of malicious demons. While powerful practitioners of magic like Earth's first Sorcerer Supreme, Agamotto, and the latter-day Ancient One could slip easily between these planes, lesser skilled mages could not. Instead, mystical novices traveled the Winding Way, a glimmering thoroughfare that weaved in and out of reality and allowed for safe passage between different planes of reality.

Astral adventures
The swiftest way for Doctor Strange to navigate the bizarre eddies of unreality was to access the astral plane and let his ghostly spirit glide along at the speed of thought. *Doctor Strange: The Best Defense* #1, Feb. 2019

Nasty neighbor
Even incursions from seemingly minor denizens of the Mystic Realms were cut off by Doctor Strange before they could develop into something far more dangerous. *War of the Realms: War Scrolls* #2, Jul. 2019

Many of the Mystic Realms that form the Inner Planes were created by the Elder Gods, Chthon and Set. The serpentine Set, whose human acolytes would go on to create the hypnotic Serpent Crown and bedevil humanity for countless centuries, established the Serpent's Sea, a realm of endless oceans populated by monstrous leviathans. The sea churned with a terrible ferocity—its tides ebbed and flowed as Set's own power and influence waxed and waned. At its peak, when Set's wizards held considerable sway over the antediluvian Earth, the Serpent's Sea was a broiling expanse of sinuous snakes and lizards, impossible to navigate safely.

Referred to collectively as the Flickering Realms, the Dark Heart of Chthon and the Dimension of the Darkhold were conjured into being by sinister Chthon. They were places of torment, as bewildering and as hostile as the Elder God himself. The landscapes constantly shifted from one form to another so that an arid desert might suddenly become a precarious ice floe. Equally dangerous were the distant mountains that seeped oceans of blood and the blistering snows that burned like fire. Inhospitable to most living creatures, the Flickering Realms were ideally suited to demonic life, and they became the abode of many bestial races, including the voracious N'Garai.

> **"The Mystic Realm is as infinite as my universe."**
> **Doctor Strange**

Weapons at the ready
To defeat the likes of the Many-Angled One, Doctor Strange drew power from mystical icons likes of the Eye of Agamotto, the Eternal Blade, or the Axe of Angarruumus. *Doctor Strange* #21, Jul. 2017, (variant cover)

Calling Chthon
Elder God Chthon has occasionally returned to the material plane, called back to Earth by worshipers like the symbiote-villain Carnage. *Carnage* #15, Feb. 2017

The mystical trinity

Oshtur, a far more benevolent Elder God, left the Earth in the days before the expulsion of her malign brethren, leaving behind her son, Agamotto, to protect the world in her stead. When she learned of Chthon and Set's actions in establishing power bases so close to the Earthly sphere, she created her own stronghold on the astral plane, a conduit through which Earth's benevolent magicians could access her wisdom and power. Later, Oshtur was joined by another mystical entity named Hoggoth, who had believed himself alone in all of creation, save for the ghosts of his fellow Old Ones, the so-called Hosts of Hoggoth. Some time later, when Agamotto passed beyond the veil of the living, he joined his mother and Hoggoth to create the Vishanti, a mystical trinity of great power and influence. Over the centuries, the Vishanti used their energies to empower the spells of magical defenders such as the frail Aged Genghis, the aptly named Ancient One, and, in modern times, Doctor Strange.

Radiant realms

In the Outer Planes of existence, scientific principles generally fell away, resulting in the creation of Mystic Realms that were based largely on colorful abstractions. The land, the air, the physical matter in each of these dimensions exuded a particular radiance, and the denizens of these lands exhibited extremes of emotion.

The Purple Dimension was ruled by the greedy and tyrannical Aggamon, who enslaved his people, forcing them to dig for potent mystical gems in the rocky foothills of the Purple Mountains. When a pair of thieves stole a similar gem from Doctor Strange's Sanctum Sanctorum, they were transported to the Purple Dimension and put to work in Aggamon's mines. Doctor Strange followed them to the Outer Planes and demanded their release. Aggamon refused, claiming, "In a thousand years, no captive has ever escaped through the Purple Veil." Refusing to be cowed, Doctor Strange challenged the tyrant to a mystical duel. In the ensuing contest, neither gained the upper hand, and it seemed that both might die from the resulting mental strain. Fearing for his life, Aggamon surrendered and allowed Doctor Strange passage back to Earth with the hapless burglars.

Vishanti tournament
Oshtur, Agamotto, and Hoggoth have anointed Earth's Sorcerer Supreme for centuries, organizing mystical combats to uncover the world's most powerful mage. *Doctor Strange* #383, Feb. 2018

Cyttorak, a demon once worshipped on Earth as a god, established himself as the absolute master of the Crimson Cosmos, sitting imperiously on a huge throne of blood-red granite. His was a harsh yet breathtaking realm, with ruby-colored volcanoes spitting scarlet ash into a seemingly perpetual sunset-sky. Pining for his lost significance and seeking to prove his worth, Cyttorak entered into the Wager of the Octessence with rival entities Watoomb, Valtorr, Balthakk, Farallah, Ikonn, Krakkan, and Raggadorr. To see who was the most powerful of the group, they each agreed to create a magical icon that would empower a human avatar, or Exemplar, when touched.

With the skill of a master craftsman, Cyttorak fashioned the Crimson Gem of Cyttorak. He hid his prize in an Earthly temple, where it languished for a thousand years. Cain Marko, the stepbrother of the mutant telepath Charles Xavier, stumbled upon the gem's hidden location. Upon grasping the rubylike treasure, he was transformed into the Juggernaut— a being possessing incredible strength and stamina and a determination to crush everything in his path. Having long been jealous of his successful stepbrother, Marko used his new powers to attack Xavier, sparking the first of many clashes with the X-Men. Eventually, the mutant heroes managed to use the Crimson Gem of Cyttorak to project the Juggernaut into the Crimson Cosmos itself, where he remained trapped for some time. Cyttorak eventually returned his champion to Earth but, when the rival Exemplars finally emerged, Juggernaut refused to participate in the competition and thwarted his rivals' planned conquest of humanity.

Crimson Cosmos
The demon Cyttorak's interference in Earthly matters sometimes led to confrontations with the X-Men.
Uncanny X-Men #542, Oct. 2011

"The (Juggernaut) is a hymn to destruction."

Cyttorak

Fascinating facets
The Crimson Gem of Cyttorak was a repository of demonic power and a conduit to the Mystic Realm of Cyttorak itself.
Amazing X-Men #15, Mar. 2015

Earthly avatar
Empowered by Cyttorak, Cain Marko became the demon's Earthly pawn—the unstoppable Juggernaut. *X-Men: Black—Juggernaut* #1, Dec. 2018

At this point, Dormammu reverted, at least in part, to his energy form, decreeing that henceforth the Flames of Faltine would always appear magically around the head of whoever was the rightful ruler of the Dark Dimension. While Dormammu busied himself with his freshly acquired kingdom, and plotted to expand his reach beyond the borders of the Dark Dimension, Umar explored what it meant to be human. She seduced King Olnar's son, Orini, and gave birth to a daughter, Clea, who would eventually become Stephen Strange's disciple and wife. Coming to believe she would make a better ruler than her brother, Umar turned on Dormammu and control of the Dark Dimension passed back and forth between the quarrelsome siblings. Both sought to subsume Earth within their territory, but neither of them was able to circumvent Doctor Strange's magical defenses for very long.

A dark turn

Far beyond the colorful cavalcade of the Outer Planes, more sinister dimensions were created when a massive plane of existence shattered into countless fragments, forming the Splinter Realms. These were vertiginous spheres that had little in common with the more tangible dimensions that spiraled closer to Earth. In some of these realities, life existed only in the form of sentient energy. Such was the case with the Realm of the Faltine. Untold millennia ago, a Faltine called Sinifer sired Dormammu and his sister, Umar. The twins were unlike any previous Faltines ever created. They were guilty of the most obscene perversion imaginable in a realm where energy was all—they lusted after the material. Gathering together matter as greedily as other Faltines absorbed energy, they fashioned humanoid bodies for themselves. In the end, brother and sister were banished by their Faltine cousins, finding sanctuary in the nearby Dark Dimension. There they aided King Olnar in pacifying the local population but ultimately betrayed the tyrant and took his throne for themselves.

Dark designs
Dormammu's appetite for conquest saw him repeatedly attempt to unleash his armies of Mindless Ones on Earth. *Doctor Strange* #388, Jun. 2018

Dream catcher
Sitting astride his stallion, Nightmare enjoyed a nightly feast of emotional turmoil as he consumed the dreams of hapless humanity.
Loki #1, Sep. 2019

Bad dreams

The Dream Dimension was close to the Dark Dimension both in terms of its location within the Splinter Realms and its metaphysical aspect. The ethereal realm was linked to, and shaped by, humanity's collective unconscious, given form and substance by the dreams and nighttime terrors of ordinary women and men. The swirling dreamscape was haunted by its ruler—the ghastly Nightmare, who patrolled his kingdom on the back of a coal-black stallion named Dreamstalker. Wild and gaunt-looking, Nightmare depended upon the dreams of humankind for sustenance. His hunger was such that he frequently exceeded his jurisdiction and breached the borders of his own realm to interfere directly with Earthly affairs. Of course, as Sorcerer Supreme, Doctor Strange was alert to such transgressions and would always be on hand to successfully cast Nightmare back into the fog of his ever-changing kingdom.

> "The realm of Nightmare … it is ephemeral—as much a state of mind as of existence."
>
> Nightmare

Spy at night
From his nocturnal abode, Nightmare frequently spied on Earth's mystical defenders like Doctor Strange.
Doctor Voodoo: Avenger of the Supernatural #2, Jan. 2010

Living space

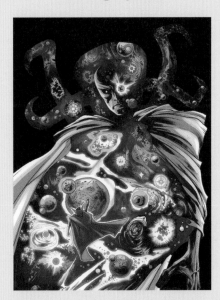

Eternity came into being at the dawn of time, an abstract entity formed from the living consciousness of the universe itself. At some point, Eternity spawned several children, equally powerful entities that personified concepts such as Empathy, Entropy, and Expediency.

As he exists on a higher plane of reality, few mortals have ever come face-to-face with Eternity. One of the earliest recorded encounters involved Doctor Strange who petitioned the ethereal being for aid following an attack upon the Ancient One by the rogue mystic Baron Mordo. Using his magical relic, the Eye of Agamotto, Doctor Strange entered Eternity's realm, where the universal being generously assumed human form, his vast body seemingly alive with swirling galaxies and stars. Rather than bestowing more power on Doctor Strange, however, Eternity advised that only wisdom could ultimately defeat evil.

Eternity appeared before Doctor Strange many times over the following years. He generally manifested at times when reality, and his own power, was threatened by villains possessing vast destructive resources, such as Thanos or Dormammu.

Unity through adversity

With the Mystic Realms home to so many hostile inhabitants, war was as frequent an event as it was in the material world. In modern times, the Vishanti became embroiled in a conflict with the rival Trinity of Ashes. Stephen Strange was expected to serve as the Vishanti's champion in this War of the Seven Spheres, but he refused and was stripped of much of his power. He soon relented and spent the next 5,000 years fighting to defend the Mystic Realms from the enemy. Eventually, with the Vishanti victorious, Doctor Strange was returned to Earth at the exact point in time of his departure, having aged only one year.

Some time after the successful conclusion of the War of the Seven Spheres, the Splinter Realms were once again visited by war. It started in Nightmare's Dream Dimension, a ferocious maelstrom that toppled everything in its path and spat out black blades that cut through buildings and beings alike. As the tempest surged through the Splinter Realms, demons and other entities scrambled to escape the deadly onslaught. Many made their way to the borders of the Infernal Domain known as the Otherplace. Amanda Sefton, a powerful sorcerer and onetime disciple of Doctor Strange, was currently serving as custodian of this limbo, and at first, she refused entry to the massed demons scrambling at the gateway to her palace. However, when Dormammu arrived to petition for aid, Sefton realized the severity of the situation. She went on to sound the Horn of Harrowing, thus unifying the denizens of the Splinter Realms for the first time in living memory.

Eventually, it transpired that the tempests were being controlled by an unfathomable bio-mechanical creature from the far future called the Archenemy. Sefton had recently created a magical computer program designed to catalog all the arcane knowledge in the universe, and it emerged that the Archenemy was the distant progeny of this AI search engine. It had traveled back to the past to ensure its own birth but was easily defeated when Sefton pulled the plug on her experiment.

A magical feast

The entirety of the magical dominions, as well as the balance of the universe itself, was threatened when Galactus was expelled from the rational universe by an extraterrestrial mystic called Zoloz. Seeking to protect his home from the mighty World-Devourer, Zoloz stole a portion of Doctor Strange's power and used it to

Queen of the damned
With the aid of the X-Men's Nightcrawler, sorceress Amanda Sefton united the demons of the Splinter Realms into a single army. *X-Men: Magik* #1, Dec. 2000

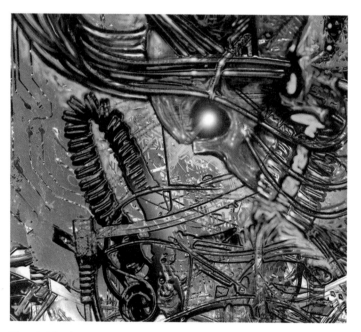

Fearful fusion
The Archenemy threatened to obliterate the Splinter Realms and their mystic inhabitants. *X-Men: Magik* #4, Mar. 2001

Silent witnesses
Eternity and the Living Tribunal observed changes to
the Mystic Realms but refused to intercede directly,
despite entreaties from Doctor Strange.
Doctor Strange #15, Aug. 2019

"I have become one with the Mystic
Realms. The ultimate symbiosis of
technology and magic.**"**
Galactus

The cosmic entities known as the Living Tribunal
and Eternity looked on as Doctor Strange performed
reconstructive surgery on reality itself, restitching the
timeline so that the World-Devourer was never banished
to the Mystic Realms, and thus science and sorcery were
kept as two distinctly separate universal forces.

The Mystic Realms have always existed outside the
experience of everyday humanity, as close as thought
yet as far away as a distant star. Nevertheless, their
influence has been felt on Earth for untold generations.
The great churn of magical energy has had a profound
effect, subtly altering the course of human history and
knowledge. Demons have inspired Earthly worshipers,
while tyrannical entities have viewed the Earth with a
jealous eye, forcing heroic mages like Doctor Strange
to wage an unseen war to keep the planet safe from the
madness-inducing monsters that exist just beyond the
borders of the mundane world. ◼

banish Galactus into the depths of the Mystic Realms.
There, the insatiable giant consumed vast quantities of
mystical energy, the unusual food source slowly driving
him insane. Galactus's gluttony also had profound
ramifications beyond the Mystic Realms. His actions
disrupted the natural order of things and caused the laws
of physics to be corrupted by magic. In the end, with the
universe facing catastrophe, Doctor Strange petitioned the
Hell-lord Mephisto for help, willingly bartering away a part
of his own soul in exchange for enough magical power to
tame ravenous Galactus and restore the proper balance
between the Mystic Realms and the tangible world.

United front
Umar and Clea rallied the sorcerers
of the Mystic Realms to help propel
Galactus back to the universe.
Doctor Strange #16, Sep. 2019

Evil Abodes

There are many different Hells, each one ruled by a devilish overlord who is but a small part of a far greater expression of evil. They are the last places in the universe any sane individual would want to visit, even for a brief moment. For a brief moment in Hell brings an eternity of torment.

Billions of years ago, a new class of higher demons was spawned from the primal energies of the original Elder Gods and their degenerate offspring. Shaped by the fears of early humans, these emergent beings were the embodiment of pure evil, and they each staked a claim to their own infernal realm, creating volcanic underworlds that were separated from the mortal plane by the thinnest of thin inter-dimensional veils. Capitalizing on the mortal belief in a single lord of evil, they all claimed to be the one true Satan, referring to their individual domains as Hell.

As might be expected, the Hell-lords were bitterly jealous individuals, vying against one another for the souls of recently departed mortals. Souls were currency in the netherworlds—the more souls a Hell-lord amassed, the more powerful they became.

Of all the Hell-lords, Mephisto was perhaps the most competitive. However, rather than use brute force or terror to achieve his ends like his infernal rivals, he used guile and trickery. Where the likes of Thog were base individuals, no different than the lowly demons from whom they had evolved, Mephisto was a master planner and strategist. He was the consummate dealmaker, and, over the centuries, he gained countless souls via promises of immortality, power, material wealth, or physical desire. His was the art of temptation, and he knew just what to offer any particular individual in order to ensure that they first teetered on the edge of his infernal pit and then tumbled into the flames. Invariably, Mephisto used trickery, some sleight of hand or slip of his forked tongue, to ensnare his victims, and they would almost always end up writhing in torment in a sea of lost souls in Hell. A deal with this particular devil was always a bad deal.

Soul takers
For all time, gods and demons have sought to ensnare human souls in their diabolical domains. Competing Hell-lords have spent eons filling their infernal realms with the spirits of pitiful victims, amassing great power and influence in the process. Each Hell is but a small fraction of a far greater evil and, at the very bottom layer of reality, is torment personified, the One Below All.

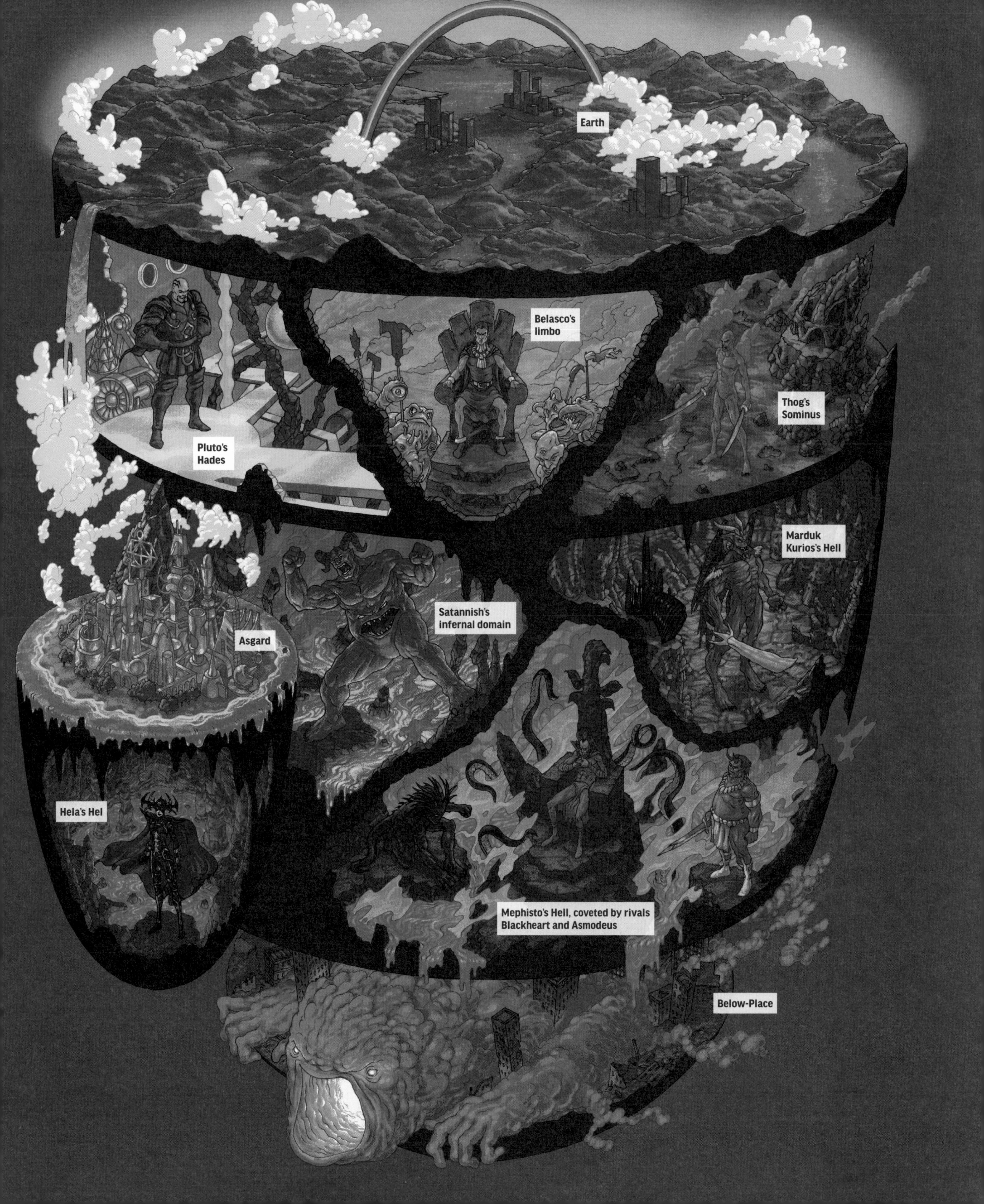
Earth
Belasco's limbo
Thog's Sominus
Pluto's Hades
Marduk Kurios's Hell
Satannish's infernal domain
Asgard
Hela's Hel
Mephisto's Hell, coveted by rivals Blackheart and Asmodeus
Below-Place

Infernal contraption
Mephisto runs his version of Hell with businesslike efficiency, siphoning off souls to power himself and his domain. *Journey into Mystery* #642, Oct. 2012

A favorite trick of Mephisto's was to bond a desperate individual with an unruly Spirit of Vengeance. Seeking to avenge some terrible injustice, these people would accept the hellfire powers offered and be transformed into Ghost Riders—restless spirits on a seemingly endless quest to avenge wrongs and deliver the guilty into Hell. The first Ghost Rider was created a million years ago when Mephisto appeared before a young man in the form of a snake. The youth's tribe had been slaughtered by a Wendigo, and Mephisto offered the teen the power to avenge his people in exchange for guessing his name correctly. "Mephisto," whispered the youth, who was then promptly consumed by hellfire. Sitting astride a huge mammoth, the newly ignited Ghost Rider defeated the Wendigo and went on to join All-Father Odin, Firehair, and other remarkable individuals as a member of the Prehistoric Avengers.

Over the following millennia, Mephisto anointed other Ghost Riders, including stunt cyclist Johnny Blaze, as well as his half brother Dan Ketch. The deal was always the same—power in exchange for bondage. The Ghost Riders all believed that they were still masters of their own destiny and could shake off the devil when the time came; however, their lives were invariably thrown into chaos by Mephisto's infernal pact.

"Hell only has a few rules. Everyone suffers."
Ghost Rider (Johnny Blaze)

Heroes in torment

In recent years, Mephisto became captivated by the super-beings that proliferated on Earth and throughout the cosmos. The pure spirit of the Silver Surfer sparkled like a freshly cut diamond, and Mephisto tried repeatedly to add the former herald of Galactus's soul to his collection. He tempted the Silver Surfer with the usual inducements—power and pleasure—and even promised to reunite the extraterrestrial hero with his lost love, Shalla Bal. All failed. However, upon learning that Mephisto had trapped Shalla Bal in Hell, the Silver Surfer willingly offered his soul in exchange for her freedom. Yet Mephisto turned him down! It seemed, in the years since leaving Galactus's side, the Silver Surfer's soul had become tarnished, the shine dulled by the necessity of moral compromise, and it was no longer the prize it had been.

In contrast, the soul of Cynthia von Doom proved to be a particularly valuable acquisition. A witch from the isolated European nation of Latveria, Cynthia had

Devilish delight
Mephisto has frequently entrapped unwary individuals in his web of lies and then sat back to delight in their misery.
Thanos #16, Apr. 2018

House call
Doctor Strange and Doctor Doom had to best Mephisto's demons before they could rescue Cynthia von Doom from the devil's clutches. *Doctor Strange and Doctor Doom: Triumph and Torment*, Jul. 1989

petitioned Mephisto for magical power to aid her in her fight against tyranny. Unfortunately, when she inadvertently killed innocents, Mephisto was able to claim her soul for his domain. Unable to accept his mother's terrible fate, Victor von Doom vowed to retrieve Cynthia from Hell, and he embarked on a journey that would ultimately lead to his becoming the despotic Doctor Doom. Entering into a deal of his own, Doctor Doom would duel with the devil each Midsummer's Eve, his mother's soul the prize for victory. Eventually, Doom teamed with Doctor Strange to journey to Hell in person and free Cynthia's spirit so that it could move on to a higher plane.

Interfering in the happiness of families was one of Mephisto's favorite pastimes. So when Spider-Man's Aunt May was mortally wounded by an assassin's bullet meant for the arachnid hero, the Machiavellian devil contracted to save her life—at the cost of Peter Parker's happiness. Mephisto overwrote reality so that Peter's beloved Aunt May survived but Parker never married the love of his life, Mary Jane Watson.

Devil masks

While Mephisto was the personification of temptation, his fellow Hell-lords wore other masks when interacting with mortals. Belasco, the ruler of the ethereal kingdom of limbo, aka Otherplace, was the pretender. His past was as mist-shrouded as his infernal realm. Supposedly a 13th-century sorcerer given immortality by the Elder Gods, Belasco delighted in confounding humankind and posed as the devil when it suited his needs. Was he a demon or a man of immense power and ambition? Perhaps his cruelest act was to kidnap a young Illyana Rasputin and torment her for years in his underworld lair. Illyana was ultimately freed from Belasco's corrupting influence by her brother Colossus and his fellow X-Men, but she would return to limbo to rule in the Hell-lord's stead for a time.

In contrast to Belasco, there was no artifice to Satannish whatsoever. Originally thought to be an aspect of the same fundamental force of evil as Mephisto and many of the other Hell-lords, he was later revealed to be the spawn of the Dark Dimension's Dormammu and had been placed among the infernal rulers to act as a spy. Satannish's realm reflected his harsh personality and was a landscape of jagged peaks and seemingly bottomless chasms that resembled the open maw in his abdomen. He represented the devil's insatiable appetite, as did the demon Asmodeus. However, while Satannish had earned much of his fearsome reputation, Asmodeus had not. A relatively minor demon, Asmodeus held sway over his own kingdom within Mephisto's domain. He used this unique position to promote himself as a full Hell-lord. However, Asmodeus's ambition far outstripped his capabilities and, when the demon sought to usurp the power of Ghost Rider Johnny Blaze, Mephisto stripped him of his privileged position.

Limbo's leader
Although deposed several times, the mysterious Belasco has always managed to reclaim limbo as his personal dominion.
New X-Men #37, Jun. 2007

Raucous rivalry
Competing Hell-lords like Marduk Kurios and Mephisto would meet at the Devil's Advocacy and seek support from the throngs of lesser demons.
Journey into Mystery #627, Nov. 2011

Hell's heirs

While avowed rivals, the Hell-lords often came together to further schemes that required their combined power and guile. They discussed such alliances in the Devil's Advocacy, a nether region where the individual infernal domains intersected each other on the metaphysical plane. Satan's empty throne lay at the center of the Devil's Advocacy—as if to tempt one of the Hell-lords to proclaim himself the true dark lord and take the seat and its power as his own. None ever did, although the demon Marduk Kurios was always the most vocal in claiming to be Satan himself.

Seeking to further their power over humankind, some Hell-lords—Mephisto, Thog, and Satannish among them—came together in modern times to produce mortal heirs who would serve as living batteries capable of storing the energy produced by humankind's sinful acts and dark impulses. The plan was to use this power to further weaken the walls between the worlds and allow the Hell-lords to launch a full-scale assault upon the mortal realm. Using Marduk Kurios as a surrogate for their combined essence, the Hell-lords seduced the mortal Victoria Hellstrom and successfully fathered a son and daughter, Daimon and Satana. While Daimon ultimately rebelled against his heritage, battling demonic entities as the exorcist Hellstorm, Satana was as mercurial as her devilish fathers, sometimes preying upon humanity, sometimes protecting it. She was even brazen enough to conspire against the Hell-lords themselves in an ultimately failed bid to become the undisputed ruler of all the underworlds.

Perhaps in an attempt to outmaneuver his devilish partners and establish an individual line of succession, Mephisto created progeny of his own in the form of Blackheart and Mephista. Regardless of his motivations, both children proved to be disappointments. Blackheart explored the nature of evil under his father's tutelage but ultimately turned on him, replacing him as Hell's ruler for a brief time. Mephista also opposed Mephisto, declaring herself humanity's defender when he sought to unite the infernal kingdoms under his rule.

Seeking consensus
Satannish, Dormammu, Mephisto, Hela, and Blackheart would sometimes convene to discuss mutual matters of concern.
Captain Britain and MI13 Annual #1, Aug. 2009

Vacationing in Hades

For millennia, the souls of the recently departed had to pass through the mist-shrouded region of Erebus to reach Pluto's Hades. That changed when the power of Olympus was shattered and the gods were forced to seek sanctuary on Earth. Erebus was relocated to the American Atlantic City on the Jersey Shore, the entrance concealed behind an innocuous-looking casino owned by the Olympus Group.

On a mission to retrieve Zeus's soul from Hades, the demigod Hercules and the genius teen Amadeus Cho visited the casino. Despite the urgency of their quest, they couldn't pass up a chance for some fun, and they spent an evening at the tables—a short vacation from all their recent trials and tribulations.

While enjoying themselves, they were amazed to witness the souls of recently departed heroes like the Wasp and Union Jack playing the slot machines. Things descended into chaos, however, when Cho was accused of cheating and Hercules was forced to let loose the three-headed dog Cerberus. Pursued by security, the heroic duo hopped a ride on a river boat piloted by Charon and were soon deposited in Hades, on the shores of Tartarus.

> **"(Below-Place is) Creation's secret reflection, vaster than we can see or know."**
>
> **Brian Banner's soul**

Gods of the underworld

Although not strictly evil, the death gods of the Asgardian and Olympian pantheons were also considered Hell-lords and thus had voices in some convocations of the infernal powers. Hela, who ruled over Hel in the Asgardian realm of Niffleheim, was as frosty as her kingdom. Considering herself a necessary part of the cycle of life, the Goddess of Death generally objected to plans that involved the indiscriminate use of force or the senseless waste of valuable souls. Pluto, on the other hand, was not necessarily averse to joining forces with the devils of Hell, especially if it provided an opportunity for him to escape his onerous duties as Lord of Hades.

Underpinning the different versions of Hell was a region known as the Below-Place. Seemingly the bottom layer of all reality, this blasted landscape was home to a malevolent, amorphous creature called the One Below All. A dark reflection of the ultimate creator of the universe, the One Below All had a single ambition—to become the last living thing in all of creation. Although supremely powerful, the One Below All could affect only the material world through a host form, and it would invade the psyches of weak or mentally wounded individuals and force them to do its bidding.

The bomb that irradiated Bruce Banner with gamma radiation and turned him into the Hulk also blew a hole in the fabric of reality and formed a gateway to the Below-Place. This in turn caused the One Below All's essence to become permanently bonded to gamma rays, making him the root cause of Banner's transformation.

Hulk in Hell
The large-mouthed One Below All tormented the Hulk in a nightmarish hellscape.
Immortal Hulk #12, Mar. 2019

Years later, acting through the soul of Banner's deceased father, the One Below All lured the Hulk to his domain in a bid to use Bruce Banner's Gamma-irradiated body as a conduit to ascend to the world above. Fortunately, the Hulk's rage was so all-consuming that he was strong enough to fight off the malign deity as well as a horde of demons to escape the terrors and horrors of the Below-Place.

Breaking free

In recent years, as Earth's Super Heroes have faced ever more complex challenges, the meaning of Hell has shifted subtly. In addition to being a literal place or places, it is now also a state of mind, a sense of ennui and hopelessness that Mephisto and his underworld brethren are particularly well suited to exploit. When Las Vegas was destroyed during a Hydra takeover of North America, the entire city and its inhabitants were condemned to Mephisto's Hell. Doctor Strange was wracked with guilt at his failure to prevent this colossal injustice and, in the wake of Hydra's defeat, he sought to rectify the situation by resurrecting the city, pulling it out of Hell.

Unfortunately, Mephisto came along for the ride. As Doctor Strange's retrieval spell reached its apex, an edifice burst through the streets—a gaudy neon-lit monstrosity that proclaimed itself to be the Hotel Inferno. Seemingly, Mephisto had grown tired of the underworld, and he now intended to offer humankind every game and vice imaginable in his own state-of-the-art gambling complex. The only catch was that patrons would have to play the devil's games with their immortal souls as collateral against any losses. Amazingly, many people took up the devil's offer and Mephisto was able to legitimately lay claim to numerous spiritual prizes. When he sought to free the stolen souls, Doctor Strange was captured and caged in the devil's towering edifice. In response to these events, the Sorcerer Supreme's assistant, Wong, hastily gathered together a team of magic-based Super Heroes and attacked Hotel Inferno.

Among this group of Midnight Sons was Ghost Rider Johnny Blaze, who was anxious to put an end to Mephisto's corruption once and for all. Regrettably, he was no match for his former tormentor and Mephisto killed him with a flick of his hand. However, because his soul was still tainted by a Spirit of Vengeance, Blaze entered Mephisto's domain upon his death, just as Wong had planned. With Mephisto away playing games, the demon's throne was vacant and just waiting for the right spirit to lay claim to it. Defeating the demonic competition in an infernal road race, Blaze seized the chance to become the new king of Hell. The loss of sovereignty swiftly led to the loss of Mephisto's diabolical powers, and he was easily contained by Doctor Strange, caged behind mystic bars at the top of Hotel Inferno.

Hell on Earth
Mephisto abandoned his infernal pit to set up shop on Earth, opening up a hotel and casino.
Doctor Strange: Damnation #1, Apr. 2018

High stakes game
Stephen Strange gambled for the lives of innocents at Mephisto's Hotel Inferno. He lost. Of course, the house always wins. *Doctor Strange* #386, Apr. 2018

Road to ruin

Governing the raucous denizens of Hell proved easier said than done, however, and Johnny Blaze increasingly found himself overwhelmed by his responsibilities. When demons began to break out of Hell, he had no choice but to turn to Mephisto for assistance. Blaze broke the devil out of his mystical prison and, with his help, restored the natural order of things by rounding up the monstrous escapees. With Mephisto obviously better able to contain the beasts of the pit, Blaze abdicated the throne in favor of the Prince of Lies.

"Ah, it's good to be home."

Mephisto

Blaze of glory
Condemned to Hell, Ghost Rider Johnny Blaze promptly seized the infernal throne for himself. *Doctor Strange: Damnation* #4, Jun. 2018

Unruly mob
The demonic wretches of the pit were disinclined to follow Ghost Rider's rule, forcing him to employ his intimidating Hellfire powers to keep them in line. *Avengers* #24, Dec. 2019

Free to foment torment once more, Mephisto turned his attention to the Avengers and began to pull together the threads of a scheme that he had been nurturing for a million years—a bid to bring about a universal apocalypse and transform every aspect of reality into an unimaginably bleak hellscape under his sole dominion. Some of his moves were simple enough. He resurrected the deceased S.H.I.E.L.D. agent Phil Coulson and had him form the Squadron Supreme of America to act in the narrow self-interests of the United States and serve as a counterbalance to the internationally focused Avengers. Mephisto also whispered in the ears of the Avengers' most intractable foes, including Namor the Sub-Mariner and the vampire lord Dracula, encouraging them to reject compromise and sow discord.

Pleased with his progress, Mephisto lured Tony Stark to a cave in Turkey and then sprang a trap that sent the Avenger spiraling back to prehistory. Stranded a million years in the past and with his Iron Man armor running out of energy, Tony was tormented by Mephisto, the devil routinely appearing in the form of a beguiling serpent. Finally assuming his human form, Mephisto teased Tony with the powerful Time Stone, offering up the cosmic bauble as a chance for the hero to return to his own time. As they traded words, Mephisto announced that Tony Stark's soul had always belonged to him and that he was his true father. Rejecting this seemingly outrageous claim, Tony used the last of his energy reserves to tap into the Time Stone's power and escape back to the present day.

Mephisto's devious scheme was far from over—in fact, it had only just begun—but he had already trapped Tony Stark in a living hell, a nightmare of doubt and uncertainty. Regardless of his ultimate goals, Mephisto had achieved a major victory and confirmed that, wherever he walked—or slithered, for that matter—the fires of Hell would never be too far behind. ▨

Master manipulator
Mephisto pulled the strings of Count Dracula, King Namor, the Winter Guard, and the Squadron Supreme, then sent them to bedevil the Avengers.
Avengers #32, May 2020

Earth-311

Earth-2149

Earth-807128

Earth-9200

Earth-691

Variations on a Theme

What if history traveled along a divergent path? The Multiverse has spawned an infinite number of alternative-reality Earths. Some are virtually identical to the prime reality, Earth-616, while others deviate radically, offering glimpses into a chaotic future.

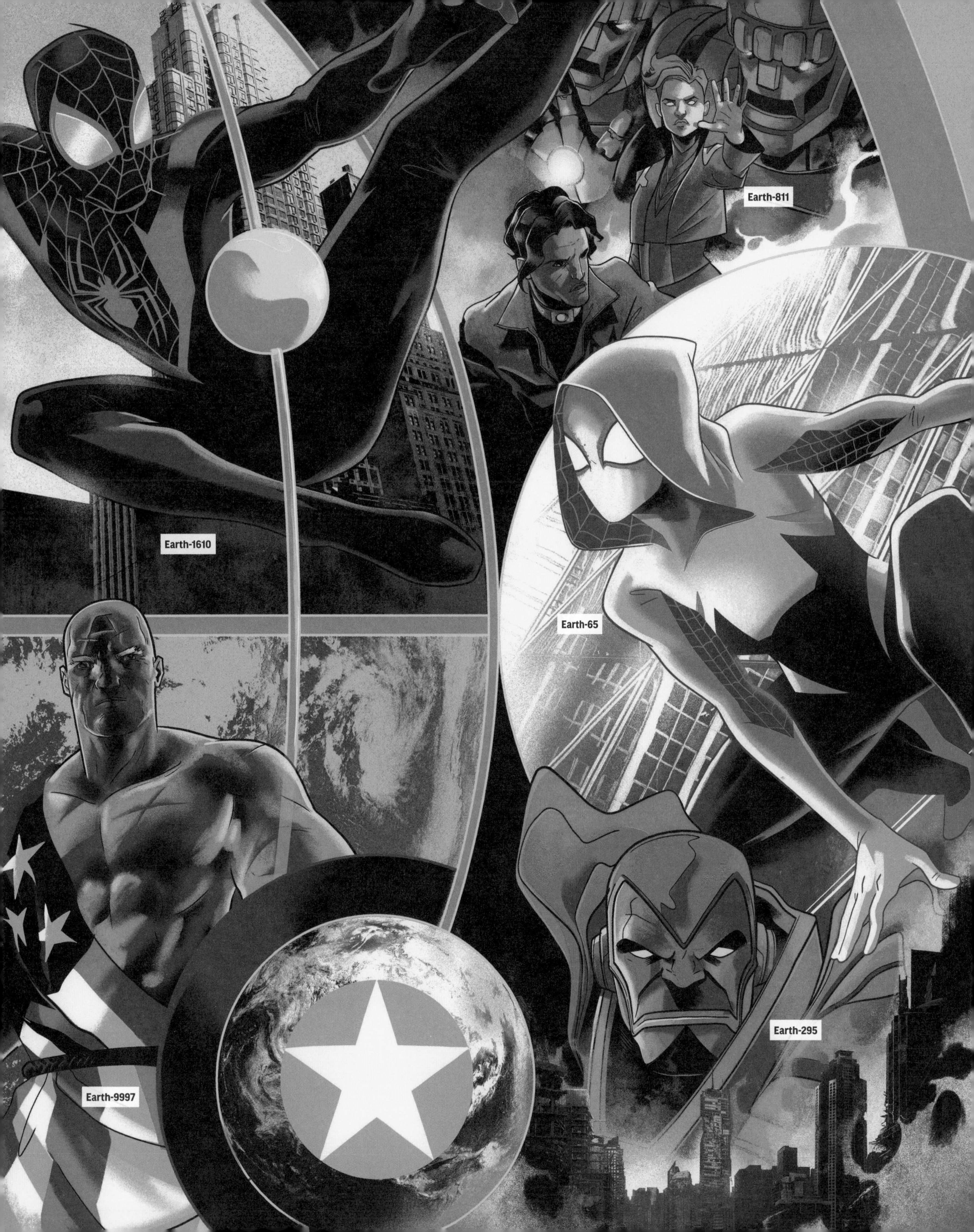
Earth-811
Earth-1610
Earth-65
Earth-9997
Earth-295

The first version of reality consisted of a single, sentient universe. Alone in the void, the First Firmament created offspring to amuse itself, bringing forth two equally powerful races: the Aspirants and the Celestials. While the former worshipped the First Firmament unconditionally, content in the knowledge that their universe was already perfect, the latter were anxious to know more about the nature of evolution, and they were compelled to study the emerging process on many different worlds. Ultimately, the two groups went to war, the conflict so all-encompassing that it shattered the universe into countless shards. The First Firmament's singular perfection was replaced by a chaotic multitude of evolving timelines and alternative realities. Where there had been a single universe there was now a Multiverse, and all future iterations of reality would be similarly structured.

The countless alternative realities were separated from each other by unseen interdimensional barriers. Thanks to a unique set of circumstances, the Earth in the universe designated as number 616 by self-appointed cosmic guardians like Merlyn, became a hotbed of superhuman activity. The planet's significance was mirrored throughout the Multiverse, with Earth often acting as the fulcrum on which sat the fate of entire dimensions. Changes to Earth's timeline could profoundly affect events even beyond the intangible barriers of any particular reality.

Solitary purpose
The First Firmament was a self-aware universe that ached for companionship, so it made plans to alleviate its isolation. *The Ultimates 2* #6, Jun. 2017

Sibling rivalry
The children of the First Firmament—the colorful Celestials and the ebony Aspirants—battled, shattering the universe and bringing about the Multiverse. *The Ultimates 2* #6, Jun. 2017

Zombies assemble
On Earth-2149, the Avengers were the first victims of a deadly disease that transformed people into flesh-hungry zombies.
Marvel Zombies #5, Jun. 2006

Originally, Earth-2149 closely resembled Prime Earth but with a few minor differences, such as Steve Rogers assuming the heroic persona of Colonel America instead of Captain America and then later serving briefly as President of the United States. Reality began to diverge significantly when the Super Hero, Sentry, arrived from an alternative universe carrying an anaerobic contagion that turned individuals into flesh-eating zombies. The Avengers were the first to succumb to the disease and, within days, the contagion had spread throughout the rest of the superhuman community. The former heroes quickly exhausted their food supply and were left roaming a seemingly dead Earth in an increasingly futile quest for sustenance. Despite their ravenous hunger, the zombies retained their human intelligence and they began to formulate a plan to travel to an alternative reality.

In a cruel twist of fate, as the zombies were creating their escape plan, the Silver Surfer made planetfall to announce the imminent arrival of the World-Devourer Galactus—the first time in this reality that this particular event had occurred. The zombies consumed the Silver Surfer and were imbued with his Power Cosmic, which they then used to overwhelm the glistening sentinel's towering master. Further empowered by Galactus's essence, the zombies took to the stars and, within 40 years, had systematically devoured all life in the universe and had passed on the contagion to cosmic beings such as Thanos and the living planet Ego. Returning to Earth, the zombies discovered that a small pocket of humans still survived. During a brief conflict, the zombies were expelled from their home reality, dispatched to Earth-91126. There, the zombies continued to spread their deadly contagion but were finally stopped when infected with debilitating nanobots by the villain Sandman. Only the zombie Sentry survived, and, hoping to create a time loop that would prevent the zombie disease from escaping beyond the two parallel worlds already devastated, Uatu the Watcher interceded to send him back to Earth-2149's past, thus starting the disastrous cycle anew.

The Spider-Verse

A psychic network known as the Web of Life and Destiny was maintained on Earth-001, linking together all the spider-powered heroes who operated throughout the Multiverse and bestowing on them their miraculous arachnid abilities. From this so-called Loomworld, the benevolent Master Weaver, an ancient spider deity, supervised the birth of Spider-Totems, allowing power to flow to select individuals in alternative realities.

The system endured for centuries but became corrupted when the vampiric Morlun and his fellow Inheritors conquered Loomworld. They used the Web of Life and Destiny to travel to other realities where they hunted down Spider-Totems and feasted on their potent life energies. Alerted to the threat by refugees from alternative realities, Peter Parker of Prime Earth joined an army of spider avatars. Together they defeated the Inheritors and restored the natural order of things.

During his adventures across the "Spider-Verse," Peter Parker encountered numerous alternative-reality doppelgängers of Spider-Man, including the so-called Ghost-Spider from Earth-65. She turned out to be Gwen Stacy, Peter's first love who had tragically died in the core timeline.

Fantastick Voyage
On Earth-311, the Super Heroic age arrived centuries early with the likes of Sir Nicholas Fury, Carlos Javier's "Witchbreed" students, the adventurous Four from the *Fantastick*, and the Thunder God Thor pooling their resources to investigate portents of the apocalypse.
1602 #4, Jan. 2004

"A person—from the future came here ... this event damaged the nature of time."
Doctor Stephen Strange

New World

Similarly, Earth-311 diverged from mainstream reality because of time travel. Plunged through a temporal rift by the villainous Purple Man, Captain America Steve Rogers found himself in the Americas of the year 1587. Effectively stranded, the hero reinvented himself as a local warrior, assuming the name Rojhaz. In this guise, he befriended the English colonists of Roanoke and helped them survive their first winter in the New World. Captain America's anomalous presence in the past created chronal ripples that spread across the entirety of Earth-311, causing many of his fellow 20th-century heroes to emerge several hundred years early.

Explorer Sir Richard Reed and his friends on the sailing ship *Fantastick* gained incredible powers after coming across strange lights in the Sargasso Sea. Doctor Stephen Strange, physician to Queen Elizabeth I of England, secretly dabbled with sorcery, while Sir Nicholas Fury ran the sovereign's global intelligence network.

In 1602, Rojhaz accompanied Virginia Dare, the first child to have been born in Roanoke, to England. Their visit coincided with a period of severe weather throughout Europe. Taken as portents of the apocalypse, the unnatural storms produced panic and were blamed on the emergent "Witchbreed"—children born with strange powers who would be considered mutants in more scientifically enlightened times. Ultimately, Rojhaz was revealed as the cause of the climate anomalies and he was dispatched back to his proper place in time by Fury. The alternative timeline of Earth-311 endured, however, even in the absence of Rojhaz, preserved in a pocket universe by the Watcher Uatu.

Hunted
When Sentinels overran Earth-811, Wolverine and an adult Kate Pryde were among the last mutants to be killed or apprehended. *Uncanny X-Men* #141, Jan. 1981

Future lawman
After years spent in hiding, an aged Logan returned to the good fight—setting out to bring the rule of law to North Amerika.
Wolverine: Old Man Logan Giant-Size #1, Nov. 2009

"(Manhattan) is rogue territory, the last place on Earth the Sentinels would expect a mutant."
Kate Pryde (Earth-811)

Dark futures

The fate of Earth's mutant population provided numerous opportunities for reality to diverge in disastrous ways. In fact, it was this factor that prompted Moira MacTaggert and Charles Xavier to establish the island of Krakoa as an internationally recognized mutant nation on Earth-616. On Earth-811, they never got that chance. In that reality, a Mutant Affairs Control Act was passed and the robotic Sentinels were reactivated to meet the perceived threat. The emotionless Sentinels determined the best way to fulfill their programming was to remove humanity from the equation entirely, and they conquered North America, hunting down mutants and other superhumans and placing them in fortified internment camps. In stark contrast to this outcome, it was mutants who achieved dominance on Earth-295, resulting in the so-called Age of Apocalypse. Following the premature death of Charles Xavier, Apocalypse seized the moment to finally conquer the United States and launch a genocidal campaign that killed millions of ordinary humans.

On Earth-9997, a veteran Captain America rallied a band of former heroes to thwart the tyrannical ambitions of a young man named Skull, who had used his mind-control abilities to conquer California. Similarly, on Earth-807128, the world was divided into fiefdoms by competing Super Villains. The Red Skull declared himself President of the United States of Amerika and promptly exterminated much of the superhuman population. The few survivors were forced into hiding. Traumatized after being tricked into killing his fellow X-Men by the villain Mysterio, Wolverine renounced his heroic calling and escaped to Sacramento, California, where he enjoyed a period of happiness with his wife and children. This Old Man Logan completely turned his back on the outside world, wanting nothing to do with the various power plays and internecine rivalries of the ruling Super Villains and their powerful henchmen. However, when his wife and children were brutally murdered, Wolverine reverted to type and brought the killers to justice before riding off into the sunset.

"This is not a world of absolutes. This is a world of confusion and of death and of misery.**"**

Ultimate Universe Reed Richards

Earthly guardians

In the alternative future timeline of Earth-691, humanity was conquered and liberated several times over. Things began to go awry in this reality in the year 2001, when hostile aliens based on Mars conquered Earth and enslaved a population already weakened by ecological collapse. Humanity rallied, however, inspired by the warrior Killraven, and the invaders were ultimately forced to abandon the Earth some time before the year 2075.

The subsequent centuries saw huge advances in science, with humankind establishing colonies on or around the planets Mercury, Jupiter, and Pluto. The emergent United Federation of Earth was a tempting prize and the alien Badoon launched a full-scale invasion of the solar system in the year 3006. Vance Astro, a 20th-century astronaut who had spent a thousand years in stasis while traveling to the Alpha Centauri star system, refused to bow down before the invaders, however. He joined with the Jovian Charlie-27, the Pluvian Martinex, the Centaurian Yondu, and the mysterious Starhawk to lead a successful rebellion against the Badoon. With the invaders driven from Earth and its colony worlds, Astro and his comrades took to the stars themselves in search of knowledge and adventure as the Guardians of the Galaxy.

While the future of Earth-691 was ultimately optimistic, events on Earth-9200 brought about a literal dystopian nightmare. Some time in the early 22nd century, a nuclear war

devastated the planet and wiped out much of the superhuman population. The Hulk was among the few survivors, left wandering across what remained of the United States of America. He was able to absorb the high levels of radiation, which, in fact, bolstered his already formidable strength. Over time, though, his mind began to warp and he became increasingly volatile. Learning that survivors had managed to eke out a paltry life in the ruins of New York, the Hulk conquered the city. He renamed it Dystopia and ruled over all as a malevolent tyrant dubbed Maestro by a fearful populace.

Future guardians
Vance Astro, Charlie-27, Starhawk, Yondu, and Martinex inspired a resistance movement that swept away the Badoon.
Guardians of the Galaxy #7, Jan. 2009

The Ultimate Universe

In many ways, the alternative reality of Earth-1610, or the Ultimate Universe as it became known, was one of the closest reflections of Prime Earth. There, just as on Earth-616, the 21st century brought with it a vast number of superhuman beings and extraordinary cosmic challenges. Bitten by a genetically modified spider, high-school student Peter Parker was transformed into Spider-Man, Reed Richards and his colleagues became the Fantastic Four after being imbued with energies from the mysterious N-Zone, and Charles Xavier formed a team of heroic X-Men to prove to all that mutants could be a force for good in a world riven with hostility and mistrust.

The Ultimate Universe was much darker than the mainstream reality, however, and its heroes often found themselves in morally ambiguous situations. On Earth-1610, rather than a team of Avengers coming together altruistically to make a positive difference in the world, a group of superhumans were conscripted into the Ultimates, a global strike force intended to promote the narrow interests of the US government.

Dark doppelgängers
The uncompromising nature of Earth-1610 produced dark reflections of the mainstream reality's major heroes—who came together under the auspices of Nick Fury.
The Ultimates #11, Sep. 2003

A new dawn
Teenager Miles Morales inspired Spider-Woman Jessica Drew and others to embrace their roles as true heroes.
Ultimate Comics Spider-Man #24, Sep. 2013

Among the great tragedies of Earth-1610 was the death of Spider-Man. A coalition of Super Villains attacked Peter Parker's home, and he died valiantly defending his family. His legacy lived on, however, in the form of Miles Morales, a second young man to receive spiderlike powers after being bitten by a mutated arachnid. The new Spider-Man became a rare symbol of hope on an Earth that seemed to grow darker by the day.

The Multiverse offered glimpses into countless alternative realities and parallel worlds, acting like a gemstone to capture certain aspects of the mainstream timeline, which it then distorted into dazzlingly original shapes. Nothing was ever constant when viewed through this prism, no event too important to be immutable. Everything could change; everything did change. On some Earths heroes rose, while on other Earths heroes fell. It was as if reality itself was trying out different scenarios to compare against Earth-616 and see whether or not they came up wanting. In the Multiverse, there was only one certainty—Earth's Super Heroes would always find themselves tested to the extreme. ■

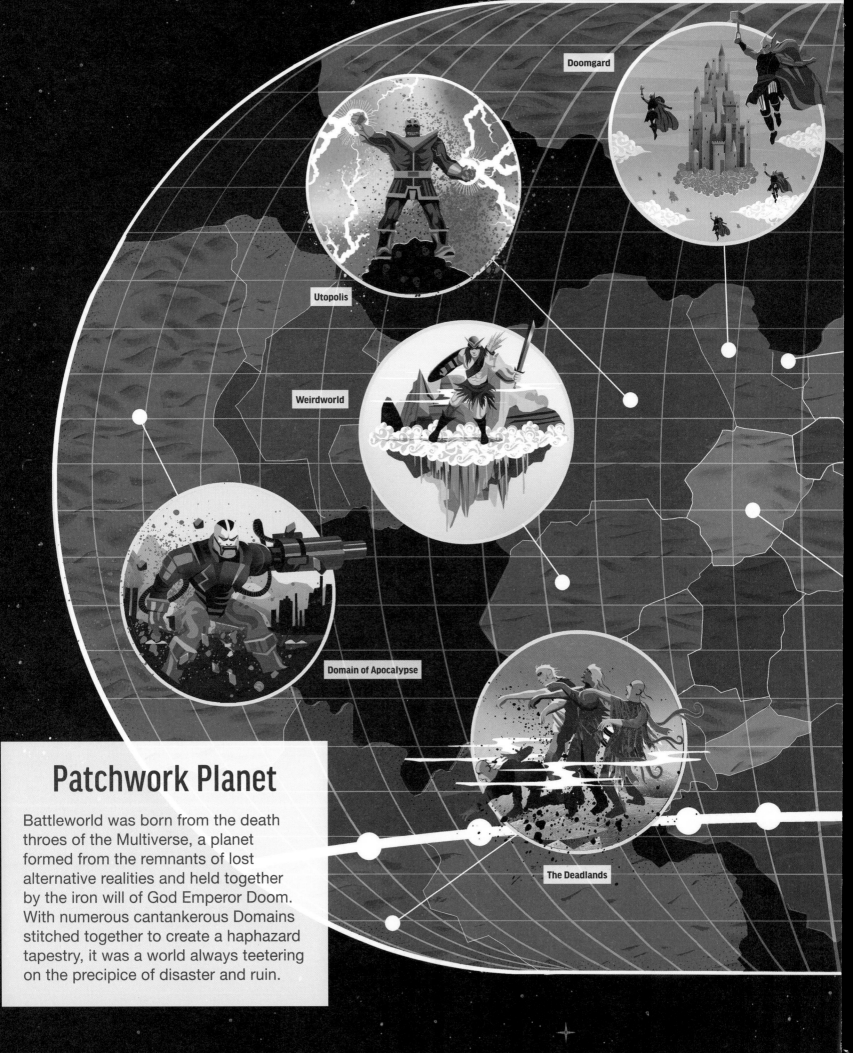

Doomgard

Utopolis

Weirdworld

Domain of Apocalypse

The Deadlands

Patchwork Planet

Battleworld was born from the death throes of the Multiverse, a planet formed from the remnants of lost alternative realities and held together by the iron will of God Emperor Doom. With numerous cantankerous Domains stitched together to create a haphazard tapestry, it was a world always teetering on the precipice of disaster and ruin.

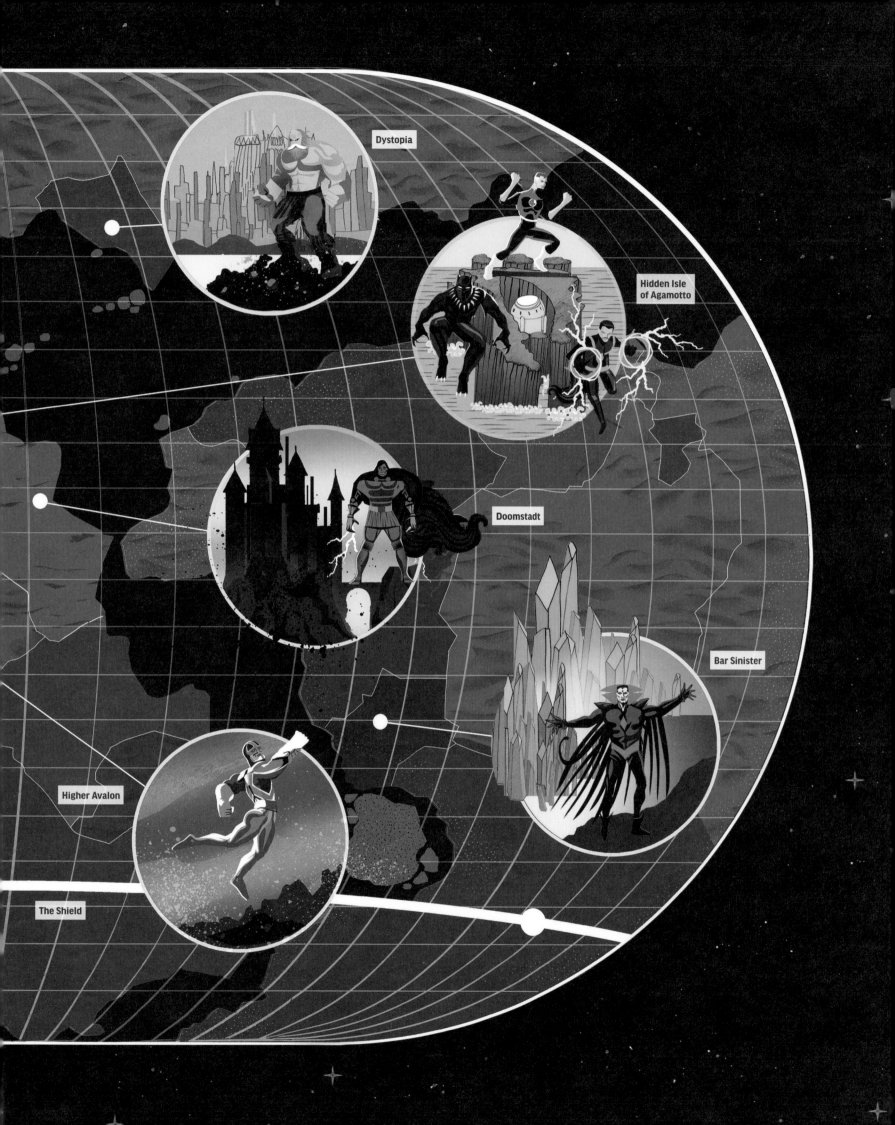

Dystopia

Hidden Isle
of Agamotto

Doomstadt

Bar Sinister

Higher Avalon

The Shield

Absolute ruler
With his wife, Susan Storm, advising from the shadows and Stephen Strange pledging absolute fealty, God Emperor Doom ruled with an iron fist.
Secret Wars #2, Jul. 2015

Next in line
Maestro—a deranged version of the Hulk who governed Dystopia—plotted to unseat Doom.
Future Imperfect #5, Nov. 2015

Battleworld emerged from the cataclysmic destruction of the Multiverse caused by the Beyonders' cosmic incursions. While the Super Heroes of Earth-616 and Earth-1610 fought valiantly to prevent the explosive collision of their alternative realities, Doctor Doom and Doctor Strange of Earth-616 confronted the otherworldly Beyonders directly. Doom had learned that the quixotic beings had created a universal singularity by placing an iteration of the same being on every single parallel Earth. The reality-warping Molecule Man was intended to be a living bomb and, when all versions of him exploded simultaneously, the resulting shockwave would destroy the Multiverse—an event the Beyonders were eager to study and catalog. However, the Molecule Man's premature death on a variety of different worlds precipitated the cascade of destructive incursions, a slower process than that which the Beyonders had intended but one that would nevertheless lead to a universal apocalypse.

Armed with this knowledge, Doctor Doom used Owen Reece, Earth-616's version of the Molecule Man, as a living conduit through which he siphoned off the Beyonders' godlike power. When the last two alternative realities in existence, Earth-616 and Earth-1610, collapsed into each other, and the Multiverse faded into oblivion, Doom used his new abilities to preserve what he could. He created a new celestial body from the remnants of the old Earths, stitching together elements from many different alternative realities to create a patchwork planet that he named Battleworld. Along with a variety of different landscapes and territories came a multitude of individuals, all salvaged from their alternative timelines by Doctor Doom's power. These people had no memories of their previous lives, and they believed they had always existed on Battleworld, where they were compelled to worship Doom as their God Emperor.

Competing kingdoms
Battleworld was split into competing Domains, with individual Barons responsible for their own kingdoms. Some, like Higher Avalon's Baron Jamie Braddock governed justly, while others, such as Dystopia's Baron Maestro planned to expand their rule beyond their own borders. While some Barons were jealous of God Emperor Doom's exalted position, none dared move openly against him. Doom's rule was law and his power absolute. Well aware of the planet's true history, Doctor Strange helped Doom maintain order as Sheriff of Battleworld, all the while maintaining a secret Sanctum Sanctorum on the Hidden Isle of Agamotto.

Castle in the sky
Doomgard, the floating citadel of Battleworld's Thor Corps, reverberated with the sounds of jousting and revelry in equal measure.
Secret Wars #7, Jan. 2016

> **"**As long as the resolute laws of Doom are followed, he permits each Baron or Baroness complete control of their province.**"**
> **Thor (Battleworld)**

Few individuals were brave enough to venture into the lands south of the Shield. In fact, banishment beyond the Shield was frequently used by God Emperor Doom as a means of punishment to control his often fractious Barons. When Baron Braddock of Higher Avalon was unjustly accused of treason by Baron Sinister of Bar Sinister, he was dispatched southward to the Deadlands. Brave Braddock leapt off the Shield, sword in hand, determined to take out as many zombies as possible before eventually falling to the massed ranks of ravenous undead.

Doomgard was home to the Enforcers of Doom's Justice, women and men recruited from across Battleworld and bestowed with the power of Thor, God of Thunder. From its floating kingdom, the Thor Corps policed Battleworld, roaring in like a sudden storm to deliver swift and certain justice to lawbreakers and disbelievers alike.

When first created, Battleworld floated alone in the void save for the orbiting satellite of Knowhere. At some point, however, the Human Torch threatened Doom's divine rule and was lifted into the heavens as punishment, condemned to burn for all eternity as Battleworld's star. In some eyes, he became a deity himself, worshipped secretly as "The Man in the Sun." Battleworld's most unruly kingdoms lay far to the south. New Xandar was a land that had fallen to the Annihilation Wave before being subsumed into God Emperor Doom's creation. Perfection was a robotic city from where the malign AI Ultron plotted the downfall of all biological life and the Deadlands was the abode of mindless zombies. All three Domains were contained behind the Shield, an enormous stone wall that circled the planet. Guarded by a contingent of Thors, it successfully held back the zombie hordes, the seasonal Annihilation Wave, and Ultron's drone armies.

Secret hideaway
Closed in by cliffs and protected by leviathans, Sheriff Strange's Hidden Isle of Agamotto was safe from God Emperor Doom. *Secret Wars* #6, Dec. 2015

Dead again
In the Deadlands, Baron Jamie Braddock tried to dispatch as many zombies as he could before succumbing to the grisly hordes. *Secret Wars* #2, Jul. 2015

Back from beyond

Eight years into God Emperor Doom's reign, Battleworld was rocked to its core by the emergence of two groups of survivors from the last two Earths to perish during the incursions. In the deserts of Utopolis, a strange craft, seemingly older than Battleworld itself, was unearthed. Under the auspices of Alex Power of the Future Foundation, a squad was sent to investigate the anomaly. During the dig, one of the worker Moloids inadvertently opened the craft, releasing the so-called Cabal from within. The Cabal was a loose coalition of villains and hostile cosmic beings that included Thanos from reality-616 and the Reed Richards of the Ultimate Universe, who had abandoned his heroic ideals to become the monomaniacal Maker.

The group had pooled their considerable resources to escape the destruction of the Multiverse and had spent the last several years in deep stasis, their escape pod buried beneath the surface of Battleworld. Freed from their ship, they murdered a member of the Thor Corps and then fled into the wastelands.

"God Doom has made a world of many wonders. I have seen mirrors of those I have known."

Sheriff Stephen Strange

Storm patrols
Reporting to Sheriff Strange, Battleworld's Thors patrolled the skies in search of dissent to God Emperor Doom's rule. *Secret Wars* #3, Aug. 2015

Rude awakening
After eight years, several heroes from Earth-616 were released from their slumber to discover everything had changed. *Secret Wars* #3, Aug. 2015

Revolution

Over the subsequent weeks, the presence of the outworlders began to destabilize the delicate balance of power on Battleworld. Cabal member Maximus, pretending to be the so-called Prophet, deployed his Inhuman mind-control powers to urge citizens to openly reject the rule of Emperor Doom. Posing as one of their number, Jane Foster slowly turned the Thors against their tyrannical master.

The twin Reed Richards set aside their differences to concoct a plan to steal Doom's godlike powers. As Maximus led his army of revolution on Castle Doom, the pair used the ensuing chaos as cover to infiltrate the dungeons beneath the castle grounds. There they encountered the Molecule Man, who had languished in a reality bubble for the past eight years. The Maker attempted to betray his heroic counterpart and steal the Molecule Man's power for himself but was easily overcome.

The villains' craft also contained a stowaway in the form of Miles Morales, who had hidden on board during reality's final moments. When everyone else had evacuated the dig site, Stephen Strange called on the teenager to finally reveal himself. Strange took Miles into his confidence and confessed that he had discovered a similar life raft some years earlier and stored it away from Emperor Doom's prying eyes in his spell-locked Sanctum Sanctorum.

Suspecting the ship also contained survivors from the times before, Strange and Miles opened it up to release a small contingent of disorientated heroes, including Reed Richards, Spider-Man, Captain Marvel, and Thor Jane Foster. Sheriff Strange immediately recognized them as his former colleagues and friends from Earth-616, and he informed them of the tumultuous events that had occurred while they slumbered in stasis.

Meanwhile, a squad of Thors had located the fleeing Cabal and engaged them in combat. Alerted to the situation, Sheriff Strange teleported himself and his heroic comrades to the scene of battle. God Emperor Doom was also made aware of the unfolding events, and he made a rare decision to intercede directly, appearing amidst the chaotic melee in a burst of power. Fearing for the safety of his friends—and wishing to spare them Emperor Doom's awful wrath—Sheriff Strange teleported both teams of refugees to parts unknown, scattering them far and wide across the surface of Battleworld. Enraged at his sheriff's seeming betrayal, Doom killed Strange instantly with a blistering surge of energy.

Stonewalled
A huge version of the Thing had formed the foundation stone of the Shield. Awakened, he emerged from the wall to confront Doom. *Secret Wars* #6, Dec. 2015

Reality reset
Possessing the infinite power of the Beyonders, Reed Richards gathered together his family in preparation for the restoration of the Multiverse. *Secret Wars* #9, Mar. 2016

Magical kingdom

Weirdworld was one of the strangest of Battleworld's Domains. Perhaps because it was composed of fragments of former magical realms such as Crystalium and Polemachus, it survived the collapse of Battleworld. It became tethered to the Earthly plane, accessed via mystical portals in places of power like the infamous Bermuda Triangle.

During Battleworld's revolution, when the fate of all reality was determined, a far more personal story unfolded on Weirdworld. Arkon, a survivor of the Earth-616 reality, had spent years exploring the magical Domain in search of his former home, the glistening city of Polemachus.

Meanwhile, on the battlefield outside the castle, Emperor Doom realized that the siege had been orchestrated as a distraction and he teleported back inside to protect his living power source. In the reality bubble, Doom and Richards fought each other, Molecule Man taking away most of the God Emperor's abilities to ensure the contest was fair. When he heard Doom confess that Richards would have done a better job with the Beyonders' power, the Molecule Man stripped away the God Emperor's last vestige of omnipotence, leaving him mortal once again.

Without Doom's will to keep everything together, Battleworld quickly became unstitched. It was replaced with something else, however, a restored version of the previous Multiverse. The Molecule Man had taken back Doom's power only to pass it on to Reed Richards, who used it to recreate what had been lost. While the new cosmos was modeled on the previous iteration of reality, some minor details were different. Key elements from the Ultimate Universe were subsumed into the core reality of Earth-616, such as Miles Morales and his family.

After establishing solid foundations for the new universe, and realizing his gifts were finite, Reed Richards embarked on a journey across the expanding cosmos with his family and the teens of the Future Foundation. He pledged to recreate the vastness of the Multiverse one reality at a time.

On the edge
Weirdworld existed in such a state of flux that Arkon was almost driven mad during his search for the lost city of Polemachus. *Weirdworld* #1, Aug. 2015

Upside down world
Polemachus was situated on the underside of the hovering isle that formed the Domain of Weirdworld. *Weirdworld* #4, Nov. 2015

Guided by an often confusing and contradictory map, Arkon finally reached what he believed to be the border of Weirdworld only to discover that the realm was actually a floating island. Polemachus was nowhere to be found and, willing to accept he had lost all, Arkon prepared to step off the cliff edge. As luck would have it, however, a dragon suddenly soared overhead. Arkon tamed the unruly beast, climbed onto it, and took off with renewed vigor to survey Weirdworld from the air.

Unfortunately, the dragon belonged to an alternative-reality iteration of Morgan le Fay, the Baroness of Weirdworld, and she declared Arkon an outlaw for stealing one of her majestic beasts. Arkon found himself hunted by Morgan's forces—troupes of ogres and Magma Men—as well as mercenaries eager for the bounty placed on his head by the Baroness. As he continued to search Weirdworld, Arkon was diverted repeatedly from his quest, propelled into one misadventure after another. He was held captive by the underwater gorillas of Apelantis, aided the crystal warrior Warbow in the restoration of the heroic Crystar, and fought the bounty hunter Skull the Slayer. Eventually, after despairing of ever finding his home again, he joined the rebellion of the Swamp Queen and her Man-Things, hoping to replace Morgan le Fay's Kingdom of the Torch with a new version of his beloved Polemachus.

During the final battle, Arkon was swept off the surface of Weirdworld and was astonished to discover his beloved Polemachus preserved in all her glory on the underside of the floating isle. He reached out for his home, but before he could touch the city's gleaming spires, Polemachus disappeared as reality was rewritten—and Battleworld itself fell apart—in the wake of God Emperor Doom's defeat at the hands of Reed Richards.

Dragon's-eye view
Arkon's quest soared to new heights when he mounted a dragon and viewed Weirdworld's confounding geography from above. *Weirdworld* #1, Aug. 2015

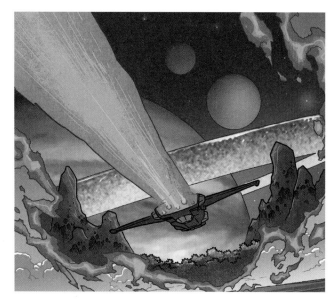

Seeking redemption
While on the run, the Black Knight stole an Avengers Quinjet and fled to Weirdworld through a portal in the Bermuda Triangle.
Black Knight #3, Mar. 2016

Land of the lost

Shortly after the restoration of the Multiverse and the establishment of the link between Earth and Weirdworld, the Avenger Dane Whitman escaped to the sorcerous realm through the Bermuda Triangle. For years, the hero had struggled to control his mystical Ebony Blade, which had been cursed in medieval times. In a confrontation with the brutal Carnivore, Whitman finally lost his battle and the Ebony Blade greedily fed on the villain's life.

The sword compelled Whitman to seek sanctuary in Weirdworld, where he deposed the evil Zaltin Tar and established the kingdom of New Avalon as a bulwark against the expansionist empire of the Fangs of the Serpent. Inevitably, the Avengers arrived in Weirdworld with the intent of taking Whitman back to Earth to face justice. However, when they saw how vital he was to the peace of Weirdworld, they allowed him to stay there, believing his service in defense of the realm was just penance for his earlier crime.

Similarly, teenager Becca Rodriguez found a fresh sense of purpose in Weirdworld. While on the way to scatter her dead mother's ashes in Mexico, Becca's plane was pulled into Weirdworld by the wizard Ogeode, who drew on the power of a mystic talisman called the Wuxian Seed to perform the incredible deed. Overjoyed at the success of his spell, Ogeode declared himself Weirdworld's mightiest sorcerer. However, a huge figure

> **"This is Weirdworld. A place where the lost can be found."**
> Goleta the Wizardslayer

suddenly emerged from behind Ogeode and killed him with a sweep of her mighty ax. This was Goleta, the self-styled Wizardslayer, who sought vengeance on all magicians following the devastation of her homeland. With no other survivors from the crash, Becca reluctantly accepted an invitation to become Goleta's squire, and the pair set off across Weirdworld, taking the powerful Wuxian Seed with them.

Weird heroes
A Wizardslayer, a catbeast, and a girl from Earth were unlikely traveling companions as they made their way across Weirdworld. *Weirdworld* #5, Jun. 2016

Dragon queen
Power-hungry Morgan le Fay used her pet dragon to intimidate supplicants like the mystic seer, Warg.
Weirdworld #1, Feb. 2016

Legendary land

The Weirdworld that existed before the incursions wiped out the Multiverse was a realm of magic, populated by diminutive creatures from folklore and myth.

Tyndall was an amnesiac elf who lived with the dwarves of Dwarf Haven. He was shunned by the townsfolk for being different and longed to learn more about his origins. Finding themselves terrorized by giant bat-monsters known as Night-Fangers, the Dwarves selfishly dispatched Tyndall to the Realm of Shadow on a quest to find and destroy the mysterious Heart of Evil and hopefully bring an end to the Night-Fangers' nocturnal raids.

After braving countless dangers, Tyndall eventually reached his destination. There he found a large egg that he assumed was the Heart of Evil. However, before he could destroy it, the egg hatched and a female elf named Velanna emerged. A delighted Tyndall welcomed his new companion, and they set off together. Over the following years, Tyndall and Velanna shared many adventures, picking up a companion dwarf called Mud-Butt along the way and finally discovering that the elves of Weirdworld originated from the floating, ring-shaped island of Klarn that dominated the sky.

Behind them, however, Ogeode's corpse stirred. From within, a strange catbeast emerged—the wizard reborn in a greatly diminished form. Catching up to Becca and Goleta, the weakened Ogeode proposed a truce. He would help Becca return to Earth if the pair first helped him retrieve his spare human body from a location beyond the legendary Fang Mountains. Terms agreed, the unlikely trio embarked on their quest. Their journey was far from easy, however, as they were bedeviled by agents of Morgan le Fay, who had sensed the Wuxian Seed and lusted after its power.

Just as the group entered the last leg of their journey, they were attacked by Morgan directly. During the encounter, Weirdworld's Baroness revealed that the Wuxian Seed was actually the Reality Stone, one of the fabled Infinity Stones. As the sorceress fought Goleta for possession of the all-powerful bauble, a stray bolt of her power shattered the Wuxian Seed, releasing a crimson aether that took on the form of a dragon and promptly fled into the sky.

Enraged at this turn of events, Morgan le Fay also retreated, leaving Becca and Goleta to count the cost of their victory. During the battle, Ogeode had been mortally wounded. As he passed, he apologized to Becca for being such a poor wizard and hoped he had been a far better cat. His last act was to declare Becca his mystical successor. With encouragement from Goleta, Becca finally accepted Weirdworld as her new home, and the pair set off in search of fresh adventures in a land of magic and wonder. ▪

Index

Page numbers in *italics* refer to comic book illustrations

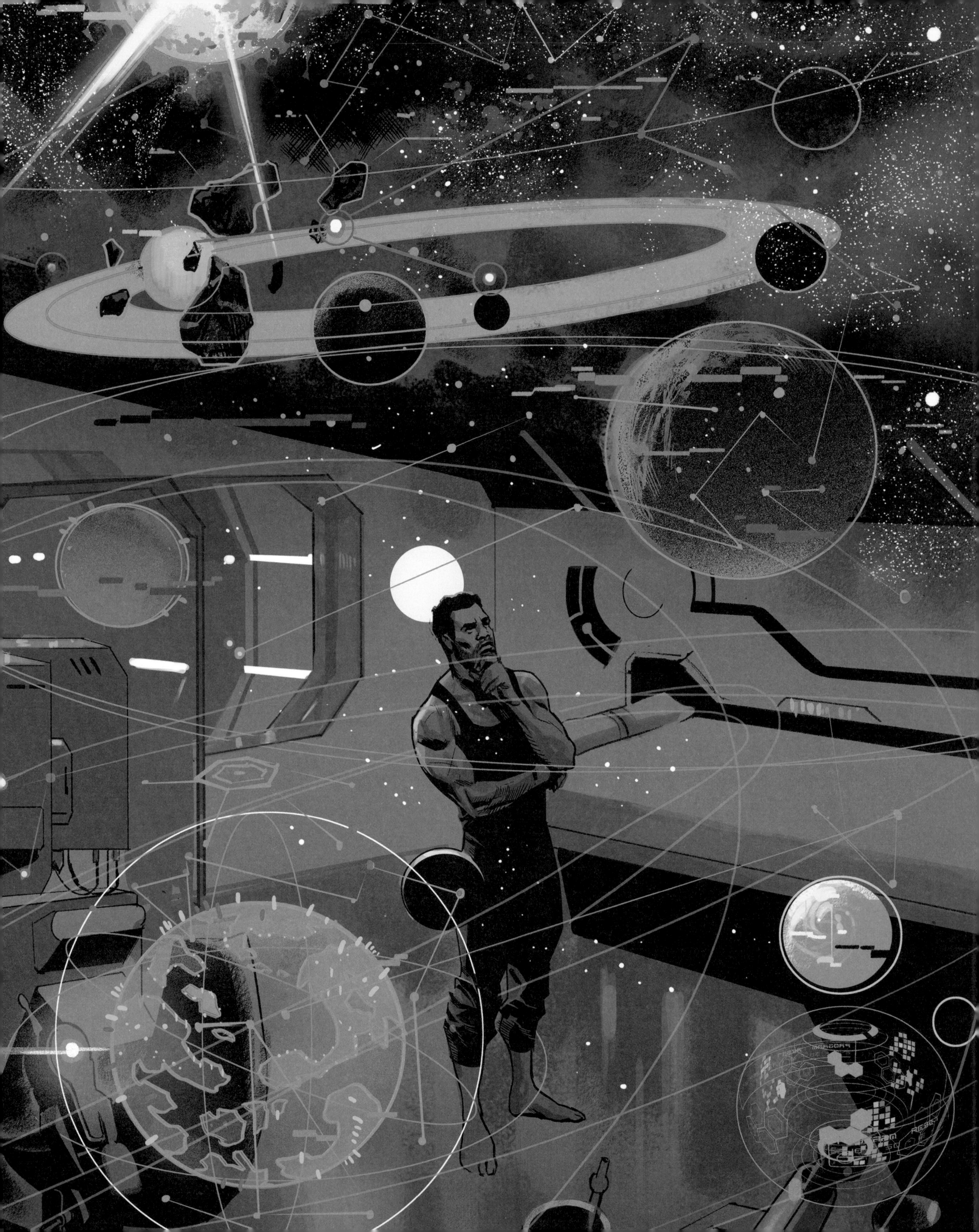